Representations of Childhood in American Modernism

Mason Phillips

Representations of Childhood in American Modernism

Mason Phillips
Fairfax, Virginia, USA

ISBN 978-1-349-70141-4   ISBN 978-1-137-50807-2   (eBook)
DOI 10.1057/978-1-137-50807-2

Library of Congress Control Number: 2016942629

© The Editor(s) (if applicable) and The Author(s) 2016
This work is subject to copyright. All rights are solely and exclusively licensed by the Publisher, whether the whole or part of the material is concerned, specifically the rights of translation, reprinting, reuse of illustrations, recitation, broadcasting, reproduction on microfilms or in any other physical way, and transmission or information storage and retrieval, electronic adaptation, computer software, or by similar or dissimilar methodology now known or hereafter developed.
The use of general descriptive names, registered names, trademarks, service marks, etc. in this publication does not imply, even in the absence of a specific statement, that such names are exempt from the relevant protective laws and regulations and therefore free for general use.
The publisher, the authors and the editors are safe to assume that the advice and information in this book are believed to be true and accurate at the date of publication. Neither the publisher nor the authors or the editors give a warranty, express or implied, with respect to the material contained herein or for any errors or omissions that may have been made.

Cover image © Clement Hurd, from *The World is Round by Gertrude* Stein Cover design by Oscar Spigolon

Printed on acid-free paper

This Palgrave Macmillan imprint is published by Springer Nature
The registered company is Nature America Inc.
The registered company address is: 1 New York Plaza, New York, NY 10004, U.S.A.

Acknowledgments

This book began as my doctoral dissertation, and each member of my committee, including Marianne DeKoven, Cheryl A. Wall, Harriet Davidson, and Patricia Crain, has shaped this project in ways both definite and indelible. It was my enormous good fortune to have Pat as a mentor throughout this process. She answered questions for me that I did not know to ask and opened doors for me that I never knew were there. One of the luckiest days of my life was when I signed up to take a class with Marianne. She is not only a renowned scholar but also a gifted teacher, an uncommonly devoted advisor, and a trusted friend.

I also owe many thanks to Michael McKeon for his meticulous feedback on earlier drafts of Chap. 4 of the book and for organizing a workshop where I received crucial encouragement and words of wisdom from Natalie Roxburgh, Sonali Barua, and Shakti Jaising. And I also must thank the Graduate Literatures in English Program at Rutgers University, including Cheryl Robinson, Courtney Borack, John Kucich, Rebecca Walkowitz, and Stacy Klein, for providing consistent and unwavering professional and financial support and for making Murray Hall one of the best places to learn and work.

I published versions of two of the chapters contained herein in *The Henry James Review* and in *PMLA*. I am grateful for the suggestions and revisions made by these journals' readers and editors, including Susan Griffin, Eric Wirth, and Nancy Bentley. I have also been fortunate to receive feedback at various conference presentations along the way. I would like to thank Katharine Capshaw for her encouragement in this context and Marah Gubar for taking the time to retool my brain in regards to nineteenth-century children's literature.

For many of these chapters, it has been my privilege to conduct research at a number of wonderful institutions and libraries. The librarians at the University of Massachusetts at Amherst, where I studied W.E.B. Du Bois's papers, went out of their way to provide me with access to materials for Chap. 6. Similarly, I have rarely met more knowledgeable librarians than those at Yale's Beinecke Library who helped guide my research on Gertrude Stein.

Last, but always far from least, none of this would have been possible without the shared sacrifices of my family. My mother, Debra, is the most patient and generous person I have ever known and extended me more than my fair share of both during this process. Tesla Miller came to my rescue on more than one occasion. Her humor and her research assistance were equally vital. Vicky and Zdzislaw Pacholec were angels who regularly took over my household so that I could work. More inspiration than I ever needed came from my daughter, Katherine Reese, who helped me, as much as anyone, to understand Gertrude Stein's children's fiction. Most of all, I want to thank my wife, Michelle, who survived with me the loss of our first born and who holds my hand each and every day.

Contents

1 Introduction   1

2 American Modernism, Childhood, and the Inward Turn   13

3 The "*Partagé* Child" and the Emergence of the Modernist Novel in Henry James's *What Maisie Knew*   37

4 An Innocence Worse than Evil in *The Turn of the Screw*   65

5 *Nightwood*: A Bedtime Story   91

6 The Children of Double Consciousness: From *The Souls of Black Folk* to *The Brownies' Book*   119

7 Drowning in Childhood: Gertrude Stein's Late Modernism   163

Works Cited   211

Index   227

List of Figures

Fig. 5.1	Henri Rousseau, *The Dream*, 1910. Courtesy of The Museum of Modern Art/Licensed by SCALA/Art Resource, NY	102
Fig. 6.1	*The Crisis* Children's Number 16.6 (October 1918) 282	132
Fig. 6.2	*The Crisis* Children's Number 8.6 (October 1914) 273	133
Fig. 6.3	*The Crisis* Children's Number 12.6 (October 1916) 275	134
Fig. 6.4	*The Crisis* Children's Number 12.6 (October 1916) 287	136
Fig. 6.5	*The Brownies' Book* 1.9 (September 1920) 272	149
Fig. 6.6	*The Brownies' Book* 1.12 (Dec 1920) 378	151
Fig. 6.7	*The Brownies' Book* 1.12 (Dec 1920) 379	152
Fig. 6.8	*The Brownies' Book* 1.3 (March 1920) 76	153
Fig. 7.1	Facsimile from Gertrude Stein's manuscript, *Geographical History of America*	184

CHAPTER 1

Introduction

By the turn of the twentieth century, childhood was in vogue. The idyllic child at the heart of poetic, Romantic discourse resurfaced in the work of twentieth-century reformers and scientists who dedicated themselves to understanding and bettering the lives of actual children. As Sally Shuttleworth observes, the child-study movement, which thrived in the early years of the twentieth century, had its roots in the core values of post-Romantic discourse (2). In promoting the belief that the entire history of human evolution recapitulates itself in the lifespan of each individual, child-study scientists validated the importance of childhood as the origin of both personal and social progress.[1] By 1930, Herbert Hoover spoke for many reformers when he argued that interventions in the problems of poverty, health, and education for just "one generation" of children would cause those problems and "a thousand other[s]" to "vanish" (qtd. in Smuts 140). Even Freud, whose theories of infantile sexuality seemed to threaten Romantic ideals of childhood innocence, underscored the essentialist line on childhood as the epicenter of the self.

Childhood played a foundational role in modern visions of individual and human history, but in many of these narratives childhood itself had no history. In the mind, childhood became a permanent fixture, a place solidified by Freud into what Carolyn Steedman calls the "timeless interiority of the unconscious" (93). For Freud and other child-study theorists, the child also served as an accessible agent of man's otherwise inaccessible, primitive past. And for reformers, childhood was the impressionable point at which and through which future history would be made.

In her 1900 treatise, *The Century of the Child*, feminist and socialist Ellen Key railed against the use of corporal punishment, factory work for both women and children, and the "idiotic" model of public school education, which, in her view, churned out (like a factory itself) identically-minded, unquestioning, and (above all) obedient children. The book became an international bestseller. Through it, Key sought to make the cultivation of the child along with its mother the centerpiece of social and political reform efforts across Europe and America (330). And, in so many respects, the early years of the twentieth-century were already en route to making Key's vision of a child-centered society a reality. Anxious parents, eager to incorporate the spirit of reform at home, enjoyed a robust body of child-rearing literature, including *Parents' Magazine* which made its debut in 1926. The psychological study of children boomed. Alice Boardman Smuts tells us that in 1918 there were only five psychologists and psychiatrists who studied childhood full time, but by 1930 there were more than 600 (1–2). 1912 saw the creation of "The Children's Bureau," which devoted its first years almost entirely to the problem of childhood mortality. In the 1890s children accounted for 40% of all deaths; by the 1920s that number had fallen dramatically to 21.7% (Zelizer 29). To help move children out of danger zones, such as the streets and the factories, public spaces were created for the child's cultivation and protection. Kindergartens grew alongside a more progressive educational model that emphasized children as active rather than passive learners. Playgrounds were beginning to become regular features of urban centers like Chicago, which built its first in 1893 (Kinchin and O'Connor 43). In the key area of child labor, however, Hugh Cunningham observes that progress in the United States was slow. Nearly all countries had passed laws regulating child labor by the end of the nineteenth century, except for the U.S. (180–181). Nonetheless, the number of child laborers in America was on the decline, from nearly 2 million in 1910 to around 667,000 in 1938 (the year the first federal regulations finally took effect) (Zelizer 65; 56).

The turn of the twentieth century was also the time of the so-called golden age of children's literature in which such classics as J.M. Barrie's *Peter Pan* (1902), L.M. Montgomery's *Anne of Green Gables* (1908), Frances Hodgson Burnett's *The Secret Garden* (1911), Kenneth Grahame's *The Wind in the Willows* (1908), Margery Williams's *The Velveteen Rabbit* (1922), and A.A. Milne's *Winnie the Pooh* (1926) appeared to work alongside Anglo-American progressives to sentimentalize childhood as a beloved space set apart from the disenchanted adult world of labor, materialism, and managed time. Anne Scott MacLeod cites an American review of *Peter Pan*, praising Barrie for having "truly kept the heart and mind of a child," as part of a larger wish on the part of turn-of-the-century adults to be themselves "as spontaneous and as innocently joyful as children" (120). Where, in times past, Anglo-American societies had concentrated on saving the child's place in heaven or its future place in the establishment, Cunningham observes that the Victorians and the moderns were also determined "to save children for the enjoyment of childhood" (137).

Representations of Childhood in American Modernism thus tells an unpopular story. It is the story of American modernism's literary efforts to disenchant adult and child readers alike of the essentialist view of childhood as redemptive, virtuous, originary, and universal. These efforts were unpopular because, as happened with Henry James, readers were frustrated by their defiant refusal to meet expectations about what children and narratives about children ought to be. One reviewer for *The New York Times* referred to James's Maisie as a "small monster," ironically echoing Maisie's depraved parents, who regularly insult their daughter in almost the same way ("Henry James's New Work" BR9). Another reviewer was more appalled by the coldness of James's approach to his subject, charging that the "author exhibits not one ray of pity or dismay at this spectacle of a child with the pure current of its life thus poisoned at its source" ("What Maisie Knew" 454). They were unpopular because, as happened with Stein, publishers and agents read modernist children's literature as "hardly being for les enfants" (Stein and Vechten 679). Like James, Stein was also guilty of failing to arouse the feelings that readers expected and desired from representations of childhood. Bennett Cerf, at Random House, rejected Stein's manuscript for *To Do: A Book of Alphabets and Birthdays* because he felt "as cold as a slab of alabaster" about the book (Stein and Vechten 697N). They were unpopular because, as happened with *The Brownies' Book*, their readership was limited in numbers and in purchasing power. The final issue of *The Brownies' Book* laments, "there are two million Brownies in the United States, and unless we got at least one in every hundred to read our pages and help pay printing, we knew we must at last cease to be" (qtd. in Johnson-Feelings 347). And they were all unpopular for reimagining the child that lay at the center of nineteenth- and twentieth-century identity, feeling, education, and reform as the source of what ails us, not the cure.

Some scholars have asserted the view that the reason there appears to be so little modernist children's literature is because modernists themselves chose not to enter the field. David Rudd, for example, has argued that the reason for modernism's minimal presence in the world of children's literature is not because children's literature denied its entry but because "modernism deliberately distanced itself from what it saw as the restrictive world of children's writing" (300). Similarly, William Gray contrasts modernist literature as an "acquired taste" most often encountered in college coursework with the populist and pleasing impulses of children's literature (28). But the image of modernists holding children's literature at arm's length mistakes an important truth: a number of modernists actively sought to widen the ways that adults think about childhood, to change the way childhood is presented to children, and to open the fields of both modernist and children's literature to make room for some of their most experimental and most unconventional contributions to twentieth-century literature.

Students and scholars of modernism routinely study the works of W.E.B. Du Bois, Gertrude Stein, Langston Hughes, J.M. Barrie, Djuna Barnes, and Henry James. But it remains the case that neither students nor experts of modernism routinely study the culture of childhood that influences a great many of their writings. Though questions about gender, race, class, and sexuality are prevalent in the field, social constructions of childhood have largely remained off-radar. Though Stein, Hughes, and Du Bois regularly wrote for children, their children's literature is not regularly included in modernist considerations of their work. W.E.B. Du Bois and Jessie Fauset were at the forefront of African-American children's literature in the teens and twenties through their combined editorial and aesthetic contributions to *The Crisis* Children's Numbers and *The Brownies' Book*, the premier children's periodical created for and by African Americans. Langston Hughes, who began his career publishing in *The Brownies' Book*, went on to write numerous books for children throughout the entirety of his career. *Black Misery*, his final book for children, was also the last book he worked on before he died in 1967. Gertrude Stein wrote a series of children's books in the late thirties and early forties, including an alphabet book and a first reader. And many other American modernists, not included in the present study, produced one or two books for children in their lifetime.[2] When we observe the dearth of modernist fiction about and for children, the question is not why modernists shunned childhood but why we as readers have neglected or denied their interest in this field.

Thankfully, this neglect has not been absolute. Scholars like Juliet Dusinberre and Douglas Mao have produced book-length studies of the child figure in modernism's adult literature.[3] And Kimberly Reynolds has taken important steps in opening up the study of modernist children's literature by showing that, although children's literature can serve conservative, mainstream interests, it has also historically served as "a breeding ground and an incubator for innovation." "Many textual experiments," she argues, "are given their first expression in writing for children" (15). Still, there have been few attempts to bridge modernism's writings for adults with its writings for children, even when both are about childhood and even when both are conceived in the same minds and flow from the ink of the same pens. What would it mean to regularly read Langston Hughes's *Dream Keeper* or *First Book of Rhythms* or his *First Book of Jazz* alongside his blues and jazz poems? How might that pairing affect our interpretations of Hughes's poetics? How might Hughes's modernist aesthetic affect our readings of his children's texts? What would it mean to insert readings from *The Brownies' Book* into the sequential study of Du Bois's writings from this period? How would our understanding of Gertrude Stein's late modernism change if *The World is Round* or *To Do: A Book of Alphabets and Birthdays* were required reading? These are among the questions that the current project hopes to answer.

Most importantly, this is a book that seeks to read the figure of the child across the history of American modernism, across authors, across decades, across genres, and across intended audiences. And in so doing, it shows that American modernism's challenge to Edenic depictions of childhood is both widespread across the movement and integral to the development of the movement itself. Henry James's child-centered works, *What Maisie Knew* (1897) and *The Turn of the Screw* (1898), are watershed texts for modernist fiction whose unconventional child characters inspire equally unconventional experiments in narrative form. After 1934 nearly every (child or adult) text Gertrude Stein produced until her death in 1946 works to deconstruct children's narratives in some form or other. Even her children's books are deconstructions of children's books. There are crucial continuities as well between Du Bois's concerns about childhood which surface in *The Souls of Black Folk* and those that remanifest in his later works for children and which contribute in meaningful ways to Du Bois's evolving thought on double consciousness and the problem of the color line. And Djuna Barnes adds an important critique not just of Romantic childhood but also of modernism itself in her late modernist novel, *Nightwood*.

Throughout, I argue that there is a child in the midst of modernism, but it is neither the child nor the modernism we are accustomed to seeing. When in 1939, Edmund Wilson, a prominent and influential scholar of modernism, was approached about reviewing Eliot's and Stein's recent children's books, he proclaimed that he "found himself baffled by the assignment." Unable to review either book, Wilson turned the task over to another reviewer but not before printing, in the place of a review, an explanation of his trouble. After confessing that he "had difficulty in getting through the Stein book" and that he was "disappointed in *Old Possum*," Wilson offers a scathing commentary on the state of modernism:

> It is perhaps worth pointing out that there seems to be something like a general tendency on the part of the more "difficult" writers to go in for children's books. Kay Boyle has done a book about a camel; and E. E. Cummings is rumored to be engaged on a book of fairy-tales. I don't know what this means—except that they evidently do not feel at the moment that they have anything better to do. (qtd. in Curnutt 115)

After pretending to pass on the job of reviewing the two books in question, Wilson presents his assessment anyway. And he does much more, reading Eliot's *Old Possum's Book of Practical Cats* and Stein's *The World is Round* as indications of a larger modernist trend. Though Wilson also feigns "bafflement" about "what this [tendency] means," he is nonetheless certain that it is both not worth the modernist scholar's or the modernist writer's time.

Unfortunately, Wilson's dismissal of modernist children's literature is just one example of the lackluster history of this literature's collective reception. Histories of childhood and children's literature have routinely skipped modernism. Jacqueline Rose brought attention to this problem as early as 1984 when, in *The Case of Peter Pan*, she argued that the conservative conventions of children's literature writing and publishing had excluded the possibility of a modernist children's literature (142). Rose may not have been aware at that time of the number of modernist children's books in and out of print, but her lack of awareness supports the observation. The vast majority of these children's books were published (when they were published) in limited numbers. But Rose is also susceptible to her own charge. Published in 1911, J.M. Barrie's *Peter and Wendy* could be read as an emergently modernist children's book, but instead Rose reads it as representative of the kind of childhood idolatry common to the field. Still, most scholars cannot be said to even struggle with the issue in the way that Rose does. For instance, James Holt McGavran's collection, *Literature and the Child: Romantic Continuations, Postmodern Contestations*, makes the decision to skip modernism self-evident.

Other studies that include early twentieth-century movements and trends skip modernism's subversive discourses in favor of the more dominant, popular discourses of the era. Hugh Cunningham describes the first half of the twentieth century, in light of new labor laws, the playground movement, and education reform, as even more committed to fulfilling the nineteenth-century promise "to save children for the enjoyment of childhood" (137). When the focus is literary, rather than social, history, the master-narrative remains the same. Focusing on widely popular golden age children's literature, *A Critical History of Children's Literature* describes the period from 1890 to 1920 (the period of modernist emergence and experimentation) as a time of "rightful heritage," when the nineteenth-century idea that children's literature "could exist for the purpose of giving pleasure and delight" was inherited and brought to "maturity."[4] Even when the focus is psychology, the early twentieth century often becomes part of a long nineteenth-century narrative of childhood. Carolyn Steedman's otherwise exceptional study of how childhood becomes central to modern ideas of human interiority extends its argument from 1780 to 1930 with little mention of modernism. Even George Boas's *The Cult of Childhood* and James Kincaid's *Erotic Innocence*, which take critical stances toward this period in the history of childhood, choose to offer modernist texts, which ironically represent the stances of the critics themselves, as exemplars of conventional rather than unconventional thinking about the child subject. Boas overlooks James's ironic representation of childhood in Maisie Farange and instead sees her as part of a lineage of "saintly children" (59). Likewise, Kincaid makes no mention of *Peter and Wendy*'s repeated criticisms of Peter Pan for his heartlessness and instead offers it as a classic case of compulsive child adoration (113–114).

Throughout much of the nineteenth and twentieth centuries, childhood became a rousing centerpiece of modern society, signifying better times past and future, even signifying one's own best self. Indeed, it appears difficult to conceive an approach to childhood at this time taking any form but these. But the writers and thinkers of American modernism did exactly this, and in so doing they were among the first to question the universality of childhood, among the first to assert the social construction of childhood, and among the first to show concern for the damage that ideals of childhood could do to children as well as adults. Writers of modernist fiction for adults, like James, and writers of modernist fiction for children, like Barrie, are forerunners to modern and contemporary critical scholarship that has sought to unveil the socially-constructed apparatus that belies notions of universal childhood.[5] Indeed, all of the writers that I examine throughout this book actually set the stage for the kinds of critical questions that Boas, Rose, and Kincaid themselves raise about society's over-infatuation with an idea of childhood, which may not be as virtuous, sustainable, or even as real as many have presupposed.

In the nineteenth century, the ideal adult was often hailed as preserving an inward connection to childhood. Well into the twentieth century, childhood, so cherished and so desired, became something to be preserved at all costs. The home, the garden, and the kindergarten set up walls around it. The mind preserved it in memory and sustained it, long into adulthood, as the key to individual authenticity. "Healing the child within" (to take a phrase from mid-twentieth-century popular psychology) meant so much more than that—it meant healing adulthood, and it meant healing the nation. But for many modernists, the modern era's extreme investment in discourses of childhood interiority comes at the price of the mature life. In Chap. 2, I examine these discourses—that hail the child in the midst as a Christlike redeemer, that imagine "the child in the house" as an emblem of protection and safe-keeping, or that remember childhood as the best time of life—in relation to several of the different discourses that modernists developed to counter them. Henry James, Djuna Barnes, Langston Hughes, W.E.B. Du Bois, and Gertrude Stein each test, in different ways, the limits of innocence, shelter, and nostalgia. In these fictionalized experiments, the child in the midst may not be able to save herself let alone anyone else; the child in the house is segregated by race as well as age; and nostalgia is an illness whose cure requires a removal of, not a return to, childhood.

In Chap. 3, "The '*Partagé* Child' and the Emergence of the Modernist Novel in Henry James's *What Maisie Knew*," I tell the story of how James's decision to represent an unconventional child led him to build a strange new apparatus around her. James was inspired by the story of two divorced parents who thereafter shared custody of the child between them. James was fascinated by the way that the divided union of the parents produced a similar division in the child who was decreed to alternate her life between them. Before he came up with the name Maisie, James referred to this child as the "partagé" (or divided) child. But the "partagé child" provided James with more than a captivating central character; it also gave him a new idea for how to write the modern novel. *What Maisie Knew* initially purports to be a story given to following the limited and evolving consciousness of this child, but the novel is most remarkable for the way that it diverts from this program and decides that it would rather be like Maisie than know her.

While James subverts notions of the "simple and confiding" child in *What Maisie Knew*, in *The Turn of the Screw*, he offers one of the most disturbing challenges to childhood innocence in modern fiction (45). Innocence has long been a hallmark of romanticized childhood, and it is the special target for modernism's disillusioned gaze. As such, I devote two chapters to two very different variations on this common modernist theme. In Chap. 4, "An Innocence Worse than Evil in *The Turn of the Screw*," I argue that James's novella fascinates both for the highly effective way that it invites readers to imagine evil and for the doubt that it casts on the value of childhood innocence. In fact, James does not place the concepts of evil and innocence in opposition to one another, as is traditionally the case, but poses them instead as analogous problems. Thoughts of the children's innocence haunt the governess's mind as much (if not more) than the two ghosts who haunt the children, if they haunt the children at all. Even if the evil spirits are real, they are not the cause of the illness and death in the novel. Rather, it is the governess's relentless pursuit and policing of the children's innocence that results in the undoing of Flora, Miles, and the governess herself.

In Chap. 5, "*Nightwood*: A Bedtime Story," I turn to the other end of the modernist timeline where Djuna Barnes's Robin Vote embodies not just the ominous innocence of James's characters but also the now equally suspect innocence of modernist art. Robin is figured as child and as doll, as blank slate and as modernist painting. Through her character's conjuncture of modernism and childhood, Barnes suggests the pitfalls of narratives of dispossession, of negation and re-invention, for the already dispossessed—for the homosexual and the Jew, the orphaned and the traumatized—on the eve of World War II. But *Nightwood* also offers a little recognized child alternative to Robin's singularly innocent child narrative. Matthew O'Connor is transgendered, a charlatan doctor, an obscene storyteller, and a doomsayer, but he is also the child with "eyes wide open" (81). Through him, *Nightwood* rejects the preservation of innocence in any form, even in the forms of modernism, and holds out instead a revised ideal of childhood disillusionment.

The narrative of innocence does not just belong to childhood, it also belongs in important ways to America's vision of itself as a new and exceptional world. The novels of James and Barnes seem most targeted toward childhood innocence, but this is not the case with W.E.B. Du Bois and Gertrude Stein who are actively invested in trying to survive the mentality of American innocence. In *The Souls of Black Folk* (1903), W.E.B. Du Bois famously writes that "the problem of the Twentieth Century is the problem of the color-line" (1). Yet, in his children's literature of the teens and twenties, Du Bois confronts a new problem for the twentieth century: the question of how to prepare black children for a lifetime of inequality. In Chap. 6, "The Children of Double Consciousness: From *The Souls of Black Folk* to *The Brownies' Book*," I argue that Du Bois's collective works for children respond to this problem by crisscrossing the line that separates youth and age. The systematic dualities of innocence and violence in these writings represent a revision of Du Bois's discussion of double consciousness in *Souls*. There it signifies an experience of race consciousness that happens suddenly to the black child unshielded by parents and home; here it represents the work of black parents and educators to actively and gradually guide the black child's entry into race consciousness, in the hopes that double consciousness may be repurposed into a homegrown model for a resilient black American subjectivity beginning in childhood.

Gertrude Stein's war-time writings clearly share in this project of troubling the lines between youth and age, but there is a violence in Stein's late modernist treatment of childhood that is wholly antithetical to Du Bois's re-constructive aims. Stein's children's narratives of this era are preoccupied with representing and with killing children, with writing and with destroying the tropes of childhood. In the seventh and final chapter, "Drowning in Childhood: Gertrude Stein's Late Modernism," I argue that Stein's anxieties about childhood nostalgia, its nineteenth-century roots and its twentieth-century hangouts in reactionary politics and in children's literature, lead her to reject sentimental representations of childhood in favor of deadpan violence. In her own works for children, Stein systematically depicts scenes of child starvation, violence, and death by drowning as a means of conveying to her child and adult readers alike the necessity, not of killing actual children, but of killing the ideals of childhood that hold actual children hostage to a culture that, Stein believes, should have been dead already.

NOTES

1. Carolyn Steedman characterizes the evolutionary theory at the root of Freudian psychoanalysis and the child-study movement as "non-Darwinian," because it signifies in each of these fields a teleological view of development, closely aligned with ideas of progress (85).
2. Djuna Barnes spent the last years of her life on a book for children, her first, entitled *Creatures in an Alphabet*. T.S. Eliot published his first and only children's book entitled *Old Possum's Book of Practical Cats* in 1939. Countee Cullen wrote two children's novels, *The Lost Zoo* and *My Lives and How I Lost Them*, which were published in the early 1940s. It is unclear when E.E. Cummings began writing his *Fairy Tales*, but that writing likely continued through the 1940s—even though the collection remained unpublished until 1965. And William Faulkner wrote *The Wishing Tree* in 1927, though it remained unpublished until 1964.
3. Dusinberre's *Alice to the Lighthouse* and Mao's *Fateful Beauty* differ from the present study in a number of ways. In addition to including children's literature as well as a special attention to unconventional representations of childhood, the present study focuses on American modernism whereas Dusinberre's and Mao's are studies primarily in the British context.
4. Elizabeth Nesbitt, "1890–1920: A Rightful Heritage," 315 and Ruth Hill Viguers, "1920–1950: The Golden Age," 437.
5. Philippe Ariès arguably launched this scholarly discourse with his *Centuries of Childhood* which claimed, radically, in 1962 that childhood is a concept with a history.

CHAPTER 2

American Modernism, Childhood, and the Inward Turn

In one of his few direct commentaries on the cult of childhood, the preeminent American psychologist and philosopher William James sets pragmatism against the proto-Romantic philosophy espoused by Jean Jacques Rousseau, most famously in his educational treatise *Èmile* (1762). *Èmile* is fiction, but despite this fact, Rousseau's efforts to imagine a childhood lovingly kept in seclusion from the adult, civilized world nonetheless set an enduring tone for a more child-centered, child-loving society. James, on the other hand, is appalled: not by the vision itself but by the gaping chasm separating the vision and the life of its creator. On the one hand, Rousseau the philosopher painted an "eloquen[t]" picture of a society bowed to its children and devoted to their care and cultivation; but, on the other hand, Rousseau the man "sen[t] his own children," five in all, "to the foundling hospital" where their deaths were all but certain. In his unsparing criticism of Rousseau's choice to love the imaginary child at the cost of the living, James also suggests that this choice may be a troubling side-effect of the philosophy itself. "There is no more contemptible type of human character," James writes, "than that of the nerveless sentimentalist and dreamer… who never does a manly concrete deed." "Rousseau," James contends, "is the classical example of what I mean," but he adds that "every one of us," who "after glowing for an abstractly formulated Good… practically ignores some actual case," such as choosing to rear the quintessential child rather than the children we actually have, "treads straight on Rousseau's path" ("Habit" 113).

© The Author(s) 2016
M. Phillips, *Representations of Childhood in American Modernism*,
DOI 10.1057/978-1-137-50807-2_2

The fact that James is more impressed by Rousseau's life than he is by his work says much about James's own approach to life and mind. Action is the wheelhouse of James's philosophy. Not only does he believe that actions produce emotions and not the other way around (arguing, for example, that we do not run because we are afraid but are afraid because we run) but he also believes in free will, a conviction that leads him in a moment such as this to argue quite adamantly that individuals are responsible for and ought to be judged by their deeds. Though William James never studied childhood personally, this may have been because the growing marriage between psychology and childhood represented in the work of G. Stanley Hall and Sigmund Freud seemed to continue in the vein of theoretical abstractions, leaving little room for the varieties of individual experience that were of particular importance to him.

James's former student and future colleague G. Stanley Hall, who shared Rousseau's idealization of childhood and its education, was at times openly hostile to James. But many of James's other students acknowledged his teachings as profoundly influential. Indeed, all of the authors in the present study, excepting Djuna Barnes, had a direct connection to William James. W.E.B. Du Bois and Gertrude Stein were both students of James at Harvard. Henry James was, of course, Williams's younger brother, but he was also an abiding fan. After reading *Pragmatism* (1907), Henry wrote to his brother that the book had first "cast" a "spell" on him, and afterwards, he confessed, "I was lost in the wonder of the extent to which all my life I have...unconsciously pragmatised. You are immensely and universally *right*" ("To William" 85). Du Bois, who called William James his "friend and guide to clear thinking," recalled with tremendous fondness how James took him under his wing while he was a graduate student at Harvard and credited James with guiding him "out of the sterilities of scholastic philosophy to realist pragmatism" (qtd. in Richardson 316). The influence between Du Bois and James went both ways. After reading Du Bois's *The Souls of Black Folk* in 1903, James was moved to write two passionate articles decrying the media's role in fueling the "monster" epidemic of lynching (qtd. in Richardson 442). One of Stein's pervasive questions in her later writings—"what is the use of being a little boy if you are growing up to be a man"—demonstrates just how much Stein's rethinking of childhood was influenced by James's theory of pragmatism which, James said, "'turns away from...pretended absolutes and origins'" toward what his biographer describes as "the recognition that activity and the consequences of activity are what matter"

(486). And Stein affectionately attributed her notion of a "complicated simplicity" to James. In her "Transatlantic Interview," she says James was "a great teacher" and her "big influence" at college and recalls how he used to say: "'Never reject anything. Nothing has been proved. If you reject anything, that is the beginning of the end as an intellectual'" (34).

If Freud's theories of the unconscious are a driving force behind the developments of British modernism and the child, as Juliet Dusinberre argues, then William James's philosophies of pragmatism and the conscious mind must be acknowledged as crucial influences on the representations of childhood in American modernism. The function of consciousness is central to brother Henry's development of Maisie Farange's point of view in *What Maisie Knew*, to Du Bois's efforts to delineate the complex double consciousness that is specific to the African-American experience growing up in a nation at odds with its own ideals, to Barnes's portrait of the "eyes wide open" awareness of *Nightwood*'s queer children, and to Stein's efforts to raise the child's own awareness of the social construct of childhood. Like William James, these writers foreground concerns, raised much later by scholars of childhood studies, that the mainstreaming of universal, priceless, and ahistorical ideas about childhood not only reduces the visibility of multiple childhood identities but also practically endangers the value of the mature life.

At the period of modernist emergence in the late nineteenth century, modernism and the "new psychology" alike were rethinking childhood, but they often did so in dramatically different ways. While Freud's theory of infantile sexuality posed a significant challenge to society's romance with the Edenic child, he nonetheless cemented even further the importance of childhood to adult, social, and cultural evolution.[1] With Freud, childhood experiences, more than ever, hold the key to adult life. On the one hand, Freud's work was radical, suggesting just how far the inner workings of childhood could be rethought, but on the other it was as normativizing, if not more so, than its predecessors. Freud's ideal child was the precursor of the white, male, heterosexual patriarch and toward his development Freud laid out strict parameters for normal (and deviant) progress.[2] G. Stanley Hall's psychology of childhood, like Freud's, was revolutionary in the early twentieth century but for very different reasons. Where Freud challenged Romantic notions of childhood innocence, Hall extended the Romantic discourse of childhood beyond the purely conceptual, aesthetic, or theoretical into arguments about the practical treatments of children. In his essay on education, Hall advises teachers that "the guardians of the young should strive first of all to keep out of nature's way...and should merit the proud title of defenders of the happiness and rights of children. They should feel profoundly that childhood, as it comes fresh from the hand of God, is not corrupt...they should be convinced that there is nothing else so worthy of love, reverence, and service as the body and soul of the growing child" ("Ideal School" 475). What this philosophy of child perfection means in practice, for Hall, is that schools should do as little schooling in a child's early years as is possible. The true goal of the school, he asserts, is to prolong childhood, not to shape it. He argues that kindergartens, for example, "should strive" above all "to kill time" (476).

In *Strange Dislocations*, Carolyn Steedman reveals how childhood became the bedrock of human interiority over the course of the nineteenth century, in part through a convergence of the new fields of psychoanalysis and history upon childhood as the key to understanding the origin and evolution of the self. Most importantly, Steedman illuminates how the significance of childhood dilated as it was converted inward into a core being inside of being. She offers the figure of Mignon as a case study for this historical phenomenon. In Goethe's *Wihelm Meister*, Mignon is a child abducted and brought up as an acrobat in the midst of a traveling troupe of rope-dancers. But despite her fictional origins, Mignon became a part of the popular imaginary of childhood in the nineteenth century. For Steedman, Mignon represents the "strange dislocation" that has abducted the child from her real context and internalized a fantasy of her elsewhere. The popularity and reach of the Mignon trope, eventually utterly dislocated from Goethe's novel, showcases how the fictional child—the Romantic child—became internalized as childhood itself in the post-Romantic era. The idea of a self within the self was a crucial modern invention that lit upon the "*littleness*" of the child as well as its fictionalized, deeply romanticized capacity for representation in order to express the past life and the inner world that each individual was increasingly believed to contain (9–11).

The possibility of prolonging childhood had enormous ramifications for the status of adult subjectivity. Anne Scott MacLeod's view that the "best" adult character represented "one that preserved most completely the qualities of childhood" suggests that the value of maturity ebbed while childhood's value was on the rise (24). This view is shared by George Boas who goes one step further in *The Cult of Childhood* by intimating that even if "the retention of childhood into maturity" as an ideal were "possible," it could hardly be "desirable" (33). Though it has become common to worry, as Neil Postman has, about the so-called disappearance of childhood, Juliet Kinchin, a Curator for the Museum of Modern Art, suggests that the worry can go both ways. In her introduction to the 2012 special exhibit, titled after Ellen Key's *Century of the Child*, Kinchin asks, "Could it be that the imprint of childish things on twentieth-century culture has been so profound that ultimately it is not children but adults who will cease to exist?" (Kinchin and O'Connor 11). In the first half of the twentieth century this may not have been a common concern, in part, because the end of adulthood was the unspoken wish that lay behind the glorification of childhood to begin with; but it was a defining question of modernism, concerned not just with what the prolongation of childhood could mean for adults but also with what it could mean for children to face this image of themselves and to live alongside adults who may themselves be pursuing the dream of eternal youth.

Though William James did not address these questions head on, his choice not to engage directly in the rising tide of child study is interesting in and of itself. In fact, by working out an approach to psychology that did not center on the child, James suggests that such alternatives are possible. In contrast to Hall, who urges teachers to keep children childlike as long as possible, William James invites teachers, in his *Talks to Teachers*, to see psychology as the common ground between adults and children. At the end of his lecture on "The Child as a Behaving Organism," James advises his audience that they "should regard [their] professional task as if it consisted chiefly and essentially in *training the pupil to behavior*; taking behavior, not in the narrow sense of manners, but in the very widest possible sense, as including every possible sort of fit reaction on the circumstances into which he may find himself brought by the vicissitudes of life" (17). Like many in the child studies movement, James believes in putting less emphasis on obedience and more on teaching that grows organically from the child's own interests, but for James these interests and this method are not exclusive to elementary education. Because James does not presume that the child is a race apart, the goal of his pedagogy is not the prolongation of childhood; quite the contrary, the goal is to develop what today might be referred to as "noncognitive skills" such as persistence and resilience that help individuals (regardless of IQ) to struggle successively through dark, uncertain, and difficult times.[3]

Throughout these talks, James appears to recognize little difference between the child and the adult mind. His signature work on habit, "stream of consciousness," and the varieties of experience all appear in these talks (11). While James acknowledges that the "new psychology" offers tempting explanatory narratives for the "nature and origin" of the inner life of the mind, he not only dismisses these as "promising speculations" but he also roundly concludes that there is no "'new psychology' worthy of the name" (11). Thus, when James speaks about "the stream of consciousness" to these teachers as "a succession of states, or waves, or fields...of knowledge, of feeling, of desire, of deliberation, etc., that constantly pass and repass, and that constitute *our* inner life," there can be no mistaking the inclusivity of the "our," placing the inner life of the child in the field of consciousness and also placing its complexity on par with that of the teachers themselves (11; emphasis added).

The importance of the "our" cannot be overstated in James's philosophy of psychology which is also his philosophy of humanity. In one of his most moving essays, "On a Certain Blindness in Human Beings," James offers an exploration into prejudice. "We are all afflicted," he writes, by an inability to feel the "the feelings of creatures and people different from ourselves" and to cognize their value as equal to our own (146). But James leans into this human limitation with a surprising force, declaring that its truth "absolutely forbids us to be forward in pronouncing on the meaninglessness and forms of existence other than our own." "Hands off," he commands at the end of this essay, reflecting that the only "superiority" any one person has over anyone else is limited to the "peculiar position in which he stands" (163). James's tone in this piece is as heartfelt as it is urgent. Though James does not mention any particular marginalized group, one can easily see how the "blind" judgements he speaks of could refer to the oppression of the poor, the black, the immigrant, the female, and the queer. Why not also the child?

It is not that the new child-centered psychology has no place in the aesthetic discourses of modernism. Indeed, both recapitulation theory and the Freudian unconscious hold hands with modernist primitivism, for example. But it is the discourse of William James, with its democratic view of complex consciousness, its interest in the mature life, and its concern for a "certain blindness" that limits people from being able to see that the same complexity that resides within them also resides inside of others, that sets the tone for American modernism's relationship to childhood. Just as scholars like Judith Plotz, Alan Richardson, U.C. Knoepflmacher, and Marah Gubar have endeavored to complicate the discourses of childhood that have dominated interpretations of Romantic, Victorian, and golden age literature, this study seeks to move the child in the midst of American modernism out from under the shadows of child-centered psychology and progressivism. Where many look optimistically to the child as a vehicle for hope, inspiration, or renewal, American modernists prove to be far more concerned with developing a pragmatic consciousness about and for the child, a consciousness that is varied and plastic enough to survive the realities of abandonment, despair, prejudice, and war.

At the turn of the twentieth century, there was remarkable momentum behind efforts to turn children inward into the security of enclosed spaces like the garden, the school, the playground, the home, and the laboratory. And, as Steedman illuminates, one of the most successful efforts to save and prolong childhood happened within the interior of the adult mind. Freud's notion of the unconscious, modern notions of nostalgia, and the return of the Edenic child as the "child in the midst" of a postlapsarian society are all iterations of a post-Romantic treatment of childhood that imagined the child's central psychosocial role as being somehow salvific, offering adults healing, reform, spiritual closeness, and artistic beauty. There is no one way that American modernists challenge these discourses of internalized childhood. Indeed, what is perhaps most important is just how many different ways writers like W.E.B. Du Bois, Langston Hughes, Gertrude Stein, Henry James, and Djuna Barnes found to question the ramifications of sanctifying, prolonging, and memorializing childhood.

The Unredemptive Child in the Midst

In the nineteenth century, the Biblical image of "the child set in the midst" enjoyed new popularity, capturing the modern Anglo-American embrace of childhood as a widely beloved and emulable style of being. In Mark (9:35–37) and in Matthew (18:1–3), Christ took "a little child" and "set him in the midst" of his disciples as a reminder and emblem of divinity. In Matthew, Christ says both that "whoso shall receive one such little child in my name receiveth me" and that "Except ye be converted, and become as little children, ye shall not enter into the kingdom of heaven" (qtd. in MacDonald 7). For the popular children's writer and minister, George MacDonald, the lesson of the parable is clear. To be childlike is to be Christlike. In one of his *Unspoken Sermons* that MacDonald titles "The Child in the Midst" (1867), he offers that childhood is a quality accessible to all ages, and it is the *"chosen type"* of heaven (9). Elsewhere MacDonald puts it this way: "He who will be a man, and will not be a child, must—he cannot help himself—become a little man" ("Fantastic" 69).

Though there were a number of competing discourses of childhood in the long nineteenth century, scholars like Judith Plotz, Alan Richardson, and U.C. Knoepflmacher have shown that it was the discourse of an essentialized and glorified childhood, heralded in the Romantic era by poets like Wordsworth and Blake and enhanced in the post-Romantic era by the likes of George MacDonald, Lewis Carroll, and John Ruskin, that increasingly dominated the cultural imaginary of childhood.[4] Wilfrid Meynell and MacDonald each make clear that by the turn of the twentieth century the child in the midst is for many less an actual child than it is an emblem of the child within humanity, the self, the divine, and art. MacDonald insists that "any human being, especially if wretched and woe-begone and outcast" would have done "as well as a child for the purpose" of the parable, but that God "employed" the image of the child "as a manifestation, utterance, and sign of the truth that lay in his childhood, in order that the eyes as well as the ears should be channels to the heart" (9). For Meynell likewise it is important to distinguish that "These are Poems about Children, not for them: gathered together for mature Readers" to give "the Child a new meaning and glory" (i). Meynell's 1892 anthology of Romantic and Victorian poetry uses the title "The Child Set in the Midst by Modern Poets" in part to highlight the role that art has played in "discover[ing] the Child" for the nineteenth century. But discovery is really only the beginning, for the true gift of these poets is not just that they embody a childlike "genius," or even that they use poetry to glorify the child, but that they also succeed in capturing and enshrining the "the child-spirit"—"caught at last and prisoned"—in poetry (vi).

As Judith Plotz observes, "what is most striking about the new embrace of childhood" in the nineteenth century "is the de-contextualizing of the child." For Plotz, what explains the "nineteenth-century idolatry toward the 'Child set in the midst,'" following several religious upheavals and the failure of the French Revolution, is the Romantic child's symbolic placement "beyond the shocks of history." The child grows in symbolic power for all that it enables in these adults, including the promise of social hope without the risk of actual social and political engagement (39). Throughout the nineteenth and well into the twentieth century, this quintessential child is not only predominantly a symbol of Edenic salvation, it is also importantly a symbol for internalization. Meynell and MacDonald each abstract the literal scene from the Bible of the child being set in the midst along two distinct lines. They read childhood as a symbolic quality accessible even to adults, and they read the child's position "in the midst" as a symbolic space of interior preservation. The child is to be embraced, taken in, enshrined, captured, and made central to every layer of spiritual, social, aesthetic, and personal existence.

The "child set in the midst" was the emergent, symbolic forerunner of popular psychology's "inner child," yet its applications were at once much looser and more narrow than this successor.[5] The image of the child in the midst resonated across a range of social, personal, and aesthetic structures, but at the same time, and regardless of context, the tenor it conveyed toward childhood was often limited to reverent optimism. In the postmodern era it became increasingly common to interrogate this child within—to challenge the potential fiction at the root of nostalgic longing. Implicit behind Steedman's and Plotz's accounts of how the Romantic discourse of childhood gains real-life status for adults while paradoxically obscuring the complex and varied lives of actual children is a recognition of the fallibility of cultural memory and internalization.

But this skepticism is not, or is not originally, a postmodern phenomenon. In the same year that Meynell married the figure of the "child set in the midst" to nineteenth-century poetry, Henry James began planning out in his notebooks a story that would invert everything this salvific narrative held dear. The idea is of a child "*divided*" between two divorced parents, since remarried. James reflects:

> Might not something be done with the idea of an odd and particular relation springing up 1st between the child and each of these new parents, 2d between one of the new parents and the other—through the child—over and on account of and by means of the child?...Best of all perhaps would be to make the child a fresh bone of contention, a fresh source of dramatic situations, *du vivant* of the original parents. *Their* indifference throws the new parents, through a common sympathy, together. Thence a 'flirtation,' a love affair between them which produces suspicion, jealousy, a fresh separation, etc.—with the innocent child in the midst. (126–127)

Though James uses words like "fresh" and "innocent," what is original in his schema for the story that will become *What Maisie Knew* (1897) is the irreverent role that he imagines for his child protagonist. Rather than bringing her parents over to the side of her virtue, Maisie is threatened by their efforts to use her as a conduit for their unseemly dramatics. Deployed in this way, Maisie's presence at the center of this society is actually pivotal to its disintegration. Her virtuous presence authorizes many an illegitimate meeting. Her good intentions amplify the messages of cruelty that are naively delivered through her lips. Implicitly, James questions the premise that a child-centered society will be a better society. The "fresh[ness]" that this child brings with her arouses her adult circle to invent new ways of hurting one another (and her) and provides them with new opportunities for parading vice as virtue. In *Maisie*, it is all too apparent that society's uncritical gaze allows the child in the midst to be just as easily appropriated for ill as for good. The child's presumed innocence may be embraced, to be sure, but it may also be exploited; it may be emulated but it may also be counterfeited.

At the other end of the modernist timeline, Djuna Barnes, like James, rewrites the child in the midst as a story of failed redemption in *Nightwood*. This dark novel about a lost and longing queer humanity features two actual (and many artificial) children. Guido and Sylvia, though minor figures, nonetheless make an impression because they show up in such strange places, unconscionably entering into the seductive, jealous, and drunken worlds of Robin Vote and her former, broken-hearted lovers. Guido, the abandoned son of Robin, accompanies his downtrodden and self-medicating father, Felix Volkbein, and the circus-performer Frau Mann on their late night tours of Vienna. "Many cafés," Barnes writes, notice "the child in the midst" of this "odd trio." The only person who does not see the misplaced child is the one person who arguably should. Barnes describes Felix as looking up at the "ceiling" or down at "his hand," actively "trying not to look for what he had always sought, the son of a once great house" (103). Evidently, Felix is more than disappointed in what his son is not, he is also anxious about what his son is: the undeniable end of the Volkbein line. Innocent and unwell, Guido is incapable of being the redemptive child that his father hoped for, but his failure is compounded by his tragic figure which serves as an unbearable reminder that there is no redemption to be had.

Sylvia is similarly invisible in plain sight. However, unlike Guido, it is unclear where Sylvia comes from or to whom she belongs. She could be any child, which allows her, in important respects, to signify childhood itself. When Barnes thrusts this allegory of childhood squarely in the midst of Jenny and Robin's toxic relationship, the effect (especially when viewed in light of the scene with Guido) is a mock reproduction of the salvific scene. Stuck in a moving carriage, crowded with Dr. O'Connor, an English woman, Robin, and Jenny, Sylvia cannot escape from the hurled insults and blows that rain around her:

"Shut up," Robin said... "Shut up, you don't know what you are talking about. You talk all the time and you never know anything. It's such an awful weakness with you. Identifying yourself with God!" [...]

Then Jenny struck Robin, scratching and tearing in hysteria, striking, clutching and crying. Slowly the blood began to run down Robin's cheeks ...

Suddenly the child flung herself down on the seat, face outward, and said in a voice not suitable for a child, because it was controlled with terror: "Let me go! Let me go! Let me go!" (66–67)

To state the obvious, no one is "God[like]" in this strange gathering. The momentum is entirely downward, as it is for all of *Nightwood*. The Dr. is "slumped" down in his seat. Jenny and Robin's bodies end up caving in on each other. Not even the child is immune from the more than earthly gravity of the scene. Rather than evincing any ability to save the adults in her presence, Sylvia clamors for escape. Even the clamor itself is empty as it is matched, not with a move toward the door, but with a movement further and more fully "down" onto the carriage seat.

For modernists the child in the midst is not an ideal, it is a problem. James ironizes the quintessential features of essentialized childhood (innocent, fresh, natural) in order to challenge their pretensions to virtue. Following James, the image of the child in the midst repeats throughout modernist literature as the ironic center of narratives and lives bent toward destruction and despair. To showcase the devolving society of *Nightwood*, Djuna Barnes positions the child of a degenerate line "in the midst" of the novel's "inverts," charlatans, and circus performers (103). To highlight the everyday anxiety of World War II France, Gertrude Stein describes youth not only set in the midst of war but also "carried off from" families and communities, removed from "in their midst" (*Wars* 86). The truest fact of wartime existence for Stein is that "there is a mingling" between "children's lives and grown up lives" (7). In her wartime writings, children die, drown, and disappear with a regular insistence that belies any cultural effort to remove them from the scene of violence. And Virginia Woolf, to capture the problem of an essentialized childhood "lodged... whole and entire" in the adult mind, never compromised or questioned, anticipates the notion of the inner child with its darkest twin. She calls this full, psychological embrace of childhood the "impediment in the centre of...being" ("Lewis Carroll" 82).

Adult-Rearing

Henry James and Djuna Barnes highlight the enormous divide that separates the symbolic child who signifies the eternal possibility of redemption and the conscious child who is burdened by these expectations without the power to meet them. These concerns are complicated for black modernists like W.E.B. Du Bois and Langston Hughes by the knowledge that black children do not even have the opportunity to try to meet the expectations of romantic childhood, and yet they are no less exposed to this ideal as a promise that does not apply to them. The prevalence of racist symbols of black childhood in literature for children motivated many early twentieth-century major Black Renaissance writers like Jessie Fauset, W.E.B. Du Bois, Langston Hughes, Countee Cullen, Arna Bontemps, and Georgia Douglas Johnson to forge a revolutionary brand of children's literature written by and for African Americans. The conscientious steps that these celebrated authors of adult literature took to address a child audience is a tradition that has endured in African-American literature, most notably through the multi-generational work of black women writers, including Gwendolyn Brooks, Alice Walker, Toni Morrison, Nikki Giovani, and bell hooks. Though many in the humanities treat children's literature and adult literature as unrelated species of the same clade, African-American culture has long taken an approach to identity and to art that is deeply concerned with transgenerational questions: questions about how the descendants of slaves can remember and pay homage to their ancestors before them; questions about how to foster feelings of belonging, beauty, and self-worth apart from the images and stories controlled and distributed by the white ruling classes; and questions about how to raise black children with all of the social and political consciousness that is required to live in a society founded on racism with, as Ta-Nehisi Coates writes, "no time for the childhoods of black boys and girls" (25).

Having the courage to be honest with children about the reality of racism in America has a long history in African-American letters. For Coates, who writes *Between the World and Me* as a letter to his 15-year-old son, it is also one of the highest forms of love that one experienced adult can share with one who must, in many respects, also be an adult, though younger and less experienced. Before Coates, James Baldwin writes a letter to his nephew, also 15, in which he moves that those most in need of honesty, which is also love, are the black communities' white "younger brothers," whom blacks must lead out of their "innocence" so that they may "see themselves as they are" and "cease fleeing from reality and begin to change it" (294). And, like Baldwin and Coates, Audre Lorde argues that the urge to shelter the child and extend the naiveté of childhood are powerful temptations that black parents must resist when it comes to raising black children in the United States. In order to survive, Lorde writes, "Black children in america must be raised to be warriors" who can "recognize the enemy's many faces" (75). "One imperfect but useful argument for honesty" between black parents and their children, Lorde asserts, is that "Whatever [is] hidden out of fear [can] be used either against the children or ourselves" (74–75).

And before each of these celebrated writers and thinkers of the twentieth and twenty-first centuries, W.E.B. Du Bois sought at the very "dawning" of the twentieth century to reduce the divide between youth and age in African-American communities (*Souls* 1). In *Darkwater* (1920), Du Bois advises black parents that they "can no longer wholly shield," the child, when to do so is to produce "wayward, disappointed children"; nor should they "realizing this, leave their children to sink or swim in this sea of race prejudice"; but they must rather chart a middle course, "between extremes," characterized by "*frank*, free, guiding explanation" alongside "every step of dawning intelligence" (119–120; emphasis added). Du Bois recognizes the kinds of flight response that any survivor of trauma might feel—to seek an escape (for and through the child) from the realities of racism or to run from the daunting task of remembering and reflecting on those traumas in order to educate black children to face them some day on their own—and seeks to encourage his readers to take a gradual approach. Du Bois wants black parents to be honest and open with their children, but he also wants this honesty to be dosed out over time, in such a way that child and parent both can bear what needs to be heard and what must be said.

Along with Du Bois, Langston Hughes was one of the earliest progenitors of this discourse of adult-rearing, and he was also one of the first African-American authors to write prolifically for children as well as adults. In his autobiography, *The Big Sea*, Hughes repeats no fewer than three times how much he regrets ever having placed his full faith in books, beginning with those he read as a child. Upon entering the second grade, he remembers how he "began to believe in nothing but books and the wonderful world of books…where almost always the mortgage got paid off, the good knights won, and the Alger boy triumphed" (16). The problem for Hughes was that his own life felt far from victorious, and his own family's mortgage "never got paid off" (16). Elsewhere, Hughes draws a similar conclusion that "lyricism" belongs to "another world" of "ivory towers"; it does not belong to him—"poor," "colored," and "stuck in the mud from the beginning" ("My Adventures" 269). The disillusionment that Hughes experienced when he came to realize his deception at the hands of fairy tales, lyric poetry, and rags-to-riches adventures must have been severe, for he relates later in *The Big Sea* how he collected all his books, which were to him "like too much reading all the time when [he] was a kid, like life isn't, as described in romantic prose," and took them aboard a ship bound for Africa, and hurled every single one of them into the sea (97–98). However dramatic this scene is, it is plain that Hughes does not really give up on America, for he soon returns. And he clearly does not give up on books either since he is, somewhat ironically, describing this experience of throwing his books into the sea in a book. What Hughes truly leaves behind at this life juncture is not a set of objects but a particular world view, one that has been authored by white Americans for a white audience. What he realizes is that he, as a black child, had no books that were actually written for him and that he and his family, as a black family in America, never actually had a chance of having a home there.

Like many African-American writers and thinkers, Hughes knew long before most that America really never did believe in the so-called universality of childhood virtue and happiness, and he also knew that children's literature was far from addressing all "children." In "Books and the Negro Child" (1932), Hughes takes up the problem of emerging black consciousness. Black children, he says, are presented with so many images of black "backwardness" in the schools and in children's books that they are not just told that they are inferior; they believe it themselves to be true. In the place of racist representations of black children like Topsy and Sambo, Hughes urges that "America's Negro children are in pressing need of books that will give them back their souls" (51). In so many ways, Hughes answers his own passionate call for a new body of literature designed for black children. In the early 1930s he collaborated with Arna Bontemps on a children's book set in Haiti, called *Popo and Fifina*, and he compiled an assortment of mostly previously published poems for a volume of children's poetry, entitled *The Dream Keeper*. In fact, Hughes composed works for children in every decade of his professional life, beginning with his first publications in *The Brownies' Book* while he was still a senior in high school and ending in the last year of his life with *Black Misery* (1969).

Many of these works represent Hughes's efforts to pull African-American children's literature out of the grip of romanticism and to find forms of address for black children which are both more honest and more useful. In *The Dream Keeper*, for example, Hughes offers a number of lyric, romantic poems for child readers in the self-titled first section of the book. Here, there are poems about the seasons, about "dreams," about "fairies," and "joy." Several of them are among the earliest poems Hughes published in *The Brownies' Book* when he himself may have still believed in the books of his youth and the romantic messages they contained. But each subsequent section of the volume, "Sea Charm," "Dressed Up" and finally "Walkers with the Dawn" introduces the child to another and older stage of experience, suggesting that the book, if read from cover to cover, might advance the consciousness of the child audience toward a fuller awareness of race prejudice in America. Where "Sea Charm" introduces readers to human suffering in other lands, "Dressed Up" brings this suffering home to black women, men, and children in America.

Though reprints, some of these poems take on new life in the context of a black child audience. The poem, "A Black Pierrot," for instance, uses a comic language that not only describes the black man, who, made to wear the costume of the clown, cannot find someone to take his hopes and dreams seriously but which also describes a common persona of childhood. In the first stanza, the black Pierrot reacts to his rejection by creeping "away into the night" which "was black, too." And then, in the second stanza, he responds by weeping "until the red dawn/Dripped blood over the eastern hills" in reflection of his heart that "was bleeding, too." But in the final stanza, the poem deviates from this pattern as the black Pierrot with his "once gay-colored soul" now "[s]hrunken like a balloon without air" goes "forth in the morning/To seek a new brown love" (31).[6] Like the stanzas themselves, each one line longer than the last, the black Pierrot grows and changes throughout the poem. His psychology is clearly far more complex than that which has so misunderstood him. Addressed now to a child audience, whom society also believes to be gay, naïve, laughing, and to-be-laughed at, the reprinted poem suggests a range of abuses experienced by African Americans of all ages.

Some of Hughes's most memorable poems, including "Aunt Sue's Stories," "Mother to Son," "I, Too," and "The Negro Speaks of Rivers," are found in "Walkers with the Dawn." In this last section Hughes addresses his audience, not as the readers of "Fairies" a few sections prior, but as members of a shared history and struggle. Indeed, "fairies" have been unceremoniously ousted from these narratives and replaced, in "Aunt Sue's Stories," with accounts taken not "out of any book at all" but "Right out of her own life" (23). One of Hughes's early revolutionary poems, "I, Too," is another reprinted poem which, like "A Black Pierrot," strikes a radically new chord in this final section of *Dream Keeper*. In the context of a volume for black children, the "darker brother," who must eat at a different table in a different room "when company comes," signifies the feelings of exile known to black children and adults alike. But as with so many of Hughes's poems about dreams kept and deferred, "I, Too" demonstrates how power is built even in the times of greatest vulnerability. Whether it is a black servant or citizen or child, Hughes's ambiguously-aged speaker uses their forced seclusion to "laugh," "eat well," "and grow strong" (46). Whether adult or child, the language of laughter and growth work in either case as tools for biding time, at once for wearing the mask of naïve contentment and for venting the outrage that builds behind it, until the strength of the oppressed catches up with and surpasses that of the oppressor.

Between Du Bois and Hughes, African-American modernism disavowed the venerable child-innocent as a representation of childhood that most assuredly did not represent the experiences of black children and which may not have even represented the dreams and ideals that underprivileged African Americans held for their children. In other words the romantic image of childhood may never have been either a universal reality or a universal dream where African Americans have been concerned. This double-disavowal is suggested in Lorde's *Sister Outsider* (1984) through an integrated reading across two of its essays, "Man Child" and "The Master's Tools Shall Never Dismantle the Master's House." If, as Lorde argues in the former, black children must learn how to struggle with the prejudice that lurks around the corners of youth, while the more privileged have entire worlds (kindergartens, playgrounds, neighborhoods) devoted to their safe-keeping and if, as she argues in the latter, different ends require different means, then it is possible that an alternative emphasis on adult-rearing might assist black Americans toward forms of knowing and strength that are unsupported in visions of Edenic childhood. This is also part of the sentiment that Coates expresses to his son in *Between the World and Me*. He writes that he is "sorry that [he] cannot save [him]—but not that sorry" (107). When the "dreamers," as Coates calls "white" America, are awoken by an unimagined violence, their entire world is shaken. If he had the choice, Coates says, he "would not have [his son] live like them" (107). The reality for Coates is that black Americans cannot afford to sleepwalk through life, but this reality has a survival-value that may be worth the price of the ticket. And in *Souls*, Du Bois recognizes set-back after set-back in the freedman's quest for freedom but he hails the spirit of "seeking" and "striving" in the face of so much disappointment as a black "oasis" in the midst of a white "desert" that has, Du Bois suggests, starved its soul for short-term gain (11).

Anti-Nostalgia

Society's increasing neglect of the negative range of experiences and features of youth is evidenced in how much the concept of nostalgia changed once it became attached to childhood. Nostalgia was originally conceived by Johannes Hofer as a diagnosis for the depressed soldier whose homesickness was so acute that it could lead to death if left untreated. In the early nineteenth century, it was also used to diagnose Africans who "threw themselves into the sea, locked in each other's arms" rather than endure the middle passage and a lifetime of slavery to follow (*Foreign Slave Trade* 83–84). The Greek roots *algos*, signifying suffering or pain, and *nostos*, signifying a homecoming, illuminate nostalgia's medical intent to encapsulate both the disease and its cure. The treatment for home sickness was a return home or to allot more time spent at home between deployments. There are a number of important differences between this largely eighteenth-century view of nostalgia and the concept's more modern permutations. What was originally conceived as an illness of soldiers, exiles, and slaves has, according to Svetlana Boym expanded into an "incurable modern condition" (xiv). Nostalgia is no longer a problem of the few who have been physically removed from a physical place; it is now a widely accepted byproduct of growing older. Where nostalgia used to identify a longing for a place, Boym explains, it now signifies "a yearning for a different time—the time of our childhood, the slower rhythms of our dreams" (xv). Robert Hemmings's work on the golden age of children's literature sums up the historical shift in this way: "By the late eighteenth century… the nostalgic yearns not so poignantly to return to the place of one's childhood—a treatment favored by Hofer—but to childhood itself" (55). The only cure for nostalgia throughout much of the eighteenth century was a physical return home, a treatment that was all too often impossible to achieve, particularly for those who had been wrenched or banished from their homelands to begin with. With nostalgia's attachment to childhood, loss became a sensation that almost anyone could experience, and because childhood had also become an internalized phenomenon, nostalgic relief, however fleeting, was only a memory away.

Nostalgia, in its pathological and normative forms, conveys the desire for and belief in the restorative powers of an originary past. The homesick soldier and the modern adult are rehabilitated by the space and time of childhood. Interestingly, contemporary scholars of the nostalgic condition almost universally convey an opposite belief—that such a return is not only impossible but that the very idea of a return is a sign without a referent. Aaron Santesso illuminates the idea of an idyllic past as one that draws less on personal, lived experience than on representations of the past, imaginative and aesthetic. Nostalgia, Santesso explains, "is not a desire for the past per se...rather, it is a longing for objects that are idealized, impersonal, and unattainable. A work may look to the past; it is only truly nostalgic if that past is idealized" (16). Though nostalgia may have begun as a medical idea, Santesso argues that it "matured as a literary device" (15). If there is a fictional component to nostalgia, then it is even more troubling that this fiction appears pervasively in the stories, fables, and fairy tales of children's literature. Echoing Santesso's discussion of nostalgia in adult fiction, Hemmings writes that "Children's books from the golden age are nostalgic also in their conspicuous construction of childhood as a personal golden age, rich in retrospective longing for a past not as it was, but as it might only have been" (57).

African-American writers, like Langston Hughes, were not alone in feeling as though the romance of childhood for children set many young readers up for grave disappointments later in life. Many of modernism's marginalized speakers—including the black, the female, and the queer—describe similar experiences of disillusionment. Djuna Barnes's queer anti-hero, Matthew O'Connor, expresses the feeling that he, like all of *Nightwood*'s underworld characters, has been "impaled" on the broken promises of the fairy tales he read as a child (114). Similarly, in an essay on Lewis Carroll, Virginia Woolf wonders about what the Rev. C. L. Dodgson had to give up in order to be the author of *Alice's Adventures in Wonderland*. She refers to the child within Carroll as an "impediment in the centre of his being" that "starved the mature man of nourishment" ("Lewis Carroll" 81–82). While Woolf is grateful for the gift of *Alice*, she seems aware that the gift has come at a price for its author. Implicitly, Woolf chooses to value maturity as the center of adult being over nostalgic memories of a prior age (in both senses of the word). In fact, in Woolf's depiction, the child within seems less like a wonderland and more like a parasitic tapeworm, "starv[ing] the mature man of nourishment."

Like Hughes, Barnes, and Woolf, Gertrude Stein describes the hypocrisies of Edenic childhood as a signature threat to twentieth-century progress. Indeed, Stein's attention to this problem, which distinguishes much of her writings from 1934 until her death in 1945, may be more extensive than that of any other American modernist. In *Wars I Have Seen* (1945), written at the height of the Second World War, Stein insists with an epic sensibility that the real target of that war is a Romantic ideology which Stein identifies as belonging to the nineteenth century and to childhood. "All" of what the nineteenth century stood for, Stein writes, was "between babyhood and fourteen," and she repeats, "It was the nineteenth century between babyhood and fourteen, and the nineteenth century dies hard" (16). Analogizing the years of a century with the first years of a life makes sense as a way of highlighting the important role that childhood played at nearly every level of nineteenth-century society, and it also makes sense given the fact that Stein herself came of age in nineteenth-century America before moving to Paris in 1903. But Stein does not just insist on how "hard" the death of the nineteenth century is, she also insists on taking credit for her part in killing it. Over and over again in *Wars I Have Seen*, Stein describes her attempts "to kill" the nineteenth century—"to kill it dead, quite like a gangster with a …tommy gun" (91), she says at one point; to render it "stone dead" (96) in another; or to kill it "dead as a doornail" in yet another (104).

Like being born in the wrong body, Stein suggests that being born in the wrong century had a significant impact on how early modernists conceived of themselves and the movement they sought to inspire and create. "I belong to the generation," she writes, "who born in the nineteenth century spent all the early part of my life in escaping from it, and the rest of it in being the twentieth century yes of course" (*Wars* 80). Once more, Stein conjoins centuries with age and with identity. Stein does not say that she spent the rest of her life being *in* the twentieth century; she says she spent her life after childhood "*being* the twentieth century" (emphasis added). Just as Stein has already equated the nineteenth century with childhood ("from babyhood to 14"), here the twentieth century is affirmed as the adult age. However, in light of Stein's long struggle throughout *Wars I Have Seen* to "exterminate" the century of her birth, the unequivocal "yes of course" victory speech that she makes on behalf of the twentieth century seems more like conceit than truth. In reality, it seems as though

Stein's disillusionment with her childhood and with its century came later in life. It was not until 1934 that Stein, who had called Paris home for 31 years, revisited her childhood home in Oakland, California and discovered that "there [was] no there there" (*Everybody's Autobiography* 298).

What Stein saw, or did not see, on this visit worried her and set her to grappling with her ideas about identity and its relationship to childhood for many years to come. As she stands at the site of her childhood home, Stein relies intensely on the nursery rhymes and lessons from childhood to make sense of her impressions:

> … the house the big house and the big garden and the eucalyptus trees and the rose hedge naturally were not any longer existing, what was the use, if I had been I then my little dog would know me but if I had not been I then that place would not be the place that I could see, I did not like the feeling… If I remember what I remember then why do I remember that. I did remember that but it did look like that and so I did not remember that and if it did not look like that then I did not remember that. What was the use. (300)

The nursery rhyme that Stein generously invokes here and elsewhere in her work of this period is the poem, titled "The Old Woman and the Pedlar." The poem tells the story of an old woman who is unwittingly attacked on her way home from the town market. After selling her wares at the market, the old woman begins the walk home but falls asleep somewhere by the side of the road before she arrives. While asleep, a peddler steals upon her and commences, in the words of the rhyme, to "cut her petticoats all round about…up to the knees." When the woman awakes, she "shiver[s]" and "shake[s]," words that suggest a visceral reaction to the cold as well as an emotional response to the assault (potentially sexual) on her person.

What follows, in the Mother Goose, as for Stein, is an identity crisis. The woman in the poem does not recognize herself much as Stein does not recognize her childhood home. The former determines that her canine companion can be a trusted judge in the matter. If she is still herself, then her little dog will know her. That he does not know her, that he sounds the alarm upon her approach, implies far more than it says—that some tragic transformation, more drastic than the mere cutting of cloth, has taken place. For Stein too the "naturally" no "longer existing" surface elements of home—of "rose hedge" and trees—seem to signify more than meets the eye. That these manifest changes may be suggestive of latent transformations, that home might not be home any longer, and indeed the sheer uncertainty of knowing whether one's memory of home was ever connected to anything actually existing, leads Stein to ask a most depressive question: "what is the use"?

Memory is notoriously unreliable in the postmodernist context, but for Stein in the 1930s, this realization strikes an epiphanic chord. Like many nostalgics, Mother Goose's protagonist has a traumatic experience away from home and hopes, like all nostalgics, that the return home will serve as a cure. That the return home fails to provide comfort in this case makes this recollection for Stein all the more apt. As with the old woman, the return home, which is also for Stein a return to childhood, becomes a gateway, ironically, to heightened anxiety. Stein attempts the application of the old mantra "if I had been I then my little dog would know me but if I had not been I then that place would not be the place that I could see ..." and reports as the result that she does "not like the feeling." As with the old woman whose dog "began to bark" and "so she began to cry, 'Lauk a mercy on me, this is none of I!'" Stein's inability to match the home of her present perception with the image preserved in her mind makes her question the validity as well as the utility of anything internalized through memory, including one's own sense of being. Elsewhere in *Everybody's Autobiography*, Stein makes the point succinctly: "And identity is funny being yourself is funny as you are never yourself to yourself except as you remember yourself and then of course you do not believe yourself...why should you, you know so well so very well that it is not yourself" (70).

For Stein, the child within is not simply a past self, lost or inaccessible, it also almost certainly a fictitious self, impossible to be felt, incapable of being believed. Identity is neither "funny" in the humorous sense nor is it simply strange; rather it is ironically unreal, a farce, a joke. It is symbolically significant that when Stein returns to Oakland she remembers not (or not just) her childhood, but she writes that she straightaway "remembered the Mother Goose." The Mother Goose stands in for her childhood and for her home as only a fictional narrative can. In mapping the story of her past self to the template of children's narrative, Stein suggests that these stories are analogous in substance as well as form. In other words, the child within may well be a children's narrative; that is, it may be a fairy tale or fantasy perspective of the past and of the self, nostalgically reified as the purest, most authentic version of both.

In seeking to work against these unreal and unrealizable memories of childhood, Stein develops an anti-nostalgic stance that repositions the beginning of life after the end of youth. In the place of America's long love-affair with innocence and youth, Stein advocates a substitution. Instead of the Edenic child, Stein recommends the internalization of human suffering as America's new psychological center. At the end of the Second World War, Stein evinces a particular hope for this exchange. When Stein meets the American soldiers who have helped to defeat Germany and to end the war, she feels encouraged by all that they have witnessed:

> A good many of the boys begin to know what the words imprisoned and persecution mean, when they see the millions in prison, imprisoned for years, persecuted for years, they begin to realize what minorities in a country are bound to lead to, to persecution and to a sense of imprisonment. When these American boys see all the instability of a whole continent imprisoned as the whole of Europe has been in prison, well somehow it does something to them, of course it does…yes they will go on, innocence and a kind heart, it worries them, they are troubled, so am I, life will begin at 30 for them, so really did mine. ("The New Hope" 145)

The worry and anxiety that have plagued Stein since the mid 1930s have become the core attributes of this post-30 subjectivity. The innocence that Stein references here is best described as a rehabilitated innocence, little resembling its ancient or modern predecessors. Stein's rehabilitated innocence is not the innocence of unknowing, of pure joy, of sheltered virtue, of immunity from wrong, or even of youth. On the contrary, these innocents are thirty-somethings, soldiers embroiled in violence, and they are Americans who are beginning to realize their and their nation's guilt in a similar system of oppression. Those who are familiar with Genesis will be struck by the image of paradise lost. In the place of Edenic innocence, Stein posits wartime consciousness as the psychological space where "Life will begin." Knowledge of evil is crucial to this new beginning. The sheltered happiness and virtue quintessential to popular nineteenth-century notions of childhood are replaced in Stein's aged-down imaginary by an anxiety and worry wrought by so much knowledge and so much exposure to suffering.

Some have described Stein's late modernist interest in child language as evidence that her writings of this period are "nostalgic" (Olson 113) or have described her criticism of Rooseveltian New Deal politics as evidence of "her nostalgia for individualism" (Bridgman 276). In these instances, "nostalgia" serves as a kind of diagnosis that has the effect of dismissing Stein's interest in childhood and children's narratives and of diminishing her politics. In my reading, and we may look to the passage just cited from "The New Hope," Stein's efforts to rescript the first 30 years of life are pointedly anti-nostalgic because they are anti-youth. Stein's extensive work of this later period challenges nostalgia's longing for a return to childhood as to a more perfect past. For Stein, this past is not the source of healing; it is the source of illness. For Stein it is not the war that hurts the soldier it is the dream that precedes the war that causes so much pain. The list of features Stein uses to describe American life before the Second World War—"easy wars, easy victories, easy success, easy money, easy eating and easy drinking and easy madly running around and easy publicity, easy everything"—captures the immaturity of a nation in denial of and out of touch with the suffering that reigns in the lives of so many others (143). By contrast, Stein hopes that the realization of suffering and imprisonment brought to light by the Second World War may lead America to come to terms with its own founding fairy tales of exceptionalism, democracy, and freedom. One cannot feel nostalgia for a past that is admittedly shameful.

Notes

1. Freud's theoretical assertions linking the unconscious to childhood were in fact highly indebted to German Romanticism. See George Makari's chapter "City of Mirrors, City of Dreams" in his *Revolution in Mind*.
2. Carol Gilligan, in her groundbreaking study *In a Different Voice*, argued that, beginning with Freud, developmental psychology throughout most of the twentieth century widely equated normative child development with male development.
3. James J. Heckman coined the phrase "noncognitive skills" to describe these attributes of success. See "The Importance of Noncognitive Skills: Lessons from the GED Testing Program."
4. See Plotz, *Romanticism and the Vocation of Childhood*, Richardson, "Romanticism and the End of Childhood," and Knoepflmacher, *Ventures into Childland*.
5. The "inner child" movement, which focuses therapeutic practice on righting the wrongs suffered in childhood as the singularly most important path to healing, was arguably most clearly articulated by Charles Whitfield and John Bradshaw in the second half of the twentieth century.
6. Unless otherwise specified, quotations of Hughes's poems come from *The Collected Poems of Langston Hughes*, edited by Arnold Rampersad and published by Random House.

CHAPTER 3

The "*Partagé* Child" and the Emergence of the Modernist Novel in Henry James's *What Maisie Knew*

"Here you are taking care of a poor little boy with one arm, and there you are sinking a ship with the other. It can't be like you."

"Ah! But which is me? I can't be two mes, you know."

"No. Nobody can be two mes."...

"Which me do you know?"

"The kindest, goodest, best me in the world," answered Diamond, clinging to North Wind....

"And you are sure there can't be two mes?"

"Yes."

"Then the me you don't know must be the same as the me you do know—else there would be two mes."

—George MacDonald, *At the Back of the North Wind* (1871), 67–68

"The little girl [was] disposed of in a manner worthy of the judgement-seat of Solomon. She was divided in two and the portions tossed impartially to

---

An earlier version of this chapter originally appeared as an article, Phillips, Mason. "The 'Partagé Child' and the Emergence of the Modernist Novel in *What Maisie Knew*." *The Henry James Review* 31:2 (2010), 95–110. © 2010 The Johns Hopkins University Press.

the disputants....This was odd justice in the eyes of those who still blinked in the fierce light projected from the tribunal—a light in which neither parent figured in the least as a happy example to youth and innocence."

—Henry James, *What Maisie Knew* (1897), 35

The universal and the simple have often been hailed as the special provinces of childhood. Writing in the post-Romantic era, beloved children's book author and minister George MacDonald communicates the logical impossibility of a divided self for his child readers. In this religious allegory, the premise that allows the boy protagonist, Diamond, to reconcile apparent tragedy with the fundamental goodness of God (the North Wind) is the certainty that there "can't be two mes" (67). Faced with two possible interpretations of the all-mighty—one merciless and the other kind—Diamond, who is himself ill and dying, is encouraged to discard his darker vision of life (and death) in favor of eternal brightness and light. MacDonald's faith in the net-good of the universe is nested in his analogous faith in the net-good of the child. His faith in a unified divinity is likewise perfectly suited for the imaginatively unified consciousness of its archetypal child purveyor.

Like MacDonald, King Solomon—millennia prior—operates on the presumption that the good, the undivided, and the child are kindred concepts. King Solomon can risk the physical division of the contested child because he can be assured of that act's impossibility. The true mother, he anticipates, will put love of child over victory in battle, will prove her rightful possession of the child through her ability to give that child up. The allusion to Solomon at the opening of Henry James's *What Maisie Knew* (1897) is a useful touchstone for James on multiple fronts. Most obviously, it highlights just how terrible Maisie's parents are. Unlike the true mother in the Biblical account who will sacrifice anything for the well-being of her child, Ida and Beale Farange readily place their daughter on the chopping block. Under the terms of her parents' divorce, Maisie is decreed to spend six horrible, embattled months in rotation with each parent. Less obviously, the allusion to Solomon, by its very ancientness, also stresses the role that deeply held cultural beliefs, both about childhood and parenthood, will play in the novel's efforts to reimagine each of these identities within the changing context of twentieth-century modernity. To the witnesses who can only "blink" in astonishment at the "odd justice" of the Faranges' divorce proceeding, these beliefs-of-old seem to have flown out-the-window where Maisie is concerned, but, in fact, they will prove to haunt her life with her parents in ways even more devastating than this initial decree. Finally, and most surprisingly, the case of the divided child takes a twisted turn in James's estimation of her. Rather than sharing the view that the prospect of a child divided is a cause for sorrow, James suggests that there may be some cause to celebrate the prospect, not just for all of the fodder that it provides the emergently modernist writer but also for the ways that it might advance society beyond a potentially unhealthy attachment to a vision of childhood more imaginary than real.

Unlike at least one of her literary precursors (MacDonald's Diamond) Maisie is not encouraged to reconcile the possibility of twoness. Rather, James writes of her that she, as ally and enemy in either parent's deeply embittered camp, develops the "art of not thinking singly" (176). On the one hand, classifying Maisie's ability to compartmentalize as an "art" implies that this kind of complex consciousness is neither an innate nor universal feature of childhood. It is a skill honed and crafted over time. On the other hand, the entire phrase "the art of not thinking singly" transforms Maisie's development of a double consciousness, in every way the equal of her conflicted circumstances, into an achievement worthy of praise. Indeed, what James early emphasized as the "*divided*" quality of his child protagonist, he later endeared in translation, re-characterizing Maisie in his notebooks as "the *partagé* child" (126; 134). In the French, Maisie's division is at once emphasized, and it is made intimate. It is a marked signal of the growing familiarity not only between author and subject but between the external event (i.e., the act of dividing) and the internal child. Where "*divided*" had described Maisie, "the *partagé* child" now comes much closer to actually naming her. Indeed, the name James actually settled on, Maisie, suggests the extent to which her identity has become synonymous with a partitioned, "maze"-like psychology (Shuttleworth 328).

Even though James posits a unified, universal child as a counter-image for Maisie, his esteem for Maisie's "art" suggests that her truer precursors may be what Marah Gubar has termed the "artful dodgers" of so-called golden age children's literature. For many, what defines this period is its presumed interest in sustaining exactly the kind of quintessentially Romantic child that Maisie is not. But Gubar shows that writers like J.M. Barrie, Lewis Carroll, Edith Nesbit, and Frances Hodgson Burnett were far more ambivalent about Romantic ideologies of childhood innocence than scholars have given them credit for. Like many of their contemporaries, these writers, at times, share a certain anxiety about childhood precocity, and yet at other times their characters are able to negotiate the challenges that life throws at them largely because they are precocious, because they are "capable of working and playing alongside adults" (Gubar 35). Like Carroll's Alice, Barrie's Peter Pan, and Nesbit's Bastable children, Maisie is a precocious child protagonist who finds creative ways to weather the storm of (her) childhood. Many American modernists owe more than their critics have liked to admit to the subversive designs of children's literature, and children's literature likewise owes a debt to the experimental scope and swagger of modernism. What really makes *What Maisie Knew* the watershed text that it is for twentieth-century literature is the way that it lifts the unconventional child protagonist out of the subversive world of children's literature and sets her down in the middle of a more overtly abrasive modernist universe. The ramifications of this new combination are striking. Not only does James push this child protagonist to the limits of unconventionality but in doing so he also pushes the novel to the limits of representation. While *Maisie* might have taken root in James's mind as an interesting idea for a provocative story, the novel becomes much more than this. It becomes a scathing critique of society's preoccupations with an unreal child figure, and it becomes a narrative petri dish for rethinking literature's own relationship to childhood.

The "Extraordinary 'Ironic Center'" of Maisie Farange

In 1895, having tried and failed for five years to achieve success on the stage, Henry James set his sights on a new method and a new novel, one which sought to merge the "scenic" method he had recently mastered as a playwright with the genre in which he had long since made a name for himself (Edel 111–112). Most directly, his inspiration for *Maisie* came from a story he overheard at a dinner with the Bryces in 1892, an apparent real life account of a child who "was *divided* by its parents in consequence of their being divorced." James describes being struck not only by the court's decision that the child "was to spend its time equally with each—that is alternately" but also by the effects of renewed marriages on both sides (*Notebooks* 126). Indirectly, James recounts in *A Small Boy and Others* (1913) an "epoch-making" event from his own childhood when he first learned the value of "scenes." At the center of the memory is his child cousin, Marie. Having traveled unhappily to Albany with his father on news of grave family illness, James watches as his uncle Augustus "expressed the strong opinion that Marie should go to bed," expressed it James perceives in hindsight with "the casual cursory humour" that was to empty it of authority if not style. Marie's response, unthinkable to James at that point in his young life, is an adamant refusal. What follows is something of a blur of retaliations, a "visible commotion," propelling Marie into her mother's arms "as for refuge," her mother refusing and imploring instead: "Come now, my dear; don't make a scene—I *insist* on your not making a scene!" As James tells it, "That was all the witchcraft the occasion used, but the note was none the less epoch-making. The expression, so vivid, so portentous, was one I had never heard…it told me so much about life. Life at these intensities clearly became 'scenes'; but the great thing, the immense illumination, was that we could make them or not as we chose" (106–107). Part of the 'immensity' of the illumination, however, is not simply that "we," or people in general, have the power to make or not make scenes but that the child in particular, a child of James's own age, "could make them or not as [*she*] chose." So much seems to depend upon the child being just so that the slightest infraction from her, a mere refusal to go to bed when told, has the ability to throw a moment into dramatic relief, to reduce her parents to uncontrolled anger and beseechment. From another angle, the child, from the sheer weight of the expectations heaped upon her, has actually an immense power. The slightest move from her to one side or the other of the line of her conventional demarcation and all order, all propriety, threatens to collapse.

Maisie, like Marie, becomes an "extraordinary 'ironic center'" for James. From the original premise of the child divided and the parents remarried, James imagines her as the center and source for dramatic complications (Preface 29). He wonders:

> Might not something be done with the idea of an odd and particular relation springing up 1st between the child and each of these new parents, 2d between one of the new parents and the other—through the child—over and on account of and by means of the child? […] Best of all perhaps would be to make the child a fresh bone of contention, a fresh source of dramatic situations, *du vivant* of the original parents. *Their* indifference throws the new parents, through a common sympathy, together. Thence a 'flirtation,' a

love affair between them which produces suspicion, jealousy, a fresh separation, etc.—with the innocent child in the midst. (*Notebooks* 126–127)

Maisie represents for James the singular and remarkable exception to the rule of symmetry that governs the narrative's larger design. In fact, he imagines her as the means for new, insidious combinations, otherwise impossible. Through her, governess and father are united. Through her, this same governess turned stepmother and Maisie's equally new stepfather meet and have a legitimate excuse to meet again. She becomes a lure and a decoy for many of her mother's adulterous suitors. And she is a source of amusement all around, at least as much is true initially. Maisie is the center that holds all of these balanced and competing extremities together. And she is the intermediary through which they communicate, connect, and of course do battle.

But Maisie is no ordinary center, no ordinary go-between, epitomizing as she does the precise opposite of that which she connects, divides, and mediates. In addition to finding herself torn between the opposing principles of parents, step-parents, and competing governesses, Maisie is also herself an opposing, ironic figure. In the preface, James expands on the idea:

> To live with all intensity and perplexity and felicity in its terribly mixed little world would thus be the part of my interesting small mortal; bringing people together who would be at least more correctly separate; keeping people separate who would be at least more correctly together; flourishing, to a degree, at the cost of many conventions and proprieties, even decencies, really keeping the torch of virtue alive in an air tending infinitely to smother it. (25–26)

Maisie's virtues are of an unconscious sort. Little more than her presence is required to unravel the superficial virtues of society and family, those of "correct[ness]," "propriety," "convention," and "decenc[y]." At every turn, James imagines her, like his cousin Marie before her, effortlessly performing an intense irony, lighting upon society's (and the reader's) most trained expectations and turning them, in the most offhand, matter-of-fact way, completely inside out. In other words, the irony carries through at every level, from the outcome, to the method, to the agent. As the bearer of indecency (which, true to his ironic design, James reads as virtue), Maisie is herself the most ironic of ironies in the novel.

Not surprisingly, these facets of Maisie's character, when noted by readers in James's time, were the subject of intense disapproval. Reviewers widely criticized the novel for its immorality. One fan of Henry James's earlier fiction is appalled by the erotic undertones: "*What Maisie Knew* is of a quality incredible in a writer whose work has heretofore been, morally, beyond reproach. In what it says, still more in what it suggests, it ranks, except for a terrible underlying dullness, with the worst schools of French fiction."[1] In the same vein, A *New York Times* reviewer calls Maisie a "small monster," repeating the preferred insult that Maisie's parents hurl at her throughout the book itself.[2] There are some exceptions to this general rebuke of *Maisie* as an immoral novel. One reviewer insists that Maisie's mind remains "unsullied" despite the depravity that surrounds her.[3] James's friend and ally, William Dean Howells, also came to his aid and defended James's later work, including *Maisie*, against readerly "enmity," which he attributed, by and large, to female readers (126).

Despite the strong feelings on both sides of the issue of James's new novel, in each of them *Maisie*'s redemption or disgrace depends upon the innocence of its central character. Though no reader would profess to desire either the unhappiness or demise of the child, both might be preferred to her unthinkable ability to "flourish" in ironic proportion to the crumbling moral foundation of her surrounding social order (Preface 25). And yet, James insists not only that Maisie's parents "both live" but that she thrives "in [their] midst" (*Notebooks* 134; 127). In truth, Maisie flourishes not through innocence or evil but through irony. Her interiority thrives by not conforming to what her parents believe the child mind is or ought to be. At first, Beale and Ida each view their daughter's consciousness as a means through which to punish each other. She becomes, for them, "a messenger of insult" (43). James writes of them first that Maisie is for them "a ready vessel," a "deep little porcelain cup in which biting acids could be mixed" (36) and later that "The evil they had the gift of thinking or pretending to think of each other they poured into her little gravely-gazing soul as into a boundless receptacle" (42). The "ready vessel," the crucible, and the "boundless receptacle" all figure as little more than a blank slate given three-dimensional form. They imagine a child with an interior, but that interior is perfectly empty, perfectly porous, and perfectly passive. It is theirs to fill, to manipulate, to corrupt, and to cull as they choose. It is an interior conceived in self-defeat, being not the property of its child host but the property of her parents.[4]

For Maisie's parents, both original and new, the hollowed child is never far from the child dehumanized.[5] Early on, Maisie observes of the various men she encounters that "all of them thought it funny to call her by names having no resemblance to her own" and of the various women that they "addressed her as 'You poor pet' and scarcely touched her even to kiss her" (57). Of these myriad inhuman appellations, Maisie is most frequently called "monster" (74; 105; 154), but she is also referred to as "you little donkey' (53), as "you little horror" (177), and as "a dreadful dismal deplorable little thing" (178). In retrospect of these multiple repeated attempts to dehumanize Maisie, Ida's early pronouncement "Poor little monkey!" which served as the "epitaph for the tomb of Maisie's childhood," may have new meaning (36). On the one hand, it may suggest that such epithets about childhood are partly responsible for the death of childhood; on the other hand, it reinforces the sense that Maisie may well have been fortunate to bury her childhood if such is the inferior-feeling stuff that it was meant to be made of.

Thankfully, Maisie's parents and the notions of childhood that they project onto their daughter are consistently undermined by the narrative and by Maisie's role within it. As Maisie's parents attempt to monstrify Maisie, they are themselves narratologically transmogrified. The narrative intensely follows, for instance, Beale's teeth, always prominent and always "such a picture of appetite," (159) as well as Ida's "huge painted eyes," similarly phantasmagoric, like "Japanese Lanterns swung under festal arches" (124). Together with their big eyes and their big teeth, Maisie's parents form an unmistakable resemblance to the wolf in "Little Red Riding Hood," except in this case they are truly her parents; they are her parents, and they are the wolf in bed. The narrative battles with the Faranges over how best to describe Maisie's interiority in an earlier instance as well. Their efforts to pour their hatred for one another into Maisie, "as into a boundless receptacle," fail in part because they misidentify their target. The "as" tells the reader that the boundless receptacle is what they mistake Maisie for and as such probably conveys more about them than it does about her. Indeed, in the same sentence, the narrative offers Maisie's "gravely-gazing soul" as a deeply human counterweight to the metallic void. Though Maisie does not speak, she yet sees "too much" (42–43).

Although Maisie's parents succeed in using her as "a messenger of insult," they fail in their larger aim of converting her to their respective enemy camps. Her parents conclude that "either from extreme cunning or from extreme stupidity, [Maisie] appeared not to take things in" when taking things in is precisely what children are renowned for (43). The white paper of the eighteenth century was believed to so readily absorb the ink of life that Sir Roger L'Estrange opened his edition of Aesop's Fables with the warning that "Children *are but* Blank Paper, *ready Indifferently for any Impression, Good or Bad (for they take All upon Credit) and it is much in the Power of the first Comer, to Write Saint, or Devil upon't, which of the Two He pleases*" (ii). L'Estrange's concern for the easy and lasting impressionability of childhood is echoed in the nineteenth century where, as Gillian Brown illustrates, one can see an "oscillat[ion] between admiration for and anxiety about children's absorptions" (20). The concern of Maisie's parents, therefore, that "she appeared not to take...in" their improprieties underscores theirs as a parental status antithetical to parenthood (43).

They are, of course, also partially mistaken. Maisie, we later find out, has apparently been taking everything in but on a temporary basis only. From ages six through eight, Maisie lives entirely for and within whichever household chooses to claim her. With "that lively sense of the immediate which is the very air of a child's mind," James writes, "the past, on each occasion, became for her as indistinct as the future." In effect, Maisie's is a mutable childhood. Moved as she is from place to place, hers is an interior which keeps pace with the back and forth, back and forth between her parents. When it comes to her parents' evil messages, hers is not a boundless receptacle but a temporary post box. For two years, Maisie "faithfully reports" (absent full understanding) the "missive[s]" of her "beastly papa" to her "horrid pig" of a mother and vice versa; these drop "into her memory with the dry rattle of a letter falling into a pillar-box" where they are "as part of the contents of a well-stuffed post-bag, delivered in due course at the right address." Whether as "messenger" or as the "little feathered shuttlecock they could fiercely keep flying between them," Maisie's early life is very nearly airborne, and her sense of interiority is similarly transitional: everything passes through her but nothing sticks (*Maisie* 42).

Maisie's Method

When things do begin to settle in Maisie's mind, her former unconscious ability to alternate her psychology completely between first one household and then the other gives way to a series of more conscious methods for psychologically containing the divided reality of her existence. What starts to recur in Maisie's mind, time and time again, is an image of home as a "domestic labyrinth" (90). Maisie begins to perceive that hers is a world full of the unknown, the mysterious, and the clandestine. Using the interior architecture of the domestic world that she knows so well, Maisie now imagines that life is "like a long, long corridor with rows of closed doors." "Everything," she concludes, "had something behind it" (54). In place of openness and intimacy, Maisie's own interiority models itself on these spaces of domestic secrecy. In the "childish dusk" of her mind, Maisie finds a "dim closet" where "images and echoes" are stored in "the high drawers, like games she wasn't yet big enough to play" (41). And with her doll, Lisette, Maisie's own games are "lessons" in secrecy. In the "darkness," Maisie seeks to reproduce upon her doll the "impression" of her mother, "of having mysteries in her life…of shading off, like her mother, into the unknowable" (55). Though Maisie gains little of use from her parents in general, she does learn early on from them that the dependent state of childhood is a disempowered one. Thus, in play, she casts her doll Lisette in her own role, as the unknowing child, and claims for herself Ida's role, as the unknowable mother. As important, Maisie's play reveals that she has actually learned that there are two pathways to power which are often unavailable to children. The first is age; the second is secrecy. In fact, Maisie claims power over her doll not by pretending to be older but by pretending to be "mysteri[ous]" and "unknowable" like her mother.

James pushes the point to an early climax, conferring on Maisie the necessity for an interiority which is actively, defiantly opaque. After two years of divided existence, Maisie experiences a sudden "new feeling… of danger," a realization that she has been deployed as "a messenger of insult…that everything was bad because she had been employed to make it so" (43). Maisie's sense of her own subjectivity does not emerge as a matter of developmental course. It springs up in her as a matter of survival. Faced with this threat that she has been used for ill, the "new remedy that [rises] to meet it" is none other than the "idea of an inner self," an inner self synonymous with "concealment." And from that moment:

> Her parted lips locked themselves with the determination to be employed no longer. She would forget everything, she would repeat nothing, and when, as a tribute to the successful application of her system, she began to be called a little idiot, she tasted a pleasure new and keen. When therefore, as she grew older, her parents in turn announced before her that she had grown shockingly dull, it was not from any real contraction of her little stream of life. She spoiled their fun, but she practically added to her own." (43)

Maisie claims for herself an interiority not reserved for children. She closes off porous entry by "lock[ing]" her previously "parted lips"; she rejects passivity with her "*determination* to be employed no longer"; and she defies an empty ideal by embracing its persona—acting the "idiot" to conceal her "concealment." Again, Maisie's parents express the conventions as to what their daughter and all daughters should be. Maisie's "accomplishment" of "keep[ing] [her] thoughts to [herself]" becomes "just the source of her mother's irritation." Mrs. Farange, "liking as she did, for her own part, a child to be simple and confiding" is faced with a child anomaly of opacity, gravity, and silence (45).

The idea that children are or should be "simple and confiding" sounds strange coming from this most unmotherly of mothers because it arguably represents the collective desire that many, far more competent, parents have for their children. In Maisie's precocity, James implicitly offers a challenge to the Romantic ideals of childhood immaturity circulating in nineteenth- and twentieth-century society. But in making characters like Ida and Beale Farange the mouthpieces for these ideals, James appears to ridicule much of mainstream adult society, including his adult readership. As Maisie defies the gold standard of childhood immaturity, her parents represent outlandish caricatures of these same conventions. The word "game" appears no fewer than 25 times in the novel, and only rarely does it apply directly to Maisie. Rather, it typically identifies the sinister amusements and strategies of Maisie's parents and of Mrs. Beale. So accustomed to the "frolic menace" of adult games (53), of being played back and forth between her parents like the "little feathered shuttlecock" (42), or of being the center of a "frightening game," a flirtatious "merry little scrimmage" between father and governess (53), Maisie "from her earliest childhood, had built up in her the belief that the grown-up time was the time of real amusement" (69).

In these hyperbolized adult-child interactions, James suggests a full-blown condemnation of immaturity at every age. There is something in the idealized immaturity of childhood that allows the adults in the novel to act like children. In contrast to "these persons," who are, Maisie "disconcerting[ly]" discovers, "not of the age they ought to be," Maisie is herself in reverse proportion not of her age either (84–85).[6] In the absence of parental assistance and security, Maisie becomes the central supporter and protector of the novel. In fact, Maisie's method for interior protection soon expands beyond the scope of self-preservation to include, most especially, the protection also of Sir Claude and Mrs. Beale; and, what is more, with this wider aim, Maisie's method accrues more diverse means for its achievement, expanding beyond silence to include secrecy and diversion.

One of the secrets that Maisie contains is the knowledge of her mother's latest infidelity, this time against Sir Claude with the Captain. The scene where Maisie and Sir Claude cross paths with Ida and the Captain is one of two which James himself offers as an exemplar of Maisie's growing ability (Preface 29–30). At this chance run-in, disaster appears immanent as Sir Claude and the Captain seem bound to meet. Their romantic illusions are saved in large measure because of Maisie's determination to act, ironically, as their protector. Diverted to occupy the Captain (while Ida intercepts Sir Claude), Maisie becomes a strange confidante for the Captain's confessions. Stranger still for Maisie (and for the reader) are the terms of love and devotion that the Captain somehow manages to apply to Maisie's mother. Maisie's heart goes out to both of these men, so much so that in Sir Claude's subsequent interrogation of her, Maisie determines to play the fool for the sake of peace. To his question "Well, who in the world *is* the fellow?" Maisie feels herself "flooded with prudence" and replies, "Oh I haven't found out!" (133). Recalling times past when for "the ugliness of seeming disagreeable…her father, for her blankness, called her a dirty little donkey, and her mother, for her falsity, pushed her out of the room," Maisie assents to the test of "her young endurance," resolving to "bear the sense of Sir Claude's displeasure," in order that she might not "feed [the] love of battle" as she had done so unwittingly in the past (133–134).

But Maisie's "kept silence" has really expanded in this instance to the level of a kept secret (133). Maisie faces Sir Claude's prolonged withdrawal, but this prospect of punishment:

> had no power to make her love him less; so she could not only bear it, she felt as she drove away—she could rejoice in it. It brought again the sweet sense of success that, ages before, she had had at a crisis when, on the stairs…she had met a fierce question of her mother's with an imbecility as deep and had in consequence been dashed by Mrs Farange almost to the bottom. (134)

Because of her age, Maisie can believably play "the perfection of a dunce," as Sir Claude proclaims her in this scene, but such a performance does not come easily to her. James insists on what Maisie chooses to "bear" with her silence as well as what she is willing to sacrifice, that is to take upon herself, for the peace and protection of others. Maisie's interiority proves far from empty in these moments. Where her silence had served to set formal boundaries between her interiority and the external threat of parental violence, in this case, it means withholding the improprieties of her mother so that Sir Claude's own emotions may be contained, so that, oddly enough, her mother may find a more permanent, virtuous happiness (with the Captain) apart from her. And in this latter instance, Maisie's withholding is self-directed. Though she is infected with the Captain's expressions of love for her mother, the picture of happiness she imagines does not include herself, so certain is she that her mother "won't have [her]," not "now" and not "in any place" (131).

Maisie is the quintessential noun made verb; from the sense of child interiority as container, she accrues the subsequent capacity to contain, an ability which, in the presence of so much ominous excess, is no longer even chiefly self-serving but which actively loans itself out, as it were, for the benefit of others. As Maisie shifts from silence to secrecy, her interiority likewise dilates to include, strangely enough, the interiorities of others. The silence that meant her failure as a messenger between her parents now means her success as a bearer of secrets for and from them. Following on the heels of the Captain's secret confession, Maisie finds herself faced with another. With Mrs. Beale, Maisie becomes privy to the "rare secret," to the "wretched truth," which the former governess "had to confess," of frequent, clandestine meetings with Sir Claude. In a dramatic emotional display, complete with "a wonderful outbreak of tears," Mrs. Beale, like so many of the adults in Maisie's life (indeed, like so many characters out of the Victorian novel), seems positively compelled to revelation. As if the secret were being literally pulled from her, James writes that she "had to bring out in a manner that seemed half an appeal, half a defiance" the startling fact that "'Well yes, hang it—I *do* see him!'" (135). Surprising still is the concomitant revelation that Sir Claude's absence has owed something in part to his desire not to have Maisie "mixed up" in his and Mrs. Beale's sordid affairs (141). Nothing, in fact, could be more natural to Maisie's mind than to be thusly mixed. She does not share Sir Claude's fear of her "being compromised" since from her earliest childhood Maisie "knew as well…that a person could be compromised as that a person could be slapped with a hair-brush or left alone in the dark, and it was equally familiar to her that each of these ordeals was in general held to have too little effect" (141). The passage echoes the novel's opening spoiler that though much would undoubtedly go into the tainting of Maisie's soul, "nothing ill" would yet be made of it (37). While the weapon of compromise has been easily wielded upon Maisie, it has not with such ease made a lasting impact. Sir Claude apparently has yet to learn what the reader and now

Maisie do know which is her ability to be "in the midst" without being lost (*Notebooks* 127).

With these grownups then, Maisie not only detects the "overflow of their difficulties" (162) but she also frequently attempts to take the burden of difficulty from them. Maisie resolves in this last instance to take on Sir Claude's "scruple"—willingly filling the mixed position which was, arguably, already hers—in order that she "might simplify" things for him (141). And, what's more, her abilities for detection become increasingly subtle; they become less and less reliant on that which is visible or confessed. Maisie, whose interior has developed alongside closed doors and over-laden closets, develops something of an interior line of sight, one that seeks to read the invisible word. With her "sharpened sense for latent meaning," she ever maneuvers to peer behind the curtain of the verbal and bodily gesture to register in her own thoughts the actual thoughts of others (189).[7]

The second scene which James identifies as a particular testimony to Maisie's abilities is none other than the counter to the first. The scene with the Captain and Sir Claude is mirrored in Maisie's reunion with her father while they wait for the Countess (or, as Maisie identifies her, "Papa's Captain" (157)). After an immense absence on Beale's part, after in fact, having only accidentally come upon Maisie and his wife at the exhibition, Maisie deeply registers his "restless[ness]." "[S]o well could she privately follow his difficulty in being specific to her about anything" that Maisie knows without being told that Beale needs her to help him "pretend" that he knows anything at all about her life (148–149). Beale's difficulty is a matter of his deficiency. He struggles to address Maisie as his child in part because he has been willfully absent from her life. Taken up by Maisie, these difficulties accrue new dimensions. As Maisie follows the mental laborings of her father, the narrator, as closely, follows Maisie's own. In wanting nothing more than to "give a better turn to the crisis," Maisie wonders "what particular thing she could do or not do, what particular word she could speak or not speak, what particular line she could take or not take" (149). Unlike her father who says nothing because he has nothing to say, Maisie thinks strategically about the advantages of silence as one option among many. Indeed, in the further spirit of restraint, she determines an exception; she is willing to do or not do anything but surrender Sir Claude and Mrs. Beale.

In the tortured light of Maisie's mentally considered approach, her father's method seems embarrassingly "abrupt" and coarse. In suddenly accosting Maisie with the question of what she knows about her "brute of a mother," Maisie notes the surprising coincidence between the subject of his question and his way of asking it, namely the resemblance between his abruptness and her mother's similar manner of "free flight." On the heels of this insight, a new "inspiration" strikes. Maisie proclaims, "'Oh yes, I know everything!'" feeling "pressingly, that the more she should be able to say about mamma the less she would be called upon to speak of her step-parents" (151). As before, Maisie's aim is fundamentally protective, though her means have grown significantly more complex than the days of mute unresponsiveness. And, as usual, it comes at the cost of an immense effort, an immense exchange. Where Maisie's silence as a much younger child had plainly opposed her parents' own penchant for verbal assaults, her oppositional acrobatics in this instance aim to fly beneath Beale's radar. Here, instead of locking her lips, Maisie endeavors to keep them moving. On the surface, her exclamation, "Oh I know everything," followed by the revelation of her Kensington Garden encounter, resembles the excessive, compulsory revelations of mother and father. But, in reality, Maisie's inspiration is one which practically merges her options of speaking and not speaking. In short, she is inspired by the idea of a diversion. Where she had kept the secret about the Captain in order to protect Sir Claude, here she reveals it in order to achieve the exact same end.

Neither Maisie's method nor her selfless intent is mirrored by her father who, with his plans for an American voyage with the Countess, is most fearful of his own exposure. Beale makes a show of inviting Maisie to travel with them but quickly assumes her refusal, thus enabling him to preen: "You can't say I don't put it before you—you can't say I ain't kind to you…Mind you never say that, you know" (152). By his warning, Beale confirms his own "limited consciousness" in the form of a self-interest that is so totalizing that he cannot see that he is instructing a master of silence and secrecy to watch her words. Unlike Maisie, the narrator baldly[8] reveals exactly how unkind Beale is by noting "a dryness in the way" he replied to Maisie that showed that "it didn't matter what she thought," a failure of conscientiousness for her in the way he begins "to smoke in her face," and a lack of affection in his "awkward," "flounder[ing]," "clumsy," and "so stupid all through" manner with her (148–149). Maisie's growth has been unmarked by her father. Like her mother who, at the inception of her silent method, read silence as imbecility, Beale takes hers to be a transparent, literal consciousness. Ostensibly, he places the offer before her and in doing so thinks she will know no better than to report it as such. In actuality, it takes only for Beale to rub "his beard against her cheek" "in the most inconsequent way in the world" for Maisie to perceive:

> as well as if he had spoken it that what he wanted, hang it, was that she should let him off with all the honours—with all the appearance of virtue and sacrifice on his side. It was exactly as if he had broken out to her: "I say, you little booby, help me to be irreproachable, to be noble, and yet to have none of the beastly bore of it. There's only impropriety enough for one of us; so *you* must take it all." (153)

In addition to the familiar metaphors of empty and boundless receptacles, fun and amusing shuttlecocks, of transparent minds and blank slates, it is as if we can now add religious confessional to the list. For in this scene and in the prior scenes—with the Captain and with Mrs. Beale—it is truly as if Maisie's interiority has become a space for the sordid to unload their burdens of sin and to imagine themselves as utterly absolved by the exchange. In a manner at last wholly unconventional, Maisie's various parental figures see her interiority not as a source for moral solutions but rather as a repository for unwanted complications. The child, ironically, offers these adults, a space where they can displace and store their troubles so that they are the ones who can continue to travel through life unfettered.

But if there can be a development more striking than this parental strategy for the manipulation of the child, it is the child's comprehension of it. James enters Beale's thoughts in this instance not through the means of an omniscient or even attendant narrator but through the "expanding consciousness" of Maisie (24). It is she, with her ever-more subtle interior sight, who bypasses manifest expression to discern the latent uses her father would make of her. In other words, Maisie's insight is a kind of metaperspective where what she perceives is none other than her father's perception of her: as container, as confessional, as scapegoat—as someone to "take…all" impropriety and leave him ironically innocent (153). But, in point of fact, this meta-comprehension is not new to Maisie, for from the start, her silent method was borne out of her distinct awareness that she was being made "a messenger of insult" (43). Thus, Maisie surpasses the adult figurations of her as container (whether conventional or no) by the mere fact that they become part of the very thing she contains. By implication, what Maisie bears, and indeed she ever bears more and more, is not as important as how she bears it. In contrast to the adults in her life who prove unable to think beyond their own irresponsible self-interests, Maisie's method splits upon her core objectives of peace and protection, strategically giving and withholding by turns.

The Divided Child and the Emergence of Modernist Fiction

"Nothing was less new to Maisie," we are told by the end of this sequence, "than the art of not thinking singly" (176). The weight of James's diction as applied to Maisie, and as otherwise to the adults in her life, falls on the side of consistency. Where silence and secrecy spoke to Maisie's as a divided and segmentable consciousness capable of adapting to the demands of the moment, the proposition here is of a child consciousness cemented in division. More than the suggestion of stability and indeed durability—"nothing" being "less new" to Maisie than this form of consciousness—James insists too that Maisie has honed this way of thinking into an "art." In the place of the familiar metaphors of childhood, James identifies an unconventional child interiority that is divided, restrained, and perhaps most especially, authorial. Many scholars have noted that *What Maisie Knew* is an emergently modernist novel and many others have noted that James's new novelistic method, one which centers itself on individual consciousness, begins with *Maisie*, and many have noted that this method (whether they attribute it to *Maisie* or not) is at the very forefront of what takes shape as the modernist novel, but none, so far as I know, has given Maisie her full due by unifying these separate observations in one.[9] Together, they illuminate the link between emergent efforts to reimagine childhood interiority and the emergence of modernist fiction.

In the preface to *Maisie*, James himself outlines the symbiosis between his own efforts to reconceive both the child mind and the modern novel. And he does this interestingly through an extended metaphor that places both entities—child and text—on the same boat. James begins this passage by describing Maisie in navigational terms as a ship, as his "light vessel of consciousness, swaying in such a draught." He extends the metaphor by imagining Maisie as a child craft constructed "without extravagance" as a "slip of a girl," and yet also invested with empathic sails "easily and almost infinitely quickened." As a ship, Maisie appears in these depictions to be small, fast, light, designed to weather stormy seas. And yet as the metaphor continues to expand it becomes clear that Maisie also carries an enormous freight which is the weight of the novel itself. James concludes this passage by extending the ship metaphor from the child to the novel. Thus "fitted out," he writes, this child "vessel of consciousness" "might well see me through the whole course of my design" (26). Of course, metaphors linking the child mind with the act of writing are not new. Locke's *tabula rasa* metaphor arguably popularized the concept. Yet, James complicates this classic vision of the child as "white paper or wax to be molded and fashioned as one pleases" (Locke 161). James may be punning on the word "vessel," as container and ship, but it is a useful pun. Not only does he hereby emphasize that Maisie does have a mind capable of containment but he also emphasizes that she, like the ship, has some agency to move through and navigate her world. What's more, he suggests that both of these senses of "vessel" are central to the novel's own design. While it is evident that the interiority of the novel is to an important degree the interiority of Maisie, it is far less evident that the novel's design joins also with Maisie's method (of containing, withholding, and redirecting knowledge) in order to achieve its own end-game.

In other words, the phrase "vessel of consciousness" aptly captures Maisie's dual role as a character in the novel and as a method of novelization. As a character, Maisie is a child equipped to survive the careless self-indulgence of her parents and step-parents. As a method, Maisie offers a way of revealing these excesses without resembling them. In the preface, James depicts Maisie's economical design as her and his novel's saving grace. She is a mere "slip of a girl," buoyantly "light," and outfitted "without extravagance" (26). And by siding with her (against her "*immense* and awful" parents) James boasts that he achieves "an *economy* of process" that is "interesting in itself" (29; emphasis added). James highlights the pinhole-like smallness of Maisie's perspective as the keyhole through which the reader (less naively) witnesses the grotesque horrors of her reality. In James's words, his signature epiphany with Maisie was "to make and to keep her so limited consciousness the very field of [his] picture" (26). With typographical verve, James emphasizes the idea at the point of discovery: "EVERYTHING TAKES PLACE BEFORE MAISIE. That is a part of the essence of the thing—that, with the tenderness she inspires, the rest of the essence, the second of the golden threads of my *form*" (*Notebooks* 238). The nineteenth-century novel for adults became synonymous in the modernist imagination with a prescriptive and descriptive excess which, to borrow from Virginia Woolf, said pages and pages (sometimes volumes and volumes) more about people's houses than about "the human beings who live[d] there" ("Mr. Bennett" 32). By using the metaphor of the ship, James highlights Maisie's ability to float, that is to survive, in a sea of trouble, but he also underscores how different her "design" and his novel's "design" (through her) are from the surrounding waters. For Maisie these waters are the adults who tyrannize her; for the novel these waters are the conventions of nineteenth-century fiction. Both threaten to overwhelm the mind of the child, to overflow the banks of an era, to overwrite the boundaries separating youth and age. Maisie/*Maisie* succeeds (if she succeeds) because she refuses to follow in these rather large (forgive the pun) footsteps.

Across the vast body of scholarship on this novel, James's characterization of Maisie's as a "limited consciousness" has nearly always been taken to describe a world view that is naturally deficient and naïve. Nearly all who seek clues to the fulfillment of the apparently unfulfilled promise of the novel's title, to identify the "what" of *What Maisie Knew*, rest on Maisie's consciousness as a limited, partial register of events. There are readings which focus, for instance, strictly on what Maisie actually sees and/or on what she actually, physically feels as being the central line of the novel and, usually too, as being the key to the riddle of her knowledge.[10] There are readings which determine that there is more, because of her limitations, that Maisie, in fact, does not know than the other way around and interpret the title, therefore, ironically.[11] While all of these readings fail to appreciate Maisie's appreciation for absence (for silence and secrecy), they also hold up better in the novel's first half than in the second, where Maisie comes to know more and more what is "latent," comes to understand more and more what is not presented to her (189).

The full sense of this accumulation is clearly visible in the scene following that between Maisie and her father at the Countess's where, it will be recalled, Maisie not only "follow[ed] his difficulty" in speaking to her, but through a mere brush of his beard, osmosis-like, registered his unspoken thoughts in her own mind (148). In the next chapter, Maisie is en route with Sir Claude to Folkestone when she realizes a change in her own mental habits. It has always been the case with her, she thinks, that "to be with Sir Claude was to think of Sir Claude"; however, somehow, her thoughts have now turned from presence to absence. Now, with Sir Claude-without-Mrs. Beale, what presents itself "into her dizzy head" is the "long-lost image of Mrs Wix." "It was singular," James writes, "but from this time she understood and she followed, followed with the sense of an ample-filling out of any void created by symptoms of avoidance and of flight" (162). Really, the old governess has done nothing less than Maisie has done her whole novelistic life; she has removed herself, detached herself from the situation in order that she might have a better affect on it. She has worked on Sir Claude the importance, as Maisie has already learned, of "sacrifice" and convinced him to give up Mrs. Beale for "the real good of the little unfortunate" (163).[12] From her own method of detachment, Maisie comes to appreciate and understand it in others. The narrator underscores the significance of the scene with the acknowledgement that though "Maisie had known all along a great deal," she never knew "so much as she was to know from this moment on" (162).

And yet at this moment of Maisie's most dramatic intake of knowledge, the narrator interrupts the revelatory trajectory. He interrupts and he fast-forwards both at once, proclaiming with regard to this newfound knowledge that "I shall have no room for the goal if I attempt to trace the stages." This declaration not only arrests the momentum of the scene, not only wrests the narrative line from Maisie's consciousness to the narrator's own, but most importantly begs the question as to what has been the goal after all if not to trace the stages of Maisie's knowledge (162). Though James challenges the conventions of childhood from the novel's outset, his title and his epistemological method for much of the novel have promised, at the very least, a Victorian ending: a most satisfying revelation as to what, however unexpected or sinister, Maisie at last does know. The novel drives home as its central purpose the following of Maisie's "expanding consciousness" and thereby seems to guarantee that Maisie's initially "limited consciousness" will be finally unlimited; she will know what should, by the conventions of her age, be off-limits, and we, as readers of her, will know what that something is (Preface 24; 26).

That there might be another goal to *Maisie* is suggested by the novel's general failure to ever identify what Maisie in fact knew. The last thoughts are of Mrs. Wix expressing that that line of inquiry at last has no goal, has no end, for there is "still...room," she feels, "for wonder at what Maisie knew" (266). To the extent that there is any satisfaction via this ending, it is not the satisfaction of revelation but of tautology, of having arrived precisely where the novel began. What is truly interesting in this moment is not what it reveals but the manner in which it does not reveal. It was one thing for the attendant narrator to divert the narrative line from Maisie's evolving consciousness, but it is another thing to follow in its stead the consciousness of Mrs. Wix, to supplant with her "wonder" the wonder of the child. In a novel whose first law is that "EVERYTHING TAKES PLACE BEFORE MAISIE" (*Notebooks* 238), the last line manifests a striking exception, following as it does "the sidelong look" of Mrs. Wix, neglecting the look *from* Maisie to look *at* her instead. If one has taken as central to the novel the twin threads of tracing the child's epistemological growth and of doing so by seeing only what the child also sees, then this will likely seem an ending to a different novel.

What most bothered reviewers in James's own time about the novel was its failure to meet expectations, not only according to nineteenth-century conventions but according to James's own novelistic reputation. Its style is described as "labyrinthine" in the place of James's "earlier" (and one also senses more welcome) "lucidity."[13] It is, one reviewer writes, a "bewildering blur of motive and action which has the same effect of irritation on the mind as an ill-focused photograph upon the sight."[14] Caroline Levine has recovered for Victorian literature what she terms "the serious pleasures of suspense" or the way in which Victorian fiction often unsettled its readers' expectations in order to make room for unconventional thought. However, even Levine acknowledges that the Victorian reader, however willing to subject herself to the mental rigors of suspense, nonetheless expected and was satisfied to receive the gift at the end of the novel of its theretofore closely-guarded secrets (2). For reviewers of *Maisie*, James constructed a new frustration, a difficult novel without any apparent reward. "To read 'What Maisie Knew,'" one reviewer writes, "is to go through an experience almost or quite as remarkable as that of his unfortunate little heroine." For him, the "author's cynical refusal to answer the conundrum in the propounding of which he has used up every one of his 470 pages" produces the inevitable question as to whether the difficulty of reading the novel has, after all, been "worth while?"[15]

Maisie's is a modernist ending not only for what it refuses in terms of readerly insight but for the manner of its refusal. What it promises with one hand, it denies with the other, and in fact the denial is more sharply felt because of the original promise. By the end of the novel, Maisie's cognitive limitations (whatever these may have been) have been supplanted by a growing willingness to limit others' access to her cognitive process. In a strange way, James's description of Maisie as possessing a "limited consciousness" remains true across the full arc of Maisie's development (Preface 26). Both Maisies (beginning and end) possess a "limited consciousness"; it is just that somewhere along the way her "limited" point of view stops being the involuntary byproduct of youth and becomes an appointed vehicle for her own (and the novel's) self-fashioning. What begins as an exploration of the child's limited, partial comprehension of her world expands over the course of the novel to signify a consciousness restrained and recognizing restraint, an interiority divided and limited by choice rather than by necessity.

This choice, of course, is not Maisie's alone. Within the fictional world constructed by James, Maisie would not have this agency vis-à-vis the reader without the cooperation of the narrator. Though invisible, the narrator is in some ways a minor character in the novel whose purported role is to shadow Maisie's consciousness, to present and "amplif[y]" her perceptions for the sake of an enthralled adult audience (Preface 28). And yet like everyone else in the novel at one point or other, we find ourselves on the receiving end of a powerful deception. We thought the narrator was working for us, but in the end this appears to be a great—perhaps *the* great—illusion of the novel. Though James tells us—in the lead-in to the novel—that the narrator was created to fill in the inevitable "gaps and voids" of the young child's perception, by the end we are faced with the reality that our guide is either impressively flawed or substantially unreliable (27).[16] From the moments leading up to Maisie's "crossing" from England to France to her return voyage with Mrs. Wix at the novel's close, the narrator falls increasingly behind in the race to know what Maisie knows (162). The sensation upon the reader is palpable. Somewhere the novel has changed. We turned a page or pages and left one novel and entered another.

This narrative break carves itself most sharply in the scene with Maisie and Mrs. Wix at the *plage*. To Mrs. Wix's consternation, Maisie has defended Sir Claude and Mrs. Beale, driving the old governess to ask incredulously whether or not the child "really and truly" has "*any* moral sense" (211). Maisie finds herself unable to put together an articulate answer, but it little matters. By way of their "quiet conjoined apprehension," Maisie knows that Mrs. Wix can see with her the "appalling" truth (212). The narrator continues:

> This marked more particularly the moment of the child's perceiving that her friend had risen to a level which might—till superseded at all events—pass almost for sublime. Nothing more remarkable had taken place in the first heat of her own departure, no act of perception less to be overtraced by our rough method, than her vision, the rest of that Boulogne day, of the manner in which she figured. I so despair of courting her noiseless mental footsteps here that I must crudely give you my word for its being from this time forward a picture literally present to her. Mrs Wix saw her as a little person knowing so extraordinarily much that, for the account to be taken of it, what she still didn't know would be ridiculous if it hadn't been embarrassing. (212)

Alongside Maisie, Mrs. Wix is a figure who has risen to new heights. Now, the narrator juggles her consciousness along with Maisie's. In noting their "conjoined apprehension," he prefigures the difficulty in this passage of separating theirs into individual consciousnesses. In addition to getting another instance of what Mrs. Wix "saw" as opposed to and in addition to what Maisie sees (for the implication is that this is another instance of Maisie seeing what others see in her), there is also a crucial uncertainty as to who is being "figure[d]" in this most "remarkable" event of Maisie's sojourn in France. Is the remarkable figuration Mrs. Wix's new sublime position in Maisie's eyes, or is it an instance where Maisie, once more, epiphanically perceives the way in which she herself has figured in the lives of others?

Coming at the end of a sentence with multiple "her"s, clearly referring to Maisie, following a sentence which as clearly magnifies the stature of the old governess, the "she" of "the manner in which she figured" is tortuously ambiguous (212). Purposefully so, it seems, for as the narrator nicely acknowledges, confusion has a way of compounding itself in this passage. And yet the confusion also has a way of communicating. As a product of convergence, the ambiguities of this moment reveal in part the difficulties of the narrator meeting Maisie, of their being able to follow and understand her at this late point in her epistemological development. In one sense, the difficulty speaks to Maisie's growth, to her having even surpassed the frame that initially contained her as one with knowable, pre-set limits, as one whose destiny could be summed up from the very first as childhood epitaph and resistant goodness. In contrast to much that has come before, the narrator in this instance turns from confessing for Maisie to confessing for themselves. Their method is "rough," their means "despair[ing]," their word "crude" (212). Coming as it does at the close of a novel where the narrator has consistently amplified Maisie's consciousness, from its earliest misapprehensions to its growing silences, secrets, and diversions, this is a striking recognition of a fundamental role reversal, for here it is the narrator, not Maisie, who is self-professedly limited.

But in another sense, the difficulty speaks to the growth of the novel through Maisie. Though it separates from Maisie's interiority, though it "traces" that interiority rather than revealing its contents, the novel that bears Maisie's name comes also to employ her method. Detracting from the narrator's "despair of courting [Maisie's] noiseless mental footsteps" is the nearly simultaneous salesmanship that yet promises knowledge and insight into her. In another telling first person intervention, the narrator "crudely give[s]" us "[their] word for its being from this time forward a picture literally present to her," where the "its" and the "picture" are at once guaranteed but undisclosed (212). Whether through "tracing" or fast-forwarding, the directive in both instances seems to be nothing less than the overwriting of the child's interior in favor of the child's method for sustaining the interior as such. Maisie's silences, secrets, diversions, and all of her various withholdings find a second life in the form of their telling, or not telling as the case comes at last to be. As Ida was faced with an unconventional child who by her silence refused to be "simple and confiding," so the reader of *Maisie* comes to face an unconventional novel that frustrates for precisely the same reasons and in precisely the same ways. James's narrator, in despairing over their inability to follow Maisie's presumably advanced thinking, claims an imbecility in this last scene matched only by Maisie's silent ploys before them. In ever concealing what they know or do not know, the narrator proves able to keep a secret as well as she. In shifting to the consciousness of Mrs. Wix and what she sees or does not see in Maisie, the narrator diverts from the novelistic object no less than has Maisie with her exchange of the Captain's secret for Sir Claude's.

Readings which have persisted in either perceiving a hidden revelation in the ending of *Maisie* or in continuing to seek clues for some such, often, I believe, have in their periphery a nineteenth-century novel ideal. To read Maisie or Maisie's knowledge as the center of the novel, as obvious as that will no doubt seem to many, is not unproblematic, arising as it does from a basic novelistic assumption that places plot at the forefront of that genre's interests. But this is a priority which the modernist novel frequently seeks to destabilize and disorder. From the novel's midpoint to now, from the beginning of Maisie's journey with Sir Claude to this beach scene, the suggestion of the narrator has been, despite all prior appearances, that there is a different goal for the novel, one not centered on the stages of Maisie's knowledge, one not even centered on that knowledge itself. What Maisie surmises at the end of this scene is "that if her whole history, for Mrs. Wix, had been the successive stages of her knowledge, so the very climax of the concatenation would, in the same view, be the stage at which the knowledge would overflow" (212–213). Maisie at last sees what the novel itself has seemed heretofore to be, the tracing of "the successive stages of her knowledge"; I say "seemed" because now, through Maisie, the narrator projects this narrative line onto the traditionally-minded caretaker. It is Mrs. Wix who would turn Maisie's "history" into the cup that runneth over, who would map her story onto the familiar overflowings Maisie has already encountered. Such is not, it is implied, the history of Maisie that the narrator would tell, and it is certainly not, Maisie's anxiety reveals, the history she wishes for herself.

What begins as one of the first realist depictions of child psychology, one of the first imaginings of a childhood interiority belonging to the child (rather than to the nostalgic adult), comes at last to resist the ends of the maturational, which is also the epistemological, trajectory. In contrast to the "inevitability" of the well-trod path to knowledge which Mrs. Wix and even the reader anticipate, the novel yet resists overflowing revelation, for rather than follow Maisie's consciousness down that "road to know Everything," the narrator follows instead the contours of her method (213). This is not to say, however, that the two, method and consciousness, are unrelated. In following Maisie's method, by which I mean both tracing and imitating it, James activates a feedback mechanism, whereby what is not revealed cannot have overflown. Such also has the effect, therefore, of pressing at the limits of verisimilitude; rather than imitate life, James imitates form and thereby suggests a new life, a new subjectivity in the form of a modernist child. To follow Maisie's method is to control and conceal (the two are nearly synonymous concepts for James) an interior which is the novel's no less than the child's, and it is to set Maisie firmly within the landscape of fiction.

Many are tempted because of Maisie's growth within the novel to view her as a person, as a real child, but the novel itself increasingly pushes Maisie into the realm of art. Maisie, by yet another development in her method, defies once more the weight of compounding expectations. To Sir Claude who proposes that Maisie "give [Mrs. Wix] up," to Mrs. Wix who expects that she will, with her newfound moral sense, refuse such a request, to Mrs. Beale who expects just as strongly the reverse, to them all Maisie's response is novel and strange: it comes in the form of a "condition." Maisie makes her now familiar sacrifices contingent upon another's. She will sacrifice her relationship with Mrs. Wix if Sir Claude will reciprocate in kind by giving up Mrs. Beale. The merger between Maisie's method and the novel's is registered by Sir Claude who sees that her response has defied ordinary probability and has instead like "some lovely work of art…been set down among them" (262). And like a modernist work of art, Maisie's method, whether through her silences, secrets, diversions, or now, conditions, helps to separate her from, rather than connect her to, her surrounding order. At the close of this scene, Maisie is "again dropped and divided," but as Sir Claude attests, being so dropped and being so divided can in the given context mean a new kind of freedom, a freedom in this case from the unencumbered, unconditional (261). In the notebooks and in the preface James insisted that Maisie would be "rescue[d]" (*Notebooks* 240), that "the small expanding consciousness would have to be saved" (Preface 24). To his contemporaries and to mine, no expression could be more common than "saving the child," but what James seeks to save is, as with Maisie's own efforts, wholly other to expectation. Saving children, past and present, has typically meant "saving them for the enjoyment of childhood": warding them off from experience, from exploitation, from responsibility and encapsulating them in a space and time of simplicity, innocence, freedom, and play (Cunningham 137). But for James no one plays more or is more singular or more free than *Maisie*'s adult society. To save the divided child is to keep her, in part, from succumbing to singularity, to preserve hers as the unconventional interior of art, if not someday of life.

The "*partagé* child," the child of divorce, for James embodies "the art of not thinking singly." James's form, the form of a developing modernist fiction, emerges out of the reconceptualization of hers. Because of the weight of expectations placed on the conceptual child, the slightest "turn of the screw" (a phrase which James uses for the first time in *Maisie*) with regard to her is capable of producing the most dramatic, ironic effect (97). James flips the switch on various disempowering images of the child (as white paper to be written or as an empty container to be filled) and presents instead a child mind that defies both simplicity and transparency. And as goes this child, so goes the novel. The narrator that initially "attends and amplifies" Maisie's consciousness ends by corroborating its disassociation and containment. Her method becomes the narrator's own; her form becomes the form of the emergently modernist novel. From her earliest realization of an "inner self, or in other words the idea of concealment," one can dimly discern on the dim horizon a modernist figure, the inheritor of the child and her novel's newly locked lips.

Notes

1. "What Maisie Knew," *The Literary World; a Monthly Review of Current Literature*" 28.25 (December 2, 1897): 454.
2. "Henry James's New Work: 'What Maisie Knew,'" *New York Times* 27 November 1897: BR9.
3. "Mr. James New Novel" in *Current Literature* 22.6 (Dec 1897): 505. This same reviewer buttresses his/her defense by also asserting that even if sense of immorality is present, the story is "so well" told that "the sense of its unpleasantness is forgotten in the reader's admiration of the author's fine restraint."
4. Though Maisie's parents may seem like monstrous exceptions to the rules of parenting, their views of Maisie's interiority are amazingly conventional. Referring to such popular Victorian metaphors of childhood as "The Child of Wax, The Ceramic Child," and "The Child Botanical," James R. Kincaid argues that "Over and over, this child-rearing discourse transfers the being of the child to the parent…reaching for a variety of metaphors to suggest openly that the 'child' is nothing more than what it is construed to be, nothing in itself at all" (*Child-loving* 90).
5. Prior to Locke, who made a central case for the child's capacity to reason, there was little to separate the child from the animal. See Michael Witmore's *Pretty Creatures: Children and Fiction in the English Renaissance*.
6. Pifer also notes the adult characteristics of Maisie and argues that the novel thereby collapses the gap between child and adult. This conclusion, however, does not, to my mind, account for the dematuration of the adults in the novel. In other words, it seems to me that the gap is sustained—but it is inverted.
7. That this ability for internal perception (to see one's meaning even when that meaning is either not verbalized or is contrary to what is) is not equally shared by the adults in Maisie's life is highlighted by the further details of this late exchange between Sir Claude and Mrs. Wix. It is Maisie who follows Mrs. Wix's circuitous charge, "that there must at last be a *decent* person" in Maisie's life, as an implicit critique not of Sir Claude, who is the most immediate, visible target, but of the absent Mrs. Beale. Sir Claude, Maisie is surprised to see, misses this indirection and takes the remark as personal insult (192).
8. James uses the phrase "limited consciousness" to describe Maisie earlier in the novel (26). In this scene, he uses the phrase "dim perception" to capture Beale's ignorance (149). The latter clearly recalls the former and suggests, yet again, just how dramatic the role reversal between child and adult has been.
9. Walter Isle identifies the cluster of shorter texts that James wrote following his failure in the theater as experimental and as the direct precursors of the

"involutions and obscurities" of James's "so-called 'late style'" (11). Sergio Perosa agrees with Isle and draws a further distinction between the thematic experiments in James's fiction pre-1890 and the technical experimentation, the merging of his interest in the dramatic method with a new limited point of view, central to his novelistic endeavors immediately following his failure in the theatre (5–6). And most recently, Christina Britzolakis argues that *What Maisie Knew* serves as an "'experimental' precursor of modernism" as well in that it "constitutes a key moment in the refinement, specialization, and elaboration of a technique of fictional looking devised to negotiate the shocks of urban modernity" (370).

10. John C. McCloskey argues that Maisie's is a traceable empirical development with a very restricted environment. Jeff Westover traces Maisie's as a path from passive dependence to active autonomy through the novel's various physical laying on of hands. And Christina Britzolakis's brilliant analysis of the phantasmagoric qualities of Maisie's vision nonetheless restricts Maisie's perception to literal sight, arguing that there remains throughout the novel a fundamental disjunct between what Maisie physically sees and what she cognitively understands (383–384).
11. Susan E. Honeyman argues that the inaccessibility of childhood is precisely what allows James to develop his late method, a method which dramatized the novel's struggle with representation. And Dennis Foster challenges the basic assumption that Maisie knows anything at all by showing that Maisie more often than not takes up the language of the adults around her in an attempt to please and impress them without really understanding the words themselves.
12. The line explicitly echoes the earlier expression that Maisie's parents should do something for "'the real good, don't you know?' of the child" (42). In that instance the expression proves a lie for as "any spectator" of the proceedings could see, Maisie's parents "wanted her not for any good they could do her, but for the harm they could, with her unconscious aid, do each other" (36). The second such manifestation, though not false, nonetheless proves equally futile, at least with Sir Claude as the agent of the child's good.
13. "Some Tendencies in Contemporary Fiction," *The Living Age* 223.2891 (Dec 2, 1891): 587.
14. "The Novels of Mr. Henry James," *The Living Age* 236.3061 (Mar 7, 1903): 578.
15. "Henry James's New Work: 'What Maisie Knew,'" BR9.
16. Barbara Eckstein makes a persuasive argument for narrative ambivalence in *Maisie*, based to large extent, on the narrator's restricted, humanly deficient omniscience.

CHAPTER 4

An Innocence Worse than Evil in *The Turn of the Screw*

'The way I flew! Do you know, Jane, I sometimes wonder whether I ever did really fly.'

…'Why can't you fly now, mother?'

'Because I am grown up, dearest. When people grow up they forget the way.'

'Why do they forget the way?'

'Because they are no longer gay and innocent and heartless. It is only the gay and innocent and heartless who can fly.'

—J.M. Barrie, *Peter and Wendy* (1911), 148.

Though Henry James's *The Turn of the Screw* (1898) preceded even the earliest incarnation of *Peter Pan*,[1] I offer Wendy's unsettling sentiment at the end of *Peter and Wendy* as a well-known, condensed introduction to a recurring modernist problem: the problem of everlasting childhood and eternal innocence. Wendy's grown-up longing marks an unconventional modern departure not because she yearns to be young again (for what yearning could be more modern than this?) but because her longing is only partially nostalgic, naming both the wonders and the deficits of youth. As the boy who never grows up, Peter's heartlessness is repeatedly inscribed in J.M. Barrie's text: from his first "cunning" seduction of Wendy away from her London home to his carelessly forgotten promise to visit her in the spring of each year (31; 146). One cannot have a heart for what one cannot remember, and adults, as Wendy and her mother before her prove, have full minds and heavy hearts. Despite the colossal misreading that is the now iconic Peter Pan, the narrator's and Wendy's embedded criticisms of Peter suggest that there may be something less than ideal in the child object of this modern mass idolatry.[2]

A similar set of concerns surrounds the two children at the heart of Henry James's novella, *The Turn of the Screw*. Like Peter Pan who must find creative ways to survive in the world after his own mother has given up on his return home, Flora and Miles have an incredibly sad back story, filled with loss, abandonment, and possibly worse.[3] Over the course of the story we learn that Flora and Miles's father and grandparents have passed. There is no mention of any mother of any kind. We learn that they have been moved from their childhood home in India to their uncle's country estate only to be abandoned there to the care of two "infamous" servants, Miss Jessel and Peter Quint (31). And we learn that these young caretakers (if they can be called that) have also died unspeakable deaths. And yet, like Peter, Flora and Miles appear to be strangely undisturbed by this history. On the surface, they wear all of the essential features of romantic childhood—gaiety, wonder, innocence. They act as if they have had no experience of the world.

Even though much scholarship on *The Turn of the Screw* has focused on the governess's psychology and whether the apparitions that she perceives truly threaten the children or whether they are even real, the text and paratext are much more directly focused on the suspect innocence of these two children. When the governess calls out the children's "absolutely unnatural goodness" as a "game," as "a policy and a fraud," she gives voice to a deeply troubling worry that these children might be performing childhood (47). This thought gives James's novella one of its many chilling "turns," for it demands that the reader not only imagine what terrible things might have happened to these children at the hands of their former governess and valet but that the reader also contemplate a world where these travesties don't show. More than the possibility of depraved ghosts haunting the estate of Bly, it is the possibility that children might be capable of pretending to be childlike that most motivates the governess's increasingly obsessive need to know what the children truly know…if they know anything at all.

One of the core discoveries that James perceived in crafting *What Maisie Knew*, published only one year before *The Turn of the Screw*, was that childhood holds such a tender place in nineteenth-century bourgeois society that the smallest transgression against this idealized figure could produce the most dramatic effect. Against his readers, James makes a wrenching "turn of the screw" (a phrase first used in *Maisie*) by bearing down on this cultural soft spot (*Maisie* 97). Like *Maisie*, *The Turn of the Screw* tells the story of children who have been abandoned to the care of servants. Only in *Turn*, it is the servants who take over the point of view of the story, and we are dealing with not one but two children. From the beginning, James suggests that this latter move is significant. Douglas, who agrees to unveil the governess's manuscript account of the horrors that took place at Bly, builds dramatic tension for the great reveal by asking his audience: "'If the child gives the effect another turn of the screw, what do you say to *two* children—?'" The answer "'of course'" is that "'two children give two turns!'" (1). If we read this exchange as something more than playful banter, one reason for acknowledging that two children are worse than one is because they invite the audience to imagine the potential application of such horrors to all of childhood. One child may be an exception (Maisie has often been seen in this way). Two children suggest a pattern that is much harder to dismiss.

Although *The Turn of the Screw* is not the first tale where James has explored the possibility that children may perform childhood, it is distinctly given over to the broader, unbounded, and nefarious implications of such performances. It invites readers to question: if these children can perform childhood, then what are the essential, rooted features of the child as we know it? Is it possible that childhood innocence and goodness are not innate, as supposed, but are (like gender and race) socially constructed and highly policed expectations of childhood? Scarier still, if the predominant features of childhood are not essential to children, then mightn't they be available to non-children and—even more horrifying—to what ends? Some of these questions had already surfaced for James in *What Maisie Knew*, where, as Sally Shuttleworth contends, James responded to the driving assumption within the child-study movement that there is something "natural" to childhood that can be studied with a child heroine who is saved from such adult scrutiny by her ability to convincingly perform the expectations of childhood instead (Shuttleworth 325–327). In *The Turn of the Screw* James continues this interest in the performance of childhood, but it is far less clear where the reader's sympathies should lie. *The Turn of the Screw* is notoriously ambiguous and ambivalent about the many questions that it raises,[4] and in this the text is no different. There is room to feel sorry for the young Flora and Miles who have been abandoned by their only living relative. There is also room to sympathize with the young governess who clearly possesses unrequited feelings for this uncle and who bravely (if not selflessly) accepts the daunting mission of taking sole responsibility for these children whose young lives already come with a great deal of baggage. And, of course, there is room to feel no sympathy whatever either for the children who may, in fact, be maddeningly heartless or for the governess who may, after all, be their gravest threat.

In Chap. 3, I illustrated how James's efforts to think, not normatively, but ironically about child consciousness set the stage for the emergence of modernist experiments in fiction and thought with *What Maisie Knew*. However, it is with *The Turn of the Screw* that James's and modernism's interest in darkening society's vision of childhood becomes most gut-wrenchingly clear. There is a modicum of safety in *Maisie*, as in *Peter Pan*, in the prospect that these eponymous children are exceptions to the rule of the "Quintessential Child," defined by Judith Plotz as the Victorian assumption that childhood is a universal and universally sublime entity, "unmarked by time, place, class, or gender" (5). Indeed, the famous first line of Barrie's *Peter and Wendy* reads: "All children, *except one*, grow up" (5; emphasis added). On top of this Barrie's playful way of relegating the cunning and heartless Peter to an imaginary "Neverland" adds yet another way for modern readers to distance their own investment in Edenic childhood from Barrie's imaginary world of childhood seduction and tyranny. However, there are no Mrs. Darlings or Wendys or Neverlands in *The Turn of the Screw* to contain the circulation of James's counterfeit innocence.

Much of the suspense and anxiety that *The Turn of the Screw* generates comes from the sheer lack of boundaries walling children into Edenic childhood and walling both out of the hands of adult society. At the center of the governess's dilemma is her fear that Peter Quint and Miss Jessel have over-stepped natural and unnatural lines alike, masquerading (when they were alive) as master and mistress of the largely empty estate, crossing the line (after their deaths) back into the land of the living, and, most worrisome of all, scheming their way into the hearts and minds of the children. In *What Maisie Knew*, James explored the dynamic of a child cast "in the midst" of modern, adult society; here he appears to explore a similar predicament but from the opposite direction (*Notebooks*, 127). From the point of view of the governess, the problem in *The Turn of the Screw* is really about adults taking up residence in the midst of childhood. The governess depicts herself as being on the side of the children, of being "united" with them in their "danger" (27). But, of course, this entails that Peter Quint and Miss Jessel are not the only ones who have crossed over into the realm of childhood but that the governess herself has also trespassed there.

When George Boas wrote a history of ideas on the modern fixation with "childhood as the most blessed time of life" (101–102), which he termed "the cult of childhood," he questioned whether the pursuant emphasis on the "retention of childhood in maturity" was "either possible or desirable" (33). Published 68 years before Boas's landmark history, *The Turn of the Screw* asks the same question (among others) in a story where "the cult of childhood" infects or threatens to infect everyone. *What Maisie Knew* and *The Turn of the Screw* are sister texts in that each shows that the separate spheres (to use a phrase common to the era's gender divide) of childhood and adulthood are really not separate at all. Maisie, Miles, and Flora (like so many actual children) are witnesses to a secret world where adults, regardless of class status, regularly traffic in the minds and features of childhood. Although the governess believes that she and the children are "united in [their] danger," they are actually, as the story reveals in its unfolding, distinctly endangered by their union (27). Where James surprises readers of *Maisie* by suggesting ways that the child may be empowered through performances of childhood, he takes a much darker view in *The Turn of the Screw*. Here the performance of childhood threatens not just the children but every strata of society. Part of what gets lost in readings of the novella that take sides between children and servants (both the dead and the living) is just how much the performance of childhood hurts everyone involved. In fact, the concepts of evil and innocence at the heart of the story are not placed in opposition to one another but are ironically posed as analogous problems. Innocence is as haunting, as nebulous, and as suspect as are the ghosts of Peter Quint and Miss Jessel. Of all the "turns" that the novel reveals, this is by far the worst and also, I fear, the least appreciated. Even if the evil spirits are real, they are not the cause of the illness and death in the novel. Rather, it is the governess's relentless probing into the question of the children's innocence that results in the undoing of Flora and Miles. Moreover, it is the governess's own claims to innocence—even to a childlike innocence—that excuse her (in her mind at least) from mature responsibility and restraint.

Enduring Innocence

For most, to speak of innocence as a problem is to speak of its fragility or loss. This is even true for those who read the governess's interest in the children, particularly her interest in Miles, as a fictional case study in erotic innocence, a phrase coined by James Kincaid to capture the voyeuristic pleasure nineteenth- and twentieth-century adults were allowed and encouraged to take in the presence of the child's perceived purity, vulnerability, and beauty.[5] The governess's "constant joy" in watching the children (18), the "beautiful intercourse" that she imagines possible between herself and Miles (81), and the inflamed "passion" with which she holds him at the end of the story, not realizing for a full minute that he lies "dispossessed" in her arms (85), create a thinly veiled string of sexual innuendo, laced throughout *The Turn of the Screw*. Kincaid himself offers *The Turn of the Screw* as a literary exemplar of erotic innocence, but Kevin Ohi's recent *Innocence and Rapture* supplies the most thorough explication of how it is that Flora and Miles can be branded, as they are in the text, as at once "'blameless and foredoomed'" (qtd. in Ohi 125). His answer is that the child's blameless innocence is already doomed by the adult desire that sanctified and empowered it in the first place. Erotic innocence speaks to the paradox of an innocence so beloved in its most absolute and most malleable forms that it becomes part of a binary logic, making it impossible to behold such innocence without also seeing its rupture. As Ohi puts it, the "temporality of erotic innocence" is such that it "cannot contemplate purity without seeing the salacious details of its demise" (131).

The hypocrisy of an innocence that has been socially constructed for the enjoyment of adults is an important part of what is at stake in the analyses of erotic innocence offered by Ohi and Kincaid, among others. What I would like to suggest is that this hypocrisy takes place on a much wider scale for James and for other modernists after him. There are multiple types of innocence at play in *The Turn of the Screw*. These include Edenic innocence, wondrous innocence, and even erotic innocence. However, the effect of switching back and forth between these types is crucial, for it creates a very different problem than the inevitability of the children's corruption. In fact, it creates the opposite problem, which is the inevitability of innocence's survival. What is at issue in the continual handing off of one type of innocence for another is how the cult of childhood endures, not just as a virtue that adults seek to police and prolong in childhood but as a treasure that adults themselves seek to claim.

Inspired by Jean Jacques Rousseau's counsel in *Émile* to love, prolong, and reconnect with youth as the antidote to grim maturity, many prominent writers and thinkers in subsequent years reified childhood innocence as a goal of adult-kind (79).[6] In "My Heart Leaps Up," William Wordsworth famously hailed "the Child is father of the Man," and in his "Ode on

Intimations of Immortality," he drew upon memories of childhood, "of splendour in the grass, of glory in the flower," to enrich the depths of poetic creation, philosophical understanding, and human compassion.[7] For William Blake, too, childhood innocence served as a natural and spiritual light, shining the way for the receptive artist to achieve what Roni Natov terms the "higher Innocence" of art (21). The subtitle of Blake's *Songs of Innocence and Experience*, "Shewing the Two Contrary States of the Human Soul," is as interesting for what it does not say as for what it does. In labeling innocence a state of the "human soul" Blake implicitly does not label it strictly as a state of childhood, but envisions innocence—like experience—as a possibility for anyone of any age. Across the Atlantic, there was a similar association of childhood innocence with the forces of creation as well as with the sense of what it meant to be an exemplary adult. In *Nature*, Ralph Waldo Emerson celebrates the adult "who has retained the spirit of infancy even into the era of manhood" (75). And in literature, Mark Twain and Harriet Beecher Stowe (in)famously made white childhood the voice of anti-slavery and anti-racist discourses in America. Nineteenth-Century literature is overflowing with spaces for the preservation of the child's iconic innocence. Barrie's Neverland, Carroll's Wonderland, Twain's Mississippi River, and Stowe's heaven are most interesting not because they are imaginary geographies where children can be innocent children forever but because they are imaginary geographies where adults and children breathe the same salvific air.

In *The Turn of the Screw* James highlights the absurd mental gymnastics that the fantasy of childhood innocence—preserved, cherished, and shared—requires. In regards to Flora and Miles, James dramatizes in the beginning how much history must be ignored in order for the image of the children's innocence to remain untarnished. Before the governess arrives at Bly, the children's lives have been shaped by one trauma after another. They have lost parents and grandparents, home and nation (having been raised in India); they have even lost their servant caretakers, Peter Quint and Miss Jessel. This history weighs heavy on the governess's mind as she makes the long journey to Bly, but her worries are quickly annulled by the children's unmarred appearance. Flora, to the governess's delight, shows no "sign of uncomfortable consciousness" and lives "radiant[ly]" and "angelic[ally]" like "one of Raphael's holy infants" in the moment (7–8). Miles's appearance in the narrative is preceded by the dark cloud of his recent expulsion from school. Though this expulsion is the very prerequisite for his character's entrance, in the flesh as it were, his physical showing is, it turns out, all that is required to clear him. His "incredibly beautiful" emergence reveals him "on the instant, without and within." The governess proclaims that all anyone need do is "'*look* at him!'" to see that the "cruel charge" cannot live where the "sweetness of innocence" so evidently reigns (13). Flora and Miles, when the governess encounters them, appear reborn. They are like babes who have just floated off of the canvas of a Renaissance painting or down from the heavens above. Upon meeting them, the governess whitewashes everything that she knows to be true about the children, whitewashes her image of the children themselves, and concludes that they have "nothing to call even an infinitesimal history," that they have "never for a second suffered" (19).

As the narrative unfolds, it becomes increasingly clear that the governess's duty to innocence has less and less to do with the actual children in her charge and far more to do with the idyllic images of childhood that she has brought to bear upon them. Shortly after her arrival, the governess draws out from Mrs. Grose the news that the uncle's former valet, Quint, not only took full charge of the house and children in their uncle's absence but that he was, worst of all, "much too free" with everyone (25). His relationship with Miss Jessel turns her into a fallen woman and his "perpetual" society with Miles seems no less lascivious (34). And Flora, though shielded from the basest Quint, may also have felt his influence indirectly through her "infamous" governess and older brother (31). In light of this history, the governess's subsequent determination to shield the children from the influences of the (now dead) Quint and Jessel appears to defy logic. The threat that Quint and Jessel will tempt the children to untold evils is really the threat of a repeat performance, perhaps more dangerous than the first but nonetheless secondary to what has already occurred. The governess accuses Mrs. Grose of forsaking the children by not intervening when she had a chance, even though she full-knew the effects the depraved Quint could have had on their "innocent little precious lives." But, moments later, the governess herself appears to have forgotten these effects along with Mrs. Grose's negligence in her own determination to "protect and defend the little creatures" who have already been exposed (26–27). The innocence that Mrs. Grose fails to defend appears to be definitively reclaimed by the governess whose instincts convince her that the children remain helpless victims, knowing not what they have seen.

James continues to caricature the cult of childhood by repeating the pattern of innocence found, lost, and found again across scenarios that become increasingly murky. Even when the governess believes she has discovered that the children too have seen the apparitions, she somehow manages to retrace her steps back to ground zero. When the governess believes that she witnesses Flora going out of her way not to make eye contact with Miss Jessel on the other side of the Sea of Azof, her entire mission seems upended. The governess thinks she has been shielding the children from the knowledge of evil; now she perceives that it is she who has been ignorant and naïve. The children have known all along, and it is she who has been kept in the dark. Only pages after soaring on the fantasy of saving the children and living happily ever after with their grateful and aristocratic uncle, the governess sinks to a new low. She laments to Mrs. Grose: "I don't save or shield them! It's far worse than I dreamed. They're lost!" (32). The governess's disillusionment is powerful. Her monumental efforts to "save or shield" the children have been wasted. What is "worse" is that the children have evidently been manipulating her, letting her think they are innocent while all along they have been just pretending to be. In contrast to the children, whom the governess now imagines as plotting and concealing, the governess practically explodes with her newfound knowledge. She shows herself incapable of containing such horrors and of pretending not to know what she knows. And yet, powerful as this climax is, the governess astonishingly determines to walk backwards from it, erasing her mental footprints as she goes. She determines to "give to grievous fancies and even to odious memories a kind of brush of the sponge" (36). The governess's decision in this moment emphasizes not just the act of erasure but the content that is being erased. The blotting out of fancies is one matter but the forgetting of memories is another entirely. This scene suggests that the governess is working very hard in the name of innocence to bury not just what she believes but what she has experienced. It is striking too that the "brush of the sponge" is swept across the governess's mind. The children may or may not be blank slates at this point in the narrative but the governess seeks herself to be just that. Barring additional evidence, the governess says that she will give the children both a "fresh start," but in seeking to forget her own experiences, she is also giving herself a fresh start with them (37).

Even when Miles proves plotting and inconsistent (after he has colluded with his sister to sneak out onto the lawn at night in order [as he claims] to surprise the governess with his potential for bad behavior or [as she believes] to commune with the evil spirit of Peter Quint), his innocence is nevertheless swiftly restored. Again, this feat requires a kind of hypocrisy on the governess's part. Now, rather than feeling appalled by the children's efforts to pretend at being innocent, she finds Miles's struggle "to play a part of innocence and consistency" "unutterably touching." Though he no longer possesses the healthful bloom of the schoolroom poet, Miles now readily fills the shoes of the nineteenth-century charity case. With his face "framed in its smooth whiteness," he becomes "as appealing as some wistful patient in a children's hospital," for whom the governess would have given all she "possessed on earth really to be the nurse or the sister of charity who might have helped to cure him" (60–61). Having evidently crossed the line of experience, Miles remains innocent because his brand of innocence changes. The governess arrives at a new set of conditions. She decides that even if "the imagination of all evil *had* been opened up to [Miles]" there would be no "justice" without some "proof that it could ever have flowered into an act" (63). In one sense, the governess shifts toward an innocence of negation that values the child's presumed lack of agency and vulnerability. Though already exposed, little is permanent for the child whose victimization makes him as easily extracted from the scene of danger as he was led into it in the first place. But in another sense, the governess shifts outside of the realm of childhood innocence altogether. In drawing upon the judicial doctrine of "innocent until proven guilty," she expands the litmus test of innocence beyond active goodness and original creation, beyond knowledge of sex and sin, and even beyond the experience of each of these, to the standards of due process.[8] Whether on account of unmarred beauty, a lack of experience, the lack of memory of those experiences, blameless suffering, a lack of evidence, or the absence of a punishable offense, childhood innocence is as ineradicable for the governess as are the ghosts that haunt her.

Childhood Innocence and the Adult Imagination

Though there were ideologies, ranging from the Calvanistic to the Freudian, which sought to emphasize the devil in the child, salvific representations of childhood had much more cultural currency at the turn of the twentieth century in large part because of the promise of renewed feeling, imagination, and faith that they offered to world-weary adults. The governess's vision of an enduring and pliable innocence runs with the grain of modern society's new appreciation for childhood and concomitant desire to use all of the tools at its disposal to give childhood's idealized features new longevity. Unsatisfied with limiting innocence—or childhood itself for that matter—to children alone, the successors to Romanticism increasingly carved out pathways whereby the innocent and the childlike could endure the transition from youth to age. For Blake and Wordsworth the path to a second, higher innocence was narrowly forged, requiring great efforts at compassion and creativity, but as the cultural role of the child moved from the periphery to the bourgeois heart of society, efforts to extend, relive, and channel the innocent wonder of childhood grew. As Alice Boardman Smuts writes, American society before World War I celebrated the child by trying "to reform society for the benefit of the child," and American society after World War I celebrated the child by trying "to reform the child for the benefit of society" (4). In other words, the goal no longer seems, as Hugh Cunningham writes of Victorian reformers, "to save children for . . . childhood" (137). In America, at least, it seems increasingly important in the early twentieth century to save childhood for the adults who will someday inherit it.

But while many of James's forerunners and contemporaries reveled in the possibilities of idyllic childhood, he and other modernists extrapolated—through fiction—the potential damage of an innocence enshrined in the adult imagination. It is telling that nearly three decades before Ellen Key made "the century of the child" the cause célèbre of the twentieth century, James bestowed the nineteenth century with a similar title, the "Children's Century," but with the opposite intention. Instead of rallying American society toward a progressive future, James, as Muriel Shine has put it, worries about a "juvenile takeover" (47). In the voice of the forthright and outspoken Miss Sturdy in *The Point of View*, James writes:

> *A propos* of the young people, that is our other danger; the young people are eating us up,—there is nothing in America but the young people. The country is made for the rising generation; life is arranged for them; they are the destruction of society. People talk of them, consider them, defer to them, bow down to them.... Longfellow wrote a charming little poem called "The Children's Hour," but he ought to have called it "The Children's Century." And by children, of course, I don't mean simple infants; I mean everything of less than twenty. (536–537)

For Miss Sturdy, childhood in America has become doubly and dangerously expansive, absorbing years (now up to 20) and usurping prime cultural real estate from society's more mature membership. Whether or not her "point of view" toward childhood is, as Shine argues, consistent with James's own at the time, its concerns are at least partially realized in the child-centered world of *The Turn of the Screw*, where the ever-larger umbrella of childhood, while perhaps not signaling the "destruction of society," poses a no less significant threat to the person of the governess and, for that matter, to the children themselves.

The governess in *The Turn of the Screw* represents a woman whose work and identity are yoked (a touch too tightly) to child society. The early world at Bly is, the governess finds, a space of "constant joy" and "constant fresh discoveries." Here, she imagines that there will be "no grey prose," only the "romance of the nursery and the poetry of the schoolroom" (18). Like Alice in Wonderland, the inexperienced governess imagines herself as having "fallen a-doze and a-dream" into this new world, where she is led by the confiding and intrepid Flora, "with her hair of gold and her frock of blue" (the very image of Alice), "danc[ing]…round corners and patter[ing] down passages" (9). While in hindsight the governess perceives the Bly house as "a big ugly antique…half-displaced and half-utilised," when she first sets foot on the estate grounds, she says she felt as though she had entered a world so glorious as to drain "all the colour out of story-books and fairy-tales" (9).

On the one hand, the governess's entrance into Bly represents her first foray, at 20 years of age, into adult responsibility but, on the other, it represents the gift of a second childhood. Of this tension, particularly in relation to the instruction of Miles, she writes:

> I found it simple, in my ignorance, my confusion and perhaps my conceit, to assume that I could deal with a boy whose education for the world was all on the point of beginning…Lessons with me indeed, that charming summer, we all had a theory that he was to have; but I now feel that for weeks the lessons must have been rather my own. I learnt something—at first certainly—that had not been one of the teachings of my small smothered life; learnt to be amused, and even amusing, and not to think for the morrow. It was the first time, in a manner, that I had known space and air and freedom, all the music of summer and all the mystery of nature. (14)

The governess begins with a recognition of what her and the children's roles should have been in "theory," but the "charming" circumstances of Bly, paired with her own heretofore "small smothered life," combine to create a practical reversal of these roles. In the midst of this new world, the governess herself embodies the spirit of the "young" and the "untried" (5). "Confus[ed]" and "ignoran[t]" of the situation's complexities, she finds herself operating, like an innocent, under a set of "simple" assumptions (14). Indeed, instead of preparing Flora and Miles for their own entrances into adult life, they educate her in the ways of childhood romance. The governess truly comes from a different world, certainly from a different class, "the youngest of several daughters of a poor country parson" (4). Though she has perhaps experienced the "smothered" terrain of sheltered innocence, with these children, in this uniquely independent, child-centered environment, the governess feels herself initiated into the "space," the "freedom," the "music," and the "mystery" of child wonder and creativity. The governess comes to describe the children's company as offering an otherworldly "antidote" to the "pains" of her and her family's real life hardships (19) and confesses feeling that "to throw" herself into "life with Miles and Flora" was "to throw [herself] out of [her] trouble" (18).

The roles between child and adult are evidently blurred in these passages where the governess appears to exaggerate not just her affinity for but her similarities to the naïve wonder of childhood. From the beginning, it is striking just how far the governess goes to represent herself as an innocent among innocents. Her earliest breaches with the decorum of her office, as when she interrogates Mrs. Grose regarding the ghost-figure of Peter Quint, are justified, she feels, by her ability "to meet...without scruple, any degree of innocence" (21). When the governess learns of Miles's expulsion, her obsession with the cause is so desperate-seeming that it leads Mrs. Grose to ask: "Are you afraid he'll corrupt *you*?" (12). From Mrs. Grose's point of view the joke is on the governess, whom Mrs. Grose insinuates has forgotten just who is the child and who is the adult in this scenario. From the reader's perspective, however, the joke may be on Mrs. Grose who strikes closer to the truth than she realizes. Perhaps it is not the case that the governess can yet imagine Miles as a corrupting influence, but it is certainly true that she believes herself to be uncorrupted. A young woman herself, the governess sits peculiarly astride the line of innocence. She feels responsible for preserving the innocence of her charges, but she also feels herself to be an innocent among them.[9]

The governess has, in fact, long perceived herself as a member of Flora and Miles's inner circle. Earlier, she had expressed: "We were cut off, really, together; we were united in our danger. They had nothing but me, and I—well, I had them" (27). However reluctant the governess may be to admit the extent of her own reciprocal dependence, this is a statement that insists, three times no less, on her relationship with the children as one uniquely shared. The repetition of their "together[ness]," their "unit[y]," and their mutual dependence, along with the exaggerated emphasis attached to it—they are "really" alone, "really" together; they have "nothing" but each other—suggests not just the strangeness of the situation, so strange as to command excess proof, but also the pleasure to be found in it; isolation and danger appear as mere backdrops to the new intimacy and community forged to face them.

An essential aspect of the governess's cause for alarm in the novella's final contest between child and adult is that she has presumed herself to be the bearer of innocence. That innocence has become a core feature of her identity is evidenced by her narrative paralysis in the face of the alternative. At the end of *The Turn of the Screw*, the governess faces a perilous conundrum. Having at last resolved to confront her young charge, Miles, with the fact of his expulsion, having determined that the risks of such confrontation—the child's exposure and even torment—are warranted, her interrogation yet falls short of its much anticipated mark. Miles's murky confession, that he had "said things" to "those he liked," sends the governess's ship (of which she has from the start found herself "strangely at the helm" (9)) once again into unknown waters. She writes, "I seemed to float not into clearness, but into a darker obscure, and within a minute there had come to me out of my very pity the appalling alarm of his being perhaps innocent. It was for the instant confounding and bottomless, for if he *were* innocent what then on earth was I?" (83). Implicitly, innocence is a concept that both anchors and troubles the governess's world view. The if/then logic of her question is causal and competitive. If Miles had been innocent in the past (and the emphasis is on the past tense "*were*"), then the governess would herself be guilty of bringing about its end. It's competitive because it denies the possibility of being both innocent and guilty at the same time. While the governess's "appalling alarm" that Miles might, after all, be innocent speaks to the no less appalling presumption that he might be otherwise, the more striking notion is that if the governess cannot now imagine herself as being guilty, then she may have imagined herself as a competitor in the field of innocence.

Turning the Child

As Ellen Pifer has shown, there are two deaths at the end of *The Turn of the Screw*: one is the death of the child, and the other is the death of the governess's dreams of childhood (50). What begins as a fairy tale for her, governed by fantasies of a happy-ever-after, turns into a tragedy ruled by fear, suspicion, and ghosts. The fairy tale and the ghost story are defining narratives for the governess's time at Bly. They each represent their own seemingly preposterous realities, which are also seemingly worlds apart from one other. Whereas Cox and Gilbert describe the Victorian ghost story as evincing a modern "anxiety" about a potentially "vindictive past" (ix), Jack Zipes writes that a nearly universal purpose of the modern fairy tale is "to provide hope in a world seemingly on the brink of catastrophe" (1). Yet, James describes these two genres as though they are analogous forms. Indeed, in the 1909 preface he collapses these two aesthetic categories into one, writing of the "'ghost-story'" that it "has ever been for me the most possible form of the fairy-tale" (104). One key reason that James provides for placing these two genres on the same spectrum is that they each tell big stories in small containers. What attracts James to fairy tales like "Bluebeard" and "Little Red Riding Hood" (two he names in the 1908 preface) is a less-is-more quality. The fairy tale form is compressed, "compact," but the space it opens up in the reader's imagination is a cavernous "excursion into chaos" (124–125).[10]

Described in this way, the fairy tale sounds not unlike the torture device that gives the novella its title and which appears twice in the story that follows. The "screw" was a medieval torture device, a small portable vise, capable of inflicting enormous bone-breaking pain on a victim's toes or fingers. To "turn" the screw is to clamp down on a victim so that they will spill any knowledge they may contain. Most have taken James's title to refer to the governess's increasingly desperate need for a confession from the two children of all that they know and to the increasing pressure that she applies in order to obtain it, a pressure that drives one child mad and leaves the other dead. Many have also noted the ways in which this tortuous relationship between governess and children serves as a microcosm for the novella's larger relationship to its readers, who struggle to find some interpretive foothold within James's version of a narrative vise, a story buried three narrators deep, compressed into a mere 100 or so pages. Like James's vision of the fairy tale and ghost story, *The Turn of the Screw* is a narrative that is so "compact" that it compels readers to fill in with their own imaginations the great quantity of (mostly terrible) things that are never said outright.

When James prefaces *The Turn of the Screw* with the sentiment that the ghost story is for him "the most possible form of the fairy-tale," he sets a complicated mission for the text. On the one hand, he seems drawn toward the fairy tale genre, enough that he indebts the novella to it. On the other hand, he seems deeply resistant to a form that he decides is "most possible" only when merged with its darkest cousin. One way that James meets this ambivalent objective is through his adaptation of the *tabula rasa* of childhood into a vehicle for evil. When James writes in the 1908 preface to the New York edition that his "values" in the text "are positively all blanks," he may mean that the lessons of the story are left unsaid or that the story has no moral lesson to it at all (128). In the lines that follow, James suggests that he means both of these: that the secrets of the novella are at once unnamed and morally suspect.

The key to this blank method, as James describes it, is to turn over the work of detailed description to the imagination of the reader: "Make him *think* the evil, make him think it for himself, and [the author is] released from weak specifications" (128). What James takes for granted in this discussion is the link between the "blanks" he describes and the child subject. Even if a reader were wholly unfamiliar with the notion of the blank slate which John Locke used to advocate for the power and responsibility that society has to shape the content of the child's mind, it is clear that the single biggest blank in *The Turn of the Screw* is the striking absence of Flora's and Miles's points of view. The entire question of what the children know or don't know depends upon this particular gap in the narrative design. James's blank method appears to be inspired by metaphors of the child as a blank slate and by children's narratives like the fairy tale, but James is equally interested in how he can redirect these forms into new, ironic territories that will challenge his largely Victorian readership. In the case of Flora and Miles, James turns this blank method against its child muse by using it pointedly to raise doubts about who they are and what they are about.

Just as James casts a dark shadow over the fairy tale genre by aligning it with the ghost story, he likewise calls the children and all that they represent into question by placing them vaguely in cahoots with the nefarious Quint and Jessel. Though the governess perceives two ghosts at Bly, James intimates the presence of a figurative third in the multiple conflations between the child and the ghostly. Early on, the governess describes herself as being "under a charm" (14) or "under the spell" (19) of the children. Later, when she finds both children out of bed and Flora transfixed at her window, the governess and the reader too are filled with the expectation of another spectral sighting. Only, what we behold instead, alone on the lawn, is Miles. Indeed, child and ghost receive identical narrative treatment. The same phrase, "presence on the lawn," is used twice, once to describe the anticipation of the ghost and then again to describe the figure of the child himself (43). "Presence" is also used to describe Flora in the governess's final confrontation with her, with Miss Jessel "on the opposite" side of the lake (68). In all of the versions prior to the New York 1908 edition, James describes Flora's expression, "turned" on the governess, as one "of hard, still gravity," as "an expression absolutely new and unprecedented," and as one "that somehow converted the little girl herself into the very *presence* that could make [the governess] quail" (*Two Magics* 137; emphasis added). In the New York edition, the allusion relies on the governess's proclamation to Mrs. Grose (upon the apparent discovery that eight-year-old Flora has herself managed the boat across the lake) that "at such times" Flora is neither alone nor a child; she is rather "an old, old woman" (66). These confluences show case the connections between each child and his or her own respective ghostly counterpart, where Miles converges with Quint and Flora with Miss Jessel.[11]

Yet the children are in a sense more terrifying, in part because they make for very surprising ghosts. Where Quint and Jessel represent, and not unexpectedly so, the threat of an inexorable evil, an evil that simply will not die, Flora and Miles haunt the governess (and the text) in precisely the opposite and in precisely the most unexpected way, evincing a look of innocence, a "more than earthly beauty," an "absolutely unnatural goodness," that endures where it should not (47). As Quint and Jessel acted the roles of servant and teacher in life (one of the governess's key identifying features of Quint's ghost is that he looks "like an actor" [23]), the new suggestion is that Flora and Miles may also be performing, not embodying, innocence. The governess declares their innocence in one moment "a policy and a fraud" (47) and suspects, in another, that Miles is "taxed to play, under the spell laid on him, a part of innocence and consistency" (61). But innocence, where the governess is concerned—Edenic and wondrous or now ghostly and unnatural—is still innocence to be sheltered and preserved. Miles on the lawn is still "poor little Miles"; the whiteness of his visage calls the governess to save and to shield him (43). Flora's expression at the lake too is haunting in its undying show of innocence. What strikes the governess is the smoothness of the child's "small pink face" and the look, directed from her, as if to "accuse and judge" (69). In either case, the images of the children, like the ghosts, serve as haunting reminders and vigilant critics of the governess's self-perceived role—to be herself the savior of innocence—but they also together represent the monstrous possibilities for the undying dead, be it in the form of a returned evil or in the form of an enduring innocence that turns and changes but will not be lost.

Another way that James emphasizes both the expanding connection between governess and child and the problems lurking within that relation takes me back to novella's title and its two appearances in the text.

Though the vast majority of scholars emphasize "turn of the screw" as an allusion to a device meant for exerting control over another, even to the point of torture,[12] Shoshana Felman's work stands as an important exception to this trend. Felman points to the obvious, but vastly overlooked, network of meanings for the term "turn." She asks: "Does the word 'turn' here mean 'a turning point,' 'a change of meaning,' 'a turn of events,' or 'a turn of hysteria'...And if it means a turning point (a change of meaning), does it designate a simple *reorientation* or a radical *disorientation*?" (223; emphasis in original). For Felman the title metaphor signals a loss of control, a constant turning or changing of direction that defies mastery at every level. In other words, where most are drawn to the intensity of the screw's effect to secure and really pin-down its subject, Felman points to the title's equal emphasis on the turning mechanism by which the screw works, fixing a point counterintuitively by circling around it or alternatively unfixing a point by "*revers[ing] itself*" in like manner (223; emphasis in original). Thus, *The Turn of the Screw* is most notable for Felman in the way that it uses these ambiguities, these turns of meaning, to turn skeptically on meaning itself. Meaning becomes madness for the governess who ultimately loses her grip on Flora and Miles, on her post, and possibly (as many have argued) on her sense of reality. But meaning also becomes madness, Felman demonstrates, for the reader who resembles the governess by seeking an analogous hold on the text.

Still if the reader's and governess's investments in a screw-wielding mastery are mistaken, as Felman persuasively argues, then their error cannot be adequately measured without the child medium so essential to both. Missing more generally from the various interpretations of "the turn of the screw" is the turning of the child, unique to James's particular metaphorical application. Occurring only at the very beginning and the very end of the novella, the title moments invite comparison for the ways that adults in both instances find themselves on the receiving end of the experiences of childhood. The first title reference accrues out of the ghost story that opens *The Turn of the Screw* and which motivates Douglas to share his own, superior version of what happens when children and ghosts collide. The frame narrator gives an account of the tale of Griffin's ghost and Douglas's response to it:

> The case...was that of an apparition in just such an old house as had gathered us for the occasion—an appearance, of a dreadful kind, to a little boy

sleeping in the room with his mother and waking her up in the terror of it; waking her not to dissipate his dread and soothe him to sleep again, but to encounter also herself, before she had succeeded in doing so, the same sight that had shocked him. It was this observation that drew from Douglas...a reply that had the interesting consequence to which I call attention... "I quite agree—in regard to Griffin's ghost, or whatever it was—that its appearing first to the little boy, at so tender an age, adds a particular touch...If the child gives the effect another turn of the screw, what do you say to *two* children—?" (1)

The audience's response, "'of course,'" is that "'two children give two turns!'" In this opening equation nothing could be more explicit than the conceptual child's intimate, one-to-one, relationship with the narrative's sense of turning. One sense, the one explicated by Douglas, is the vivid, even visceral, effect conferred on the audience, on account of and through the child. For the innocent, impressionable child subject, it is imagined that the appearance of the ghost will produce a more terrifying, more dreadful reaction; this heightened response, Douglas expresses, is passed on to (and whole-heartedly received by) the adult audience.

But within this transference there lies another sense of turning. Beyond the emotional effect of the story, there is also an implication of an exchange, from child to adult, a turning over, a relaying, of terror from one subject to the other. One of the surprise turns of the story is the seemingly peculiar reaction of the child to the visitation of Griffin's ghost. The frame narrator reveals by his account that the child does not behave as expected, for though he wakes his mother "in the terror of it," he does so "not to dissipate his dread" but so that she can "encounter also herself...the same sight that had shocked him." In other words, the child seeks more than the dissipation of his experience; he seeks its displacement, to turn it—that is, redirect it—to the nearest adult. In both relationships, between child and mother and between child character and adult audience, the experiences of childhood prove to be terrifyingly shareable; and the child himself proves to be terrifyingly capable of sharing them.

The second title reference follows further the line by which the governess's ventures into child society (now with Miles alone) renders her dependent upon that society at the same time that it seems to push the children out. With Flora removed from Bly and with Miles now "free" from her instruction and from her self-described "inexorable, perpetual society," the governess lays out her strategy for approaching him anew (52). Facing a dilemma she feels is "revoltingly, against nature," she deduces:

> I could only get on at all by taking 'nature' into my confidence and my account, by treating my monstrous ordeal as a push in a direction unusual, of course, and unpleasant, but demanding after all, for a fair front, only another turn of the screw of ordinary human virtue. No attempt, none the less, could well require more tact than just this attempt to supply, one's self, *all* the nature. How could I put even a little of that article into a suppression of reference to what had occurred? How on the other hand could I make a reference without a new plunge into the hideous obscure? Well, a sort of answer, after a time, had come to me…Wasn't there light in the fact which, as we shared our solitude, broke out with a specious glitter it had never yet quite worn—the fact that…it would be preposterous, with a child so endowed, to forego the help one might wrest from absolute intelligence? What had his intelligence been given him for but to save him? Might n't one, to reach his mind, risk the stretch of a stiff arm across his character?" (77–78)

As strategic rationales go, this one is frustratingly opaque, evidencing, in part, the governess's growing investment in indirection as a means to know. Indeed, one general observation worth making is that the passage represents to a great extent a meditation on manipulation: on the governess's turning of nature, of reference, her relationship with the child, and the child himself. But another, culled in tandem, is that this set of manipulations also marks a strategy for compromise. "Another turn of the screw of human virtue" is an expression of these newly cooperative concerns, whereby the governess expresses both the need to fill, and to fill absolutely, the role that traditionally belongs to the child—as the supplier of "all the nature" and the need to manage that role in a most considered and artificial way, by plotting and strategizing with it—by "taking 'nature' into [her] confidence" and by administering "little" doses of it, as it were, with concealed "tact" and "suppress[ed]… reference[s]." But perhaps the more remarkable application of this new and revised sense of indirection, of turning as a compromised means to an end, shows itself in the governess's new rationale for approaching the child, whose character, she determines, might be justifiably breached for the sake of accessing his mind. The goal, in other words, of convincing the child to come clean, that is to confess, justifies the risk of his exposure in the interim.

In light of the ending, this meditation on turning (on turning herself in order that she might save the child and vice versa) represents itself as a significant turning point, supplying justification and permission in the abstract for the manifest interrogation and dispossession to come. The governess's earlier communal sentiment that she and Flora and Miles "were cut off, really, together…were united in [their] danger" (27) is echoed by this new gesture toward a "shared… solitude" with Miles, and both are precursors to her fatal inability to release Miles from his child role, which is also, in her communal view, a role that she "share[s]." Miles's request to the governess for her "to let me alone" is a plea really for the recognition of his gender, his age, and the independence conventionally suited to both (62).[13] The difference in the second communal allusion as opposed to the first is that the nature of the union has become far more egalitarian. No longer is the governess's role to sacrifice herself in order to save the children; her consideration now is as much (if not more so) for her own salvation. Not only does she now perceive in Miles an adult equal (she invites him, in the end, to the "'grown-up' dining-room" [19]), but she, more strikingly, perceives herself as an equal to the child. Her feeling that she, and not the child, must "supply herself all the nature" to childhood sets the stage for the "appalling alarm" she feels moments later that the role of the innocent may not belong to her but may "perhaps" be the child's after all (83). Each of these turns, the turning of nature and of innocence, represents a more general turning over of childhood from the child to the adult. In the end, the governess not only kills Miles, she "dispossess[es]" him (85). She imagines herself as having battled "with a demon" for the "soul" of the child, and she, in a sense, has won (82).

Many have experienced the turn of *The Turn of the Screw* as a sensation of constraint, of tension, of entrapment; but the capaciousness, what James referred to as the "plasticity," of childhood, whereby any adult might gain vicarious entry to its heightened wonders, loves, and fears, suggests a loosening, rather than a tightening, where youth and where innocence are concerned ("To Dr. Louis" 305). James always planned *The Turn of the Screw* as a combination of freedom and constraint, as a formally structured fairy tale filled, as it were, with imaginative (and imaginatively evil) blanks. But there are two notable constants in *The Turn of the Screw*: one is the persistence of evil, the other of innocence. And both endure, in large part, because of their ambiguous and, indeed, ambivalent treatment. In *The Turn of the Screw*, innocence and damnation are not treated as distinct poles in a binary display; they are each indeterminate and possibly intermixed. *The Turn of the Screw* imagines an innocence, like evil, loosed: enduring and horrifying because it can be stretched in any number of directions.

It seems simple to say that the screw that can be turned one way can also be turned another, but James employs both turns to a most complex effect. Indeed, I submit that *The Turn of the Screw* captivates in large measure because it proves that constriction would be a relief to the loose and tormenting uncertainties of the story it tells. There are many, too many, innocences in *The Turn of the Screw*. There is the angelic innocence of Bly and its child inhabitants; there is the innocence of dependency in the governess's overwhelming desire to protect the children's innocence despite all odds and evidence to the contrary; there is wondrous innocence in the governess's desires to live herself a second childhood through life with Flora and Miles despite and in conflict with her adult responsibilities toward them; there is the innocence from wrong-doing that the governess uses to acquit the children even after she encounters evidence of their corruption. *The Turn of the Screw* demonstrates just how large and artificial the territory of childhood has become by the end of the nineteenth century. Innocence in *The Turn of the Screw* endures a touch too long; it encompasses a touch too much; it is a badge worn by too many.

In a story so obviously centered on unnatural terrors, it is surprising, but of course should not be, that innocence too should prove potentially monstrous. Peter Quint and Miss Jessel might have enticed the children to enter too soon the world of adulthood, but Bly and Flora and Miles clearly get on without them. Little seems destroyed by their temptations. The real bogey man in *The Turn of the Screw* is not evil. It is innocence. There are few apparent landmines in the pathway set to lead the children out of childhood; but the governess's efforts (which reflect the leanings of modern society) to obstruct this are devastating. While they make it easier for the governess to linger in the wonderland of her own vision of childhood, they make it impossible for the children to leave in tact. Most importantly, in these efforts the governess represents a caricature of the modern cult of childhood. Though Ellen Key celebrated the coming century as "the century of the child" and though her celebratory message struck a popular chord, in *The Turn of the Screw* James highlights the costs to child autonomy and adult restraint that this new investment in the ideal child might have forfeited in the bargain.

Notes

1. Peter Pan was first introduced within J.M. Barrie's 1902 adult novel *The Little White Bird*. *Peter Pan*, the play, emerged in 1904; *Peter and Wendy*, the children's book, did not appear until 1911.
2. Jacqueline Rose has studied the alterations which popular adaptations of *Peter Pan* have made to Barrie's original versions, particularly in the way these adaptations have tended to erase the role of *Peter and Wendy*'s ambivalent narrator. But even critics are not immune to the idolization of Peter; James Kincaid's otherwise engaging interpretation of the child in history holds the line on Peter's as a model of child innocence universally and wholly (by Barrie and by society at large) desired (113). Proceeding on two fronts, Karen Coats counters Kincaid's thesis that Peter exemplifies the empty ideal of modern "Child-Loving" with the argument that Peter's is really a figure of plenitude, whose lack of a lack actually makes him increasingly a target for Victorian "child-hating."
3. The story of Peter Pan's life before Neverland is told in Barrie's "Peter Pan in Kensington Gardens," published in 1906, five years before *Peter and Wendy*.
4. Even though Edmund Wilson's much considered essay "The Ambiguity of Henry James" makes title reference to ambiguity, it does anything but embrace the concept as such, sparking a now well-known debate over the story's ghosts as realities or hallucinations. The critical affirmation of ambiguity in James's *The Turn of the Screw* is not really launched until much later with arguments such as Shoshana Felman's (that Wilson himself exemplifies the type of critic trapped by the novella's questions without answers) and Marianne DeKoven's (that the novella does more than embrace ambiguous uncertainty, it exemplifies a modernist ambivalence, actively supplying "equally powerful evidence" for both sides of the "'apparitionist'" and "'antiapparitionist'" debate) (*Rich* 48–49).
5. I am here combining observations from Kincaid's first book on this topic *Child-Loving: The Erotic Child and Victorian Culture* and his more recent *Erotic Innocence*. While the former lays out in detail the "other[ing]" of the child during the nineteenth and twentieth centuries, Kincaid does not seem to arrive at a sense of the Victorian view of innocence as being a type of innocence deserving its own name, "erotic innocence," until later. Indeed, in *Child-Loving* Kincaid moves from an assertion by Philippe Ariès that "prior to the eighteenth century...nobody worried about soiling childish innocence because 'nobody thought that this innocence really existed'" to nineteenth-century ideas of childhood innocence as "vulnerability," and even posits that "this innocent child may be a very-late-Victorian or, more likely, modern imposition" (72–73). By the time Kincaid writes *Erotic*

Innocence this view seems to have evolved to include at least the possibility for an interim and tentative "positive" innocence (among the Romantics) before the modern "negative" innocence of the nineteenth and twentieth centuries gains a full foothold (15).
6. Rousseau's influence on Romanticism is widely acknowledged, particularly where Wordsworth is concerned, but McFarland's aptly titled *Romanticism and the Heritage of Rousseau* provides a rare book-length study of Rousseau's influence on Wordsworth, Coleridge, and Shelley.
7. Alan Richardson makes the important point that while there was very little that was original in Romanticism's glorification of childhood, a point fleshed out in more detail in Pattison's history of the sentimental treatment of the Renaissance child (47–51), nonetheless it was the Romantics, "particularly Wordsworth, Coleridge, Lamb, and De Quincey," who "succeeded at popularizing" this image. Of these, the power of Wordsworth's Immortality Ode was perhaps the most far-reaching. Barbara Garlitz writes that Wordsworth's ode "was to the first half of the nineteenth century what *The Origin of the Species* was to the last half" (639), with an influence that extended well beyond the literary sphere, profoundly affecting theologians, laymen, parents, and social activists.
8. "Innocent until proven guilty" does not make a formal appearance in American jurisprudence until the 1894 Supreme Court decision in *Coffin v. U.S.*, when Justice White cited it in his opinion (108), but Kenneth Pennington places the origins of the expression in the late thirteenth or early fourteenth century when the French canonist Johannes Monachus used it in a gloss on Pope Boniface VIII's *Rem non novam* (115). Thereafter, Monachus's commentary circulated widely through numerous manuscripts and editions for the next 400 years (116).
9. The question of the governess's innocence or guilt in the corruption of Flora and Miles (and in Miles's death) is crucial to how one reads *The Turn of the Screw*. In an early, 1892, notebook entry it appears that James's earliest thinking about the governess is tied to the possibility of her innocence. He writes: "Idea of a servant suspected of doing the mean things—the base things people in London take for granted servants do—reading letters, diaries, peeping, spying, etc.; turning out utterly innocent and incapable of these things—and turning the tables of scorn on the master or mistress" (111).
10. Both the 1908 and 1909 prefaces are cited from the second Norton Critical Edition of *The Turn of the Screw*.
11. The governess, it should be said, appears at times a figurative medium for both ghosts. She replaces Quint at the window, and with her face as white as his own gives Mrs. Grose a fright. As the living replacement for Miss Jessel, she often finds herself in a mirror position with her predecessor and ghostly counterpart, as when they face each other on opposite sides of the reflective

lake. But this is more evidence, to my mind, of the narrative's attempts to link (even if it is only in the governess's own mind) governess and children as members of a strangely perceptive community. In other words, her ability to perceive the ghosts is so akin to the child's that she is, or she imagines herself to be, capable of substituting her exposure for theirs.

12. Many scholars have read the title specifically as a reference to the manner in which the governess tortures the children, epitomized by her final death hold on Miles (e.g. Blanchot 85, Edel, *Norton* 191, Pippin 121); others have read it as a more ambiguous and multivalent reference to, among other things, the tension and/or torture the narrative inflicts either on its child characters or on its readers (e.g. Sheppard 17, Bengels 323–324, Lustig 178).

13. In point of fact, Miles's plea to be let alone repeats the same request of another (older) adult male, his uncle, who earlier outlined as part of the terms of the governess's employment with the children at Bly that she "take the whole thing over and let him alone" (6).

CHAPTER 5

Nightwood: A Bedtime Story

Lying at opposite ends of the modernist timeline, Henry James's late nineteenth-century child-centered fiction and Djuna Barnes's *Nightwood* of 1936 make for strange bedfellows. They are divided by vast cultural changes and by a world war. Maisie, Flora, and Miles, like so many of James's characters, descend from the upper echelons of white Anglo-American society while *Nightwood*'s characters (some of whom are Jewish, most of whom are queer) stagnate at the bottom of the social barrel, having already suffered what Barnes terms "the immense disqualification of the public" (*Nightwood* 11). Yet James's emergent modernism and Barnes's late modernism share a striking thematic concern not just with childhood innocence but with its adult colonization. Far from overwriting the distance that separates *What Maisie Knew* and *The Turn of the Screw*, on the one hand, from *Nightwood*, on the other, I want to emphasize it as a sign of American modernism's formative struggle with the cult of childhood. Early and late, American modernism voices its disenchantment with the salvific child, but this discourse is multi-faceted and evolving. For James, thinking ironically about childhood is a goldmine for technical innovations in deceptive, unreliable, and subversive narration. But modernism's faith in the power of experimental forms to confront longstanding cultural ideologies increasingly wanes. Late modernism, in particular, is remarkably and demonstratively worried not just about what the cult of childhood means for consciousness, identity, and democracy but also about modernism's own agency to affect this meaning. Beginning with Barnes, the remaining chapters of this book illuminate some of the surprising turns that American modernist literature takes to register this anxiety, to reflect on modernism's own aesthetic history, and to engage modernism in the politics and pedagogies of childhood.

In *Nightwood*, Nora Flood, Dr. Matthew O'Connor, and Felix Volkbein all stand at the precipice of childhood nostalgia. For Nora, what has been lost is her lover and pseudo-child, Robin Vote. For Felix, it is a fabricated ancestry which he hopes, and fails, to revive through Robin (before her affair with Nora). For the transgendered, queer O'Connor, it is the fairy tale lie that for every princess there will be a Prince Charming. As Barnes's title explicitly forewarns, the sun has already set in *Nightwood*. Though many have read this as a novel of heteronormative resistance,[1] these readings reflect a progressive urge to affirm the "alternative communities" in *Nightwood* while neglecting Barnes's festering attention to the "limitations" of these communities (129). In *Nightwood*, Barnes's disapproving lens shines as much on the victims of oppression, who have all come at the time of the novel's opening to be majority participants in their own dispossession. Though O'Connor identifies as a Catholic woman, mother, and wife, he cloaks himself in the doctor's garb: not as a healer but as an abortionist. Felix Volkbein is a Jew who identifies as a Christian Baron. Nora Flood, who plays mother and host to the underworld's needy, "rob[s] herself for everyone" (47). Jenny Petherbridge, the novel's most notorious "squatter," makes a home for herself out of the stolen lives of others (58). And Robin Vote is the "perpetual child" of *Nightwood* who abandons her husband, Felix, her own biological child, Guido, and who seduces and abandons so many others, including Nora, Jenny, and Sylvia, all in a quest for innocence that drives her further and further from living, flawed humanity: into museums, into the woods, into the chapel (113).

Nightwood reads like a depressive, behind-the-scenes troll through these tortured lives. While there is much that is arguably new in the novel—like its postmodern population of characters—Barnes evinces a compelling reluctance to embrace "the new" as a fashion-forward mode of cultural resistance. Instead, as Tyrus Miller argues, Barnes is a "pathbreaker" of late modernism "whose work bears signs of her passage through the funereal spaces of modernism's demise" (13). Modernism's love affair with the new has been linked to youthful rebellion, experimentation, and innovation, but by 1936 when *Nightwood* was published, it would seem that modernism's formal alliance with these tropes of youth has not only run its course—it has gone too far. In his *Minima Moralia*, Theodor Adorno postulates that early modernists, Edgar Allan Poe and Charles Baudelaire, were willing to "plunge into the abyss, no matter whether hell or heaven" to find something, anything new (235). Indeed, Adorno could be describing James's "blank" method in *The Turn of the Screw* that invites readers to "*think* the evil" for themselves when he characterizes the origins of the modern "cult of the new" in the works of Poe and Baudelaire (James, *Turn* 128). In each, he writes, the subject would prefer to greet the unknown, potentially evil "*blank* space in consciousness," rather than continue to live in a society that "enmeshes and assimilates equally" all objects and perspectives (235; emphasis added). And while this willingness to rush headlong into the unknown might not have mattered in the hands of a handful of artists, Adorno argues that, in the hands of a mass consumer culture, the headiness of novelty has turned into an addiction that is practically and morally unsustainable (236). Worse, the dangers of what Adorno perceives in hindsight as having always been a negative ideology of modernism are borne out, for him, in the totalizing embrace of a new world order represented by fascism and the Second World War. Newness, in this view, unbound in life as in art to the limitations of reason and morality, carries with it multiple profound risks, among them the extraordinary loss of all that must be crowded out or erased in order to make room for each "new" addition (236).

What is missing from Adorno's and other studies in late modernism is the ways in which the cult of the new in modernism intersects with the cult of childhood, an intersection that apparently was not lost on Baudelaire or Walter Benjamin. In the seminal "Painter of Modern Life," Baudelaire describes the central components of the modern artist as part flâneur and part child. Because "the child sees everything in a state of newness," Baudelaire perceives that the "genius" of the modern artist "is nothing more nor less than *childhood recovered* at will" (8). Benjamin writes in the notes for *The Arcades Project* that "the task of childhood" is "to bring the new world into symbolic space," a space at least partially emblematized by the "dialectical fairyland" that is the flâneur's experience of Paris.[2] Margaret Higonnet has shown that modernism, "from the outset," developed a "metaphoric understanding of the 'new' through the child" (86). Though Ezra Pound did not provide the catchphrase for modernism ("make it new") until 1934, Higonnet provides overwhelming evidence that this association was part of the cultural currency of modernism long before. In the early visual arts of the period, numerous exhibitions featured actual child art and the perceived imaginative, free, and formal play of that art is treated as an ideal model for the likes of Roger Fry, Picasso, Klee, Miró,

Kandinsky and others.³ In the realm of narrative, Peter Brooker notes of early modernism that "Examples of sexual, social and cultural innocence or 'unknowingness' occur frequently"; and he names texts such as Ford's *The Good Soldier* (1915), *What Maisie Knew* (1897), Wilde's *The Picture of Dorian Gray* (1890), Conrad's *Chance* (1913), and *The Turn of the Screw* (1898), all texts in which youth and innocence (particularly at the level of narration) play enduring narrative roles (40). And then there are the tenets of Futurism which develop the influence of youth on modernist art into an explicit ideology. The 1910 "Manifesto of the Futurist Painters" not only addresses itself to a youthful audience but demands, through them, that modern art must "Make room for youth, for violence, for daring!"⁴

Part of what is new in *Nightwood* is the way it constructs itself around allusions to the aesthetic and to the modernist aesthetic of the new in particular, but there is little in *Nightwood* that is both new and affirmed as such.⁵ The subtitle of Adorno's *Minima Moralia* or "Reflections from Damaged Life" could double as a title for *Nightwood*, written at least 10 years prior, before World War II, by an author who was very much a part of the 1920s expatriate scene in Paris. With T.S. Eliot as one of its chief champions and editors, *Nightwood* is in many respects thoroughly modernist. But *Nightwood* also offers one of the most unsparing critiques of modernism that the period has to offer. Often called a "transitional" text between the modern and the postmodern, *Nightwood* is a late modernist novel that shifts the youthful features of modernist experimentation—invention, innocence, resistance to conventions—and makes them the subject matter of the story that the novel seeks to tell. The result is that *Nightwood* turns the lens of unconventional critique—itself rooted in modernism—onto modernism itself.⁶

As Phillip Herring has observed, "much of *Nightwood*'s humor is an insensitive probing into the grotesque ways in which people deny nature and create themselves anew" (206). For Nora and Felix in particular, Robin acts as a beacon for such transformations. At one point Nora comments that Robin "was like a relative found in a lost generation," and though some have resisted reading this as a modernist allusion, it strikes me as yet another of Barnes's many layered analogies, referencing the manifold aspects of Robin's appeal: her hollow, "lost" interior; her invitation to an immortality forged by a rift in the chronological fabric; her peculiarly detached subjectivity, signifying her appeal to outsiders as the ultimate outsider; and, related to all of these, her embodiment of something centrally modernist (129).⁷ Though Nora and Felix each perceive that, with Robin, "anything can be done," their attraction to her is misguided by a desire to resist the narratives that have been written for them (by history, by culture, and by biology) and to write, upon the blank slate that she falsely figures for them, new narratives of self-fashioning (37). These characters come to Robin as they would not only to a narrative of self-fulfillment but also to that which Robin herself embodies, a complicated narrative of resistance and re-invention.

Images of youthful and primitive innocence in *Nightwood* are quickly supplanted by images of their artificial replacement: by the doll, the toy, the circus, and art. Robin Vote is at the center of a mass effort in the novel to channel the energies that society has long stored in childhood to power Felix's, Nora's, and Robin's own desperate need to wipe the slates of their lives clean, to erase their mistakes, to erase the trauma of memory, and to start over. Robin, we are told, can play with her toys for hours. She pretends to mother a doll (even though she has given birth to a living child). For Nora, who "should have had a thousand children," Dr. O'Connor surmises that Robin "should have been all of them" (85). And, for Felix, she represents both innocence and immortality. In one moment she makes him think wistfully of "cherubs in renaissance theatres" (39) and in another moment, wistful but also disturbing, of the quintessential American wife and mother, because "with an American anything can be done" (37). Through Robin, reproductions of youthful innocence become the hopeful counterfeit property of adults seeking self renewal or re-invention. Through her, Barnes weds late modernism's troubled reflections on what Adorno calls "the cult of the new" with modernism's abounding concerns about "the cult of childhood" and suggests the problematic—indeed doomed—entanglement of the two. The central figure of *Nightwood*, Robin Vote, is not only repeatedly cast in the mold of the "perpetual" child, she is also always a work of art, an invitation to creation, a blank canvas, and a picture. Robin is the hypothetical child of modernism, offering not innocence but its artifice, not substance but its empty form.

Innocence Re-invented ("She Will Make an Innocence for Herself")

All that seems shocking in *The Turn of the Screw*—the ominous portent of the ghostly, the veiled knowingness of the child, the mental anguish, isolation, and potential madness of the adult caretaker, the illness and the death—are commonplace in *Nightwood*. And in this way, *Nightwood* takes over where

The Turn of the Screw leaves off. The dispossession that kills Miles at the end of *The Turn of the Screw* is the primary inheritance of *Nightwood*'s children. Guido Sr.'s gifts to his son, Felix, are the twin degradations of the "impossible ambition" of re-inventing himself as a Christian aristocrat and the "impermissible blood" of his secret Jewish ancestry (103; 4). Son to Felix and Robin Vote, Guido Jr. continues the downward momentum of his patronage. Before he is even born, he is estranged from the mother who carries him. Robin is angrily ill-suited to pregnancy. She reacts at first like someone in denial. She resumes her nomadic wanderings; "A lost land in herself," she goes missing sometimes for days on end (42). She begins frequenting churches, and even "takes the Catholic vow." To all, she appears not like a woman expecting, but like a child herself, not even a girl but a "tall boy" (43). And so when Guido is born, sick and ill-equipped for the life that awaits him, it is not really surprising that it is Robin and not the child who is "delivered" by the cutting of the cord (44). Like Guido and like Felix, *Nightwood*'s other child character, Sylvia, also seems unmothered and displaced. A girl of unknown origins, Sylvia appears on the scene as one of Jenny Petherbridge's many collected and co-opted relations, but unlike any other object or person in that collection she proves expendable. Though the novel calls her a "little girl," like just about every other adult in the novel, she has the unfortunate experience of being seduced and abandoned by Robin (98).

More than the child, the performance of childhood prevails in *Nightwood*. The doll, the toy, and the fairy tale all make many more and many more apparently lasting impressions than do *Nightwood*'s actual child characters. Robin, we are told, can spend entire days playing with "her toys, trains, animals and cars to wind up, and dolls and marbles and soldiers" (122), toys that make an important reappearance in the final chapter as objects laid by her at the altar in Nora's backwoods chapel (139). In each of these scenes, Barnes stretches the already substantial distance between the narrative point of view and Robin. The cataloguing of Robin's toys objectifies a world that is for her deeply intimate. Even calling these objects "toys," when to Robin they are anything but, manifests how at odds the narrative is with its central character, and the inclusion in the list of "cars to wind up" and "marbles" makes Robin's behavior seem more infantile than innocent. But it is the second appearance of these toys, laid on the altar, which forces readers to grapple not just with the absurd but with the disturbing ramifications of Robin's excessive adult identification with childhood. For Robin, these items make for a worthy sacrifice. Giving up Guido was easy. Giving up her toys is hard.

Rather than the child to whom she gave birth, Robin mothers a doll—first with Nora and then again with Jenny. It is Nora who expresses the feeling that it is the doll, internalized in childhood as the duplicate for childhood, that has sabotaged her relationship with Robin. She reflects, "We give death to a child when we give it a doll—it's the effigy and the shroud; when a woman gives it to a woman, it is the life they cannot have, it is their child, sacred and profane" (118). In both cases, whether given in childhood or adulthood, the doll appears to represent a false idol. For the child—for girls most especially—this may be the mismatch between themselves and the image of themselves that has been presented to them. For the inverts of *Nightwood*, it is a reminder of the price for their deviance from the social norms that police gender, sexuality, and family. At first, blaming the doll seems like a back-handed way of blaming Robin (herself so doll-like) for the fallout of their relationship. But Nora's tone is one of such immense regret that it is evident that she is searching for her own role in what went wrong in this affair and that she, the gifter, may be more to blame. Yet, she also suggests, through the universal pronoun in "*we* give death to a child when *we* give it a doll," that her error is the error of adults everywhere (emphasis added). The reader may look on this scene with confusion or horror; but if Nora is right, then Robin is the child of our collective creation. In other words, "we" may also be responsible for her.

In so many respects, Robin Vote is the embodiment of this mistaken "gift" to childhood. In her, the ramifications of this empty preservative of childhood take on living, breathing form. In the reader's first encounter with her, Robin is characterized as a kind of child automaton. The novel identifies her as a "born somnambule...meet of child and desperado" and with that begins to paint a picture of her as someone who careens thoughtlessly and dangerously through life (34). For O'Connor Robin represents "a sort of first position in attention; a face that will age under the blows of perpetual childhood" (112–113). Not only does Robin take on the bodily posture of the doll in this portrait of her, rigidly fixed in the "first position" of (an aestheticized) childhood, but she ages in the way that a relic ages, from being frozen in one time and one space while the rest of the world has moved on. Earlier in the novel, Felix uses similar imagery when he likens Robin to an "old statue in a garden" whose worn condition "symbolizes the weather through which it has endured" (39). He also perceives a "density...of youth" in Robin that is not unlike the force of "perpetual childhood" that O'Connor witnesses in her (101). In each of these assessments, the preservation of childhood signified by Robin conveys something that is aesthetically pleasing but also self-annihilating. In the first, the image of the unconscious innocence of the "somnambule" is undercut by the image of the unlawful, potentially unconscionable violence of the "desperado." For O'Connor, Robin's open-endedness seems to suggest, as equals, the possibilities for beauty or destruction. His image of her combines, as analogous, the "first position" of the ballerina and the readiness "in attention" of the soldier. And though Felix had imagined Robin's as an innocence bound to past traditions, O'Connor realizes in hindsight that hers is an opportunistic innocence that will survive through any means necessary.

The attested desperation, density, and perpetuity of Robin's innocence suggest not just an excess but a hoarding of childhood in her. Many scholars have discussed the innocence at the heart of Robin's character, but these discussions almost invariably reference hers as an "animal innocence." Phillip Herring characterizes Robin's innocence in precisely these terms because she lacks both memory and conscience (209). Teresa de Lauretis similarly argues that, from the point of view of Matthew O'Connor, "Robin embodies the sensual innocence of animals unfettered by civilized morality" (125). And Georgette Fleischer argues that Robin "achieves" a "fearful primitive innocence," pagan in its worship of a "dog-likeness" that is "god" and its/his/her reverse signification (426). Readings such as these demonstrate that innocence is a category in *Nightwood* that must be accounted for, but they also show just how difficult this challenge is to meet when the character that the novel insists on calling innocent is also arguably the most depressive and most unfeeling character in the entire book. As David Copeland argues, innocence is widely recognized as one of the most important categories in *Nightwood*, but it is also "the least understood" (117). Trying to reconcile the word "innocence" with Robin's depravity is no easy feat and really requires an open examination of how innocence is deployed in the text. Copeland undertakes such a study and observes that innocence is treated not as an "essence" of childhood but as "an adult construct" that Barnes finds baffling because it romanticizes childhood as the time of greatest happiness and leaves adults (who have created this fantasy) feeling miserable (132).

Clearly Barnes forwards a version of innocence that eschews romantic ideals of childhood, but her sensitive treatment of non-human animals makes the no less essentialized view of "animal innocence" equally worrisome. It is true that Barnes uses animals, just as she uses children, to reflect Robin's character. Robin is kindred first to the circus lioness who visibly gravitates toward her; then she is the bird that roosts in Nora's heart and turns scavenger upon it (76); and last she is the dog in church who finds and forces her mirror image in Nora's hound. Each of these animals is, in turn, similarly represented as a beast-human hybrid. Nora observes that all of the circus animals "going around and around the ring, all but climbed over at that point" where they passed Robin, and the lioness in particular reached toward Robin through the bars of her cage, and "her eyes flowed in tears that never reached the surface" (49). This latter image is especially striking because it reveals an inversion of the beast and human stereotypes in the lioness whose body is that of a predator but whose "soul" (to use a term that Barnes herself used with regard to non-human animals) contains the complex emotional depth of a sorrow that does not show ("Djuna Barnes" 190).[8] In an analogous scene, the novel's closing image of Nora's hound invokes a similarly reversed or mirror image to Robin. When Nora and her dog come upon Robin in the derelict chapel, Robin goes down before the domesticated hound as if she were herself its wild ancestor. Cornered and "trembling," the dog is said to be "troubled to such an agony" by what it sees that it actually attempts at first not to imitate Robin but to counter her. The narrative that describes her "going down" and "coming forward" toward him, describes him "rearing back" and "seem[ing]" to "ris[e] from the floor" in a futile effort to escape her (139). In other words, her efforts to penetrate his non-human sphere are countered by his efforts to become human (to stand on two legs). In each of these captivating scenes the animal who locks eyes with Robin communicates a humanity—expressed through soulful sorrow or standing terror—that seem to exceed Robin's own.

Although O'Connor reflects on Robin as animal when he says, "Ah... to be an animal, born at the opening of the eye, going only forward, and at the end of the day, shutting out memory with the dropping of the lid," this oft-quoted passage is neither as wistful as it might seem nor as isolated. Far from showing how enviable Robin is, the extended passage shows O'Connor meditating (in the preceding image) on how she will suffer "under the blows of perpetual childhood." She is less enviable still in the image that follows, as O'Connor comically considers her alongside the primitivist trend in high fashion that sees women with "feathers, flowers, sprigs of oat, or some other gadget nodding above their temples!" (113). What this sequence of images—comparing Robin to the child, to the non-human animal, and to haute couture—have in common is that each has nothing to do with nature. Rather, they emphasize just how artificial Robin's identity and appeal are. Robin is less like Guido or Sylvia—*Nightwood*'s actual child characters—and more like the doll. And she is not like the non-human animal either—whether wild or domestic. Her habitat is not the wilderness, and it is not the home either; instead, she roams the havens of the masses: the streets of Paris, the museums, the churches, and the circus.

Putting "The Cult of the Child" and "The Cult of the New" in the Same Bed

In "The Work of Art in the Age of Mechanical Reproduction" published in the same year as *Nightwood*, Walter Benjamin perceives a monumental transformation in the concept of art as it is absorbed by the forces of an emerging consumer culture. With the proliferation of photography and film in particular, Benjamin observes that the "aura" of "authenticity" that the arts once possessed as unique pieces cusped in the hands of the few cannot but be diminished now that art is being reproduced and redistributed among and for the masses (66–67). In *Nightwood*, art for the masses is very much a part of the world that Barnes's characters inhabit. The home that Nora and Robin make together is a "museum of their encounter," replete with "stage drops from Munich" and "circus chairs" and merry-go-round horses (50). Their very lives are, in many respects, reproductions of exhibits, statues, plays, paintings, and fairy tales. However, in *Nightwood* these reproductions do not demonstrate—as they do for Benjamin—how much art has changed through time; rather, they suggest depressingly how little has changed. The authenticity of art from any age, including Barnes's modernist moment is seriously called into question in *Nightwood,* which reproduces more than anything else the flaws in art. And, more than any other character, Robin Vote is the bearer of these flaws. In her, many of the novel's disillusioned images of novelty and innocence converge. Beginning with the reader's first encounter of her, Robin appears like a person in a photograph or painting, fixed in time and space. Physically, she lies unconscious in her hotel room, subject to the gaze of Dr. O'Connor, who has been called to help her, and of Felix, who has joined him. She is also objectified by the third-person point of view which makes her immobilized figure the center of a series of tableau-like images that set her in the jungle, in the artist's studio, in a fairy tale, and in a dream. These allusions invite readers to think of Robin as paintings and portraits and stories that date anywhere from the fifteenth century onward such as Aphrodite, Sleeping Beauty, or the fantasy woman in Rousseau's *The Dream*, the much admired nineteenth-century socialite, *Madame Récamier*.

Daniela Caselli has compared this first image of Robin to Boticelli's *Birth of Venus* (1480s) because Robin has the odor and appearance of a newborn woman (120). Barnes writes that "the perfume that her body exhaled was of the quality of that earth-flesh, fungi, which smells of captured dampness and yet is so dry...her flesh was the texture of plant life...about her head there was an effulgence as of phosphorous glowing about the circumference of a body of water" (34). Robin seems to have just arisen from the rainforest floor fully grown, only she is actually lying passed out in her suite at the Hotel Récamier. The hotel's name conjures with it yet another aesthetic allusion to the portrait of Madame Récamier, and both allusions figure into Barnes's third aesthetic allusion borne out of Robin, Henri Rousseau's post-impressionist painting, *The Dream* of 1910. Barnes writes:

> Like a painting by the *douanier* Rousseau, [Robin] seemed to lie in a jungle trapped in a drawing room (in the apprehension of which the walls have made their escape), thrown in among the carnivorous flowers as their ration; the set, the property of the unseen *dompteur*, half lord, half promoter, over which one expects to hear the strains of an orchestra of wood-winds render a serenade which will popularize the wilderness. (34)

This last of Rousseau's modernist paintings was acclaimed (and criticized) for its "collage-like" composition of heterogeneous plants, animals, people, and furniture to form an inauthentic image of the jungle, more reminiscent of the exaggerated jungle scenes in children's books or those arranged on public display at the Jardin des Plantes in Paris (which Rousseau frequented) than anything in nature (37) (Fig. 5.1).[9]

Of course, *The Dream*'s most striking juxtaposition lies between the painter's studio and the jungle scene. The female nude posing on Madame Récamier's studio divan might have been airlifted into the middle of a jungle "set." The painter, likewise, appears to find his double in the figure of the enchanter, who stands just right of center with her instrument and who mirrors with her internal witchcraft the external magic of the artist, who has compelled the mystical juxtapositions of this scene.

Barnes not only replicates Rousseau's painting in this introduction to Robin but she also replicates his modernist method. She, like him, merges

Fig. 5.1 Henri Rousseau, *The Dream*, 1910. Courtesy of The Museum of Modern Art/Licensed by SCALA/Art Resource, NY

the Parisian woman, the drawing room, and the jungle; and she likewise imbeds the voyeuristic mechanism of the scene. Felix and the doctor, like the lions and the elephant in the painting, seem eager to disguise their gaze. Felix, literally, "step[s] behind the palms" and peeks through, quite like the lion in the painting (34). The doctor also, much like the snake charmer, turns the encounter into a magic show, becomes "a man of magic" and makes some lipstick, perfume, and money disappear. Barnes, like Rousseau, also reveals the extent to which the entire scene has been fictitiously arranged. Each work from the *Birth of Venus* to *Madame Récamier* to *The Dream* to "Sleeping Beauty" is self-consciously revealed as an elaborate "hoax," in which "the whole fabric of magic has begun to decompose" (to quote Barnes on this scene) before our very eyes (35). Robin is no more a goddess, or an ideal of femininity, or a creature of the jungle than she is a throwback to childhood innocence, if such a thing even exists (and *Nightwood* intimates that it does not). In her, child, animal, and woman become less something represented or embodied than a spectacle of representation and embodiment.

Later in *Nightwood*, Barnes presents yet another version of the bedtime tableau. Only in this episode, O'Connor has replaced Robin as the woman reclining in bed. When Nora, despairing over her broken relationship with Robin, turns up at O'Connor's door, it is as if she has walked into a scene from "Little Red Riding Hood":

> The doctor's head, with its over-large black eyes, its full gun-metal cheeks and chin, was framed in the golden semi-circle of a wig with long pendent curls that touched his shoulders, and falling back against the pillow, turned up the shadowy interior of their cylinders. He was heavily rouged and his lashes painted. It flashed into Nora's head, "God, children know something they can't tell, they like Red Riding Hood and the wolf in bed!" (69)

O'Connor's drag reproduction at first appears sadly unlike the fairy tale heroines (including Red Riding Hood, Goldilocks, and Sleeping Beauty) that have inspired its efforts. And yet Nora's point of view must give this reading pause, for when she beholds the scene, it is as though she has "flashed" effortlessly into the mind of the child encountering the fairy tale for the first time. What she sees there surprises her precisely because the flashback is so like the physical scene she has entered into in O'Connor's room. Later, O'Connor himself reflects that all of their efforts to reproduce the narratives from childhood have been doomed from the start. "We were impaled in our childhood," he tells her, by romanticized images of androgyny, "for in the girl it is the prince, and in the boy it is the girl that makes a prince a prince—and not a man" (114). What began in the fairy tale as the well-intentioned "sweetest lie" turns into "the dark misery of the close nightmare" for those like O'Connor and Nora who hung onto it as truth (114–115). Having lost Robin, the novel's primary child/lover, Nora returns to O'Connor as to a replacement child healer. She confesses, "Sometimes I don't know why I talk to you. You're so like a child; then again I know well enough" (112). This hesitant admission is saturated with suggestion—not only that there are any number of reasons why one might find it easy to talk to children but also and more importantly that O'Connor reminds her, in his resemblance to childhood, of Robin. But O'Connor refuses this analogy, and he refuses to offer a narrative of healing for Nora. Instead he offers her a parody not just of the fairy tale but also of Robin who is both red riding hood and the wolf.

Though Robin is the central figure of *Nightwood*, she operates within it very much like the Jamesian blank in *The Turn of the Screw*, not simply because they both construct spaces of uncertainty and ambivalence but because they each function as a peculiarly preserved innocence around which the entire narrative apparatus is arranged. In an argument that could be applied nearly verbatim to the children of *The Turn of the Screw*, Karen Kaivola has observed that Robin "can be whatever we want her to be: mysterious, erotic, infantile, dangerous" because she so rarely represents herself in thought or in speech but is rather almost invariably represented by those in proximity to her (175). For a figure of such novelistic stature, Robin is, like Miles and like Flora, astonishingly silent. Horner and Zlosnik note that Robin speaks "no more than ten times in the novel" (85). And while many, including Kaivola, have placed this silence in the frame of Robin's presumed animality, it is also a feature that aligns her not just with the childlike but with the novel's sense of her as a living work of art. In addition to her unconscious slip into the posture of a Rousseau painting, Barnes describes Robin elsewhere as "a 'picture' forever arranged" (36) and in another instance as "an image" like the "stop the mind makes between uncertainties" (93). When Joseph Frank famously described modernist fiction as operating by a series of spatial fragments more akin to the modernist painting than to anything synonymous with narrative temporality, he, by his own account, was responding to the particularly "haunt[ing]" experience of reading *Nightwood*.[10] Brian Glavey, who recovers this important fact about *Nightwood*'s critical history, also highlights the ways that the novel self-consciously embodies this central modernist modality within the "queer ekphrasis" of Robin's persona, which he argues is distinctly modernist for its irresolvable resistance to interpretation—both by the many lovers who would control her and by the novel's readers who seek to understand her (757).

In so many ways, Robin is the allegorical embodiment of the modernist innocence narrative. From one vantage point she is the primitivist jungle child, from another she is the consumer capitalist doll, and from yet another she is the avant-garde narrative assemblage of a fragmented ekphrasis that is not only irresolvably queer, as Glavey argues, but which is also, in its foundational uncertainty, perpetually and repeatedly new. If *Nightwood* acts by a narrative resemblance to modernist painting, as Frank suggests, then Robin might be the novel incarnation of a kind of cubist blank slate, figuring a resistance to the epistemologies of narrative temporality and visual perspicuity. As Glavey points out, Robin's anti-narrative persona—spatial and non-linguistic—is not precisely visual either. Robin is aesthetically visualized (as photograph, as painting, as statue) but hers is a hollow, concealed, and shifting interior that eludes the hermeneutics of the visual register. Glavey likens her to a "'black hole,'" but this metaphor, while tonally apt, is nonetheless insufficient and obviously anachronistic (757). Blankness, as shown both by James's ambivalent blank method and by Adorno's concept of the blank abyss, is dark enough for modernists, early and late. Indeed, Barnes herself offers a similar view in proximal language. In a tongue-in-cheek review of, then friend, Charles Henri Ford's *The Young and Evil* (1932), she writes:

> Never to my knowledge, has a certain type of homosexual been so "fixed" on paper. Their utter lack of emotional values—so entire that it is frightening; their loss of all Victorian victories: manners, custom, remorse, taste, dignity; their unresolved acceptance of any happening, is both evil and "pure" in the sense that it is unconscious (qtd. in Herring 175).[11]

For Barnes, Ford represents what she would herself begin to represent only a year later in the first drafts of *Nightwood*—the late modernist configuration of a youth so definitively characterized by the features of "lack" and "loss" and "unconscious[ness]" as to be at once "pure" and "evil."

Whereas the governess in *The Turn of the Screw* signifies the horrifying fruition of so many "Victorian victories" with regard to innocence by preserving it across the ages (both historical and individual), Robin represents the fruition, as troubling, of a modernist dream of innocence abstracted from history and time and circumstance. Just as the governess's quest to preserve innocence is arguably too attached to and too haunted by the deeply imbedded historical and cultural accounts thereof, Robin's is too much an innocence of detachment and invention; her narrative is too much one of narrative resistance. Time and time again Barnes couples the sense of Robin's mortal and maturational resistance with a powerful suggestion of its futility and error. Not only does Robin capture the "eternal momentary" (107) but she is also one in search of the "indecent' eternal" (130); "Like something dormant," Robin's youth is "protected" and "moved out of death's way by the successive arms of women" who make of themselves tombs, museums, roosts, and living hosts for her parasitic preservation (57).

Of Robin's preservation in Nora, Barnes writes:

> Love becomes the deposit of the heart, analogous in all degrees to the 'findings' in a tomb. As in one will be charted the taken place of the body, the raiment, the utensils necessary to its other life, so in the heart of the

> lover will be traced, as an indelible shadow, that which he loves. In Nora's heart lay the fossil of Robin, intaglio of her identity, and about it for its maintenance ran Nora's blood. Thus the body of Robin could never be unloved, corrupt or put away. Robin was now beyond timely changes, except in the blood that animated her. (50–51)

Indicative of *Nightwood*'s "analogous" style, metaphor in this passage overlaps with metaphor such that Nora is associated with all things preserving (tomb, sustenance, museum, and artistic medium) and Robin with all things preserved (body, artifact, and aesthetic artifice). Metaphors of the living and the dead—of the beating heart and the tomb; of "the body of Robin" and its empty imprint—so intermix that the body becomes immortal by its emptiness, and (more ironic still) the heart becomes a hollow for its keeping. The images of Robin as fossil, artifact, or as intaglio art, all sustained by Nora's blood, invite a series of still more tacit analogies of Robin to the child in the womb of the mother or, more sinisterly, to the living dead figure of the vampire. Rather than read these seemingly contrary models as an either/or hermeneutic choice, I take the passage to offer an intermixing of the two as it does with metaphors of the living and the dead. Its unsettling tone is in part the by-product of this "indecent" concoction (130). Yet we have seen this strangely ominous child seductor before, for Robin takes us back (once again) to Barrie's Peter Pan, "gay and innocent and heartless" (148), except in this case Barnes takes heartlessness to graphic new heights, for Robin achieves perpetual, "never" to be "corrupt[ed]" innocence, by drawing for her immortality (literally and figuratively this passage suggests) upon the loves and lives of others.

Formally, this passage is striking for the way that it suggests a microcosmic extrapolation of interiors within interiors. There is Robin's interiority, Nora's, and Robin's within Nora's. By implication each of these interiors and compound interiors is encompassed by the novel whose own interiority consists of the idea of Robin and of Nora and of Robin inside of Nora. Ironically *Nightwood's* architecture of concentrically arranged interiorities remains uninhabited. Nora hollows herself out to hold Robin, who is herself a hollow woman. And like Nora, the narrative works by containing and sustaining the image of Robin without any direct or substantive reference to her, either in thought, action, or voice. That being said, it would be a mistake to equate the novel's relationship to Robin with Nora's.[12] Despite her biographical and even textually internal resemblances to Barnes and/or the narrator, Nora is not an unproblematic figure for the text. The relationship between Nora and Robin is, though central, far from a subject of novelistic embrace. This relationship, though everything to Nora, is at best half of *Nightwood*. The other half, the other child, and the other narrative option comes in the form, figure, and voice of O'Connor.

The Child "With Eyes Wide Open"

"Go Down, Matthew" is structured as a dialogue between Nora and Matthew O'Connor, but by the end, true conversation has been supplanted by what might best be characterized as two competing monologues, each vying for discursive space. Nora's posture in the chapter is one of nearly compulsive writing and speech. She says, "I don't know how to talk," and yet "I've got to" (109). She is writing a letter to Robin, a new letter in an apparently unending series of letters. The doctor prophesies a vision of Robin "tearing open a million envelopes to her end," but Nora laments again: "If I don't write to her, what am I to do?...I've got to write to her...I've got to" (106). Though the doctor has been the talker par excellence of the novel to date, Nora in this late exchange battles with him for this title. To his advice, his stories, Barnes describes Nora as at first somewhat politely having "not heard him" (113), but she becomes increasingly "unheeding" (116); later she takes up her own narrative strand "as if she had not been interrupted" (117), and finally she demands "Listen...you've got to listen"—a plea that is ironic enough given her own unilateral approach to the conversation (128).

Though O'Connor is not (and does not pretend to be) a psychoanalyst, Nora comes to him as for a talking cure. Her turn to narrative modes eschewed by Robin, those of the written and spoken word, place her, on the one hand, notably at odds with the figure she seeks to recapture, but, on the other, Nora's desperate and unheeding speech seems as impenetrable as Robin's silence. Despite the doctor's punctuated refrain "to put down the pen," Nora cannot stop writing (105). Despite his plea, at last frantic, for her to simply "Stop it!" (121), to "be done," to "give up," to "rest" (105), and again to "lay down the pen," Nora suffers from an inertia against these various ends as powerful as Robin's inert stance ever was (107). At the pitch of desperation, O'Connor retorts:

> Oh...A broken heart have you! I have falling arches, flying dandruff, a floating kidney, shattered nerves *and* a broken heart! But do I scream that an

eagle has me by the balls or has dropped his oyster on my head? Am I going forward screaming that it hurts that my mind goes back, or holding my guts as if they were a coil of knives? Yet you are screaming, and drawing your lip and putting your hand out and turning round and round!...Oh, you poor blind cow! Keep out of my feathers; you ruffle me the wrong way and flit about, stirring my misery! What end is sweet? (128)

More than the facts of Nora's experience of misery and loss—for these are facts which O'Connor shares—this is a diatribe against her resistance to the inevitable "end." O'Connor points out, what must be obvious to readers of *Nightwood* by now, that everyone is suffering. Only O'Connor has resigned himself to misery while Nora's posture (in his view) is very nearly a caricature of protest. O'Connor's image of her "screaming" and "drawing [her] lip" and "putting [her] hand out and turning round and round" suggests that Nora's narrative of resistance is like a toddler's tantrum.

In contrast to Nora, who places all of her faith in the power of writing and talking to combat her misery, O'Connor argues that there are no methods available to the "new young" that can work the magic Nora seeks. He offers her the cautionary tale of Guido: "'Very well,'" he says, "'but know the worst then. What of Felix and his son Guido, that sick lamenting, fevered child; death in the weather is a tonic to him. Like all the new young his sole provision for old age is hope of an early death... So I say, was Robin purposely unspun? Was Jenny a sitting bitch for fun?...Can't you rest now, lay down the pen'" (107). O'Connor's reference to the "new young" casts a wide net that includes Guido, first, and then spreads to include Robin and Jenny and Nora, all of whom, he intimates, might be best served by wishing for an early death. O'Connor implies that the torment that has visited the lives of all of these figures, even Robin, is out of their collective control.

Nora may not be persuaded either by O'Connor's mortal wish for an "end" or by his recurrent advice to "put down the pen," but the novel itself apparently is, for it draws rapidly and confoundingly to a close only pages thereafter. Indeed, O'Connor's allegorical voice in "Go Down, Matthew" is only a thinly veiled apostrophe from the author to herself. O'Connor repeats his wish for narrative cessation and further laments:

> Oh the poor worms that never arrive!...Haven't I eaten a book too? Like the angels and prophets? And wasn't it a bitter book to eat?...And didn't I eat a

page and tear a page and stamp on others and flay some and toss some into the toilet for relief's sake,—then think of Jenny without a comma to eat, and Robin with nothing but a pet name—your pet name to sustain her; for pet names are a guard against loss, like primitive music. But does that sum her up? Is even the end of us an account? (107)

One can no more miss the parallels between Nora's writing and Barnes's than one can miss the irony of O'Connor's pleas for an "end" to the story of Nora and Robin in the midst of a novel centered around its telling. Unlike many of the other passages in "Go Down, Matthew" which have a meta-narrative subtext, here the meta-narrative is primary. The only "pet name" we have for Robin is Robin; the bird name is ascribed to her by Barnes, not Nora. If Jenny starves for want of a comma, it is because Barnes (not Nora) has withheld narrative voice from her. But beyond Robin and Jenny, to whom Barnes had well-known biographical reasons for dispensing a certain amount of narrative poetic justice,[13] no one in this passage (and in the novel as a whole, it suggests) escapes the purview of a kind of novel damage. Though some are starving for narrative, others like O'Connor are drowning in it.

The narrative that at first seemed grounded either in Robin's innocence method, frozen outside of time and language, or in Nora's attempt to preserve that same method across time and in language, has turned gradually and peripherally to O'Connor's relentless disenchantment with both. Though *Nightwood* contains the modernist innocence narrative of aesthetic re-invention and resistance signified by Robin, its narrative technique bears little in common with this central representative of the new young. It cannot be said that *Nightwood* is silent as Robin is silent. That *Nightwood* is blank as she is blank. That it forgets as she forgets. If anything, *Nightwood* is far more like O'Connor whose speech is an exercise in excess, in the appalling and obscene, and in historical mumbo-jumbo.[14] As Barnes simultaneously acknowledges and parodies her own aesthetic forebears, O'Connor calls attention to his own duplicity. He relates in one instance how he personally took the leeches "to bleed" Catherine the Great. Even when the ex-priest admonishes, "Remember your century at least!" O'Connor insists that it is those who "look as innocent as the bottom of a plate that get you into trouble, not a man with a prehistoric memory" (135). Those who "look...innocent" is another apparent allusion to Robin and another moment where Barnes posits O'Connor's outrageously flawed persona as the narrative's alternative to her.

Barnes's narrative of excess, conditional authority, impurity, and surrender serves as the counter and the critique to Robin and to the modernist innocence narrative that her character embodies. Alongside and really in the place of Nora's hollowed containment of the blank interior that is Robin, the novel holds the narrative method and message of another—demystified and demythologized child figure. Though O'Connor speaks a debased, obscene, and fatalistic language, though he is the novel's only veteran of war, and though he is by his own admissions a charlatan and a liar, he is nonetheless *Nightwood*'s other child replacement, in addition and in opposition to Robin. In one of the novel's most important paradoxes, even though O'Connor disidentifies with "all the new young" like Guido and like Robin (whom he has said should "hope" for "an early death"), he yet identifies himself with childhood (107). More importantly, the novel substantiates the connection by showing the resemblance between O'Connor and its other, actual child character, Sylvia.

O'Connor's plea to be let go in the long passage that follows is not only reminiscent of Miles's identical plea at the end of *The Turn of the Screw*, it is the direct echo of Sylvia's entreaty at the end of "The Squatter." Stuck in a moving carriage with a brawling Jenny and Robin, "the child flung herself down on the seat, face outward, and said in a voice not suitable for a child, because it was controlled with terror: '"Let me go! Let me go! Let me go!"' (67). O'Connor, also an entrapped onlooker to the scene, later emphasizes Sylvia's expression as one "with eyes wide open," (89) a description that echoes (only pages later) his own depiction of himself as "a child with my eyes wide open" (81). Both sets of images, of Sylvia and the doctor, converge in the novel's last, late-night bar image of O'Connor:

> He began to scream with sobbing laughter. 'Talking to me—all of them—sitting on me as heavy as a truck horse—talking!...Why doesn't anyone know when everything is over, except me?...He came down upon the table with all his weight, his arms spread, his head between them, his eyes wide open and crying, staring along the table where the ash blew and fluttered with his gasping breath. 'For Christ's sweet sake!' he said, and his voice was a whisper, 'now that you have all heard what you wanted to hear, can't you let me loose now, let me go? (136)

The doctor's eyes are again, as Sylvia's have also been, "wide open and crying." He flings himself down on the bar table, staring outward, much as Sylvia cast herself on the seat of the carriage. Both despair, but neither looks away. Sylvia faces the wrath of Jenny just as O'Connor faces and inhales the ash-strewn air. Her original "let me go" has become his. But unlike Sylvia's (and Miles's) cries for release, there is nothing in O'Connor's pleadings that resembles resistance, nothing to suggest a desire for individual independence or freedom to counter the entrapment that has inspired its outburst. Quite the contrary, O'Connor identifies himself with the end of all narratives and with an acceptance of these ends.

Unlike Robin, who represents an innocence that is at odds with the realities of time and history and the body and age, O'Connor conjures an unsettling vision of a childhood wounded and spent. His child model, with "eyes wide open," entrapped and bowed by circumstance, is so clearly the child of trauma, not the child of romance. There is no innocence in his child narrative. There is no sleep, no dreaming, no forgetting. He represents and tells the story of the disillusionment that only the child can feel when s/he realizes that all the fairy tales have been a lie. His narrative, so unlike that of Robin or of Nora or of Felix, is a mortal one. It moves not in the circles of resistance but in the direction of acceptance. With Felix and with Nora both, O'Connor is a doctor who heals most by trying to counsel the limits of healing. For some illnesses there are no cures. In O'Connor's narrative there is no worship of the healed, the reborn, or the new but only a profound wish for an end. Though he has been at nearly every turn the novel's replacement for Robin, he insists at last on being no substitute for her. There is nothing affirmatively new about him, nothing aesthetically pure or blank, and nothing, certainly, to be preferred or preserved as such.

And yet, by narrative quantity if not by thematic emphasis, *Nightwood* does prefer and does preserve him. Most strikingly, perhaps downright shockingly, this is true in the novel's final images of Robin. The voices of Barnes and O'Connor converge once more in O'Connor's final prophesy: "Now...the end—mark my words—now *nothing, but wrath and weeping!*" (136). This proclamation, which is also the final sentence of "Go Down, Matthew," serves doubly to announce some future apocalypse and to introduce the ending of the novel. The "now" performatively suggests that the two are one: that the novel's last chapter will be the ending of which he speaks. The typographical flare of the sentence, the double dash and the italics, enact the author's manner of underscoring his insight, literally "mark[ing]" his words and marking them also as her own. Unfortunately, this prelude to the end offers little help in interpreting the actual ending that follows. There might be wrath, if one interprets the chapter old-testament style, and there is certainly weeping, but the novel's actual ending fails to deliver the combination of these sentiments that O'Connor's prophesy leads the reader to expect. And this is fundamentally the case because the Robin of the ending is to a great extent not the character that we or he or Nora has come to expect. Indeed, what O'Connor fails to foresee is the way that the final image of Robin going down with the dog will parallel himself.

Cornered, pursued by Robin around the narrow chapel, Nora's hound "let loose one howl of misery and bit at her…barking"; then the novel's final paragraph tells us:

> Then she began to bark also, crawling after him—barking in a fit of laughter, obscene and touching. Crouching, the dog began to run with her, head-on with her head…He ran this way and that, low down in his throat crying, and she grinning and crying with him; crying in shorter and shorter spaces, moving head to head, until she gave up, lying out, her hands beside her, her faced turned and weeping; and the dog too gave up then, and lay down, his eyes bloodshot, his head flat along her knees. (139)

Aside from the ambiguous content of this passage as to what exactly has transpired between Robin and Nora's hound and why, I want here to focus on the words, for they present a striking echo of O'Connor's last image, which was also, it will be recalled, itself an echo of the child, Sylvia. That first image of the child, "with eyes wide open," who casts herself down on the seat of the carriage, facing outward and crying "let me go!" (67) ripples through the image of O'Connor screaming "with sobbing laughter," his body also bowed down (upon a bar table), his eyes also "wide open" and "crying," his voice beseeching "can't you let me loose now, let me go?" (136). And now, it would seem, these ripples have reached all the way to Robin. She too emits a mixed laughter, "obscene and touching" as ever O'Connor's had been; her "grinning and crying" reproduce his "sobbing laughter." The hound's howl, "let loose," and her strange barking echo those calls that have preceded them—to be let loose, to be let go. Let him and let herself loose Robin apparently does, for she too "g[ives] up" and bows her body down, turns her face out in the gesture, like Sylvia's and O'Connor's before her, of a sad and yielding awareness. The dog's "bloodshot" eyes mirror the open awareness of its child predecessors, and Robin, as O'Connor predicted, cries as they all have cried.[15]

As the central child figure of *Nightwood*, this is not the Robin we have come to know. Here the ekphrastic image, frozen in and outside of time, has succumbed; here everything has given up, from the rotting chapel to the dog to Robin herself. Here the "gay...and heartless" innocence, that made Robin so like that other child who never grows up,[16] has given way to anguish and "weeping." Here the toys and the dolls that have always figured in Robin's figuration of childhood have found their way with her to the altar of this ruinous chapel. And though this last image might be read as a sign of a continued idol worship of innocence in Robin, in the light of the final parallels to *Nightwood*'s other children, I read it more as a symbol of that innocence's sacrifice. All along O'Connor has acted as a figure for the replacement of Robin; all along his abundance of speech has served to fill the void of her silence; his awareness has colored in the features of her unconsciousness; and his inability to heal along with his acceptance of that fact have sought to quell her Siren song of self-renewal and reinvention. But now it is Robin who follows him. In this final scene, the novel has changed its image of her by remaking her in O'Connor's abject image, an image that is itself a reflection of the child, Sylvia.

Nightwood has from the outset been a story about the dispossession, not the death, of childhood, and it has been a story also of childhood and narrative revision. Though modernism emerged in part out of an examination of the former narrative of dispossession, in its own unconventional ways, modernism itself participated in the dispossession of childhood. Miles's dispossession at the close of *The Turn of the Screw* is a horror and an outrage, but he is no less dispossessed by the narrative of his invention, which substitutes so many blanks and gaps for the child's point of view. In part, this is also the story of *Nightwood* where, if anything, dispossession is the default for childhood, aesthetic re-invention a topical mainstay. But *Nightwood* moves away from the narratives of resistance and negation, signified by Robin and characteristic of so much of modernism, toward a narrative of revision predicated first and foremost on a difficult acceptance—whether of a marred past, a present loss, or an unwanted life. And it likewise moves away from one vision of childhood—youthful, innocent, and perceiving the world as with "new lights"—to another which is disillusioned and which sees the world as with the blurred vision of one "with eyes wide open," tear-filled, and weary. Both James's emergent modernism and Barnes's self-critical late modernism confront and challenge the cult of childhood, but where one seeks to make something that is aesthetically new out of this challenge, the other extends the challenge further to confront also the modernist innocence narrative borne out of it. Just as the preferred child for *Nightwood* is the characteristically unpreferred—the misfit, the hopeless, the betrayed and alone—so too *Nightwood*'s preferred method is not resistant, blank, creative, or original but archival in its memory, analogous in its style, obscenely embodied in its discourse, and disillusioned in its narratives of modernism and childhood.

Nightwood's rejection of innocence in any form—in the child, in the adult, or in art—illuminates a key moment in American modernism's representations of childhood. The celebration of aesthetic novelty begins to give way in Barnes's novel to an anxiety about what, if any, role modernist art can play in altering constructions of childhood that lead to disappointment and even despair. Barnes's feeling about this, as depicted in *Nightwood*, seems bleak. But as I will discuss in the remaining chapters, there were other modernists like W.E.B. Du Bois and Gertrude Stein who shared Barnes's concerns but who found a striking source of hope in taking this critique of childhood to children themselves. Unsatisfied with abstraction and novelty, many late modernist writers return to the presumed source of their own marginalized, endangered, or lost subjectivities. It is a shift that will be played out not only in the move of many of these authors to write for children but to revise also, in the process, their own past works and the spirit of modernism vested in them.

Notes

1. In addition to Benstock, who sees the novel as a critique of patriarchy rendered through its debased internalization in the novel's characters, and Marcus, who argues that the novel represents a critique of fascism by affirming the lives of those whom that movement would come to target, Merrill Cole and Carrie Rohman are two recent critics who view the novel as offering similar kinds of critiques against historical master narratives (in the case of Cole) and against humanist (read: imperialist and masculinist) discourse (for Rohman) in favor of the "unspeakable" desires (Cole 395) and "nonlinguistic" animal subjectivity (Rohman 57) figured for the novel by Robin. Andrea L. Harris makes a similar argument about *Nightwood*'s thematic interest in the "third sex" and its own narratological inversions. Harris writes that Barnes takes the "classical binary oppositions governing Western thought and inverts the hierarchies, privileging the feminine term: the night, the irrational, the unconscious, the improper, the anonymous" (65).

2. What would ultimately grow into the idea for the unwieldy and unfinished *Arcades Project* began first as an idea for a 1927 newspaper article before it was transformed into the intermediary idea for the essay to be titled "Paris Arcades: A Dialectical Fairyland." I have quoted here from this title (873) and from the unfinished notes (390). See also Eric L. Tribunella's essay on "Children's Literature and the Child Flâneur" and Margaret R. Higonnet's "Modernism and Childhood: Violence and Renovation."
3. The collection, *Discovering Child Art: Essays on Childhood, Primitivism and Modernism*, edited by Jonathan Fineberg, includes essays on each of these facets and figures.
4. 184. Again, Higonnet's essay provides an especially in depth analysis of Futurism's relationship to youth.
5. In many ways this represents the condensation of an implicit debate between the second wave of *Nightwood*'s critical resurgence, which read the novel (largely through the lens of identity politics) as an affirmation of sexual liberation, feminist and queer identities, and carnivalesque social transformations, and the one currently underway, which has repeatedly taken this former set of readings to task by shoring up evidence for the novel's darker, dystopic, and self-critical discursive practices. Shari Benstock's *Women of the Left Bank* and *Silence and Power: A Reevaluation of Djuna Barnes*, edited by Mary Lynn Broe, and including, most especially, Jane Marcus's controversial "Laughing at Leviticus: *Nightwood* as Woman's Circus Epic" are cornerstones of the first order. The readings of Georgette Fleischer, Karen Kaivola, Robin Blyn, and Dianne Chisholm (among others) exemplify the recent countertrend, arguing respectively for the religious degeneration, sexual differentiation, freak show decadence, and profane illumination of the novel.
6. *Nightwood*'s transitional status, between modernism and postmodernism, is a point of rare consensus in *Nightwood* scholarship. Louis F. Kannenstine describes Barnes as a "transitional writer" whose approach is so intensely and "willful[ly] depersonaliz[ed]" that she must be placed in a broader tradition spanning at least "the early innovators of this century and the later generations of experimental writers" (xvii). Jane Marcus also famously recharacterizes *Nightwood* as "making a modernism of marginality" (223), of participating in a revision of modernism by its "hysterical heteroglossia" that renders it very nearly "postmodern" (222). Carolyn Burke similarly describes Barnes and Mina Loy as two women who "wrote as ex-centric or outsiders" to the period, recalling Linda Hutcheon's theorization of postmodernism as similarly "ex-centric." And most recently (and most substantially), Tyrus Miller theorizes "late modernism" as a precursor to postmodernism and devotes a chapter of that study to Barnes.

7. Plumb offers the gloss on this line that "it is unlikely that Barnes had in mind here Gertrude Stein's statement to Hemingway that his was 'a lost generation,' though Barnes herself belonged to that generation," but provides no further explanation as to why such a connection is "unlikely." Since Hemingway himself published the comment as an epigraph to *The Sun Also Rises* in 1926, it was certainly in public circulation well before Barnes wrote *Nightwood*.
8. The full title for Barnes's article, "Djuna Barnes Probes the Souls of Jungle Folk at the Hippodrome Circus," offers an allusion to W.E.B. Du Bois's collection of essays *The Souls of Black Folk*. In bulk the article seems to represent an entertainment piece about the Hippodrome Circus until the very end where Barnes rebels against her own narrative, refusing to add anymore to the man-eater storyline that excites the audience so. "The animal," she writes, "has long enough had human life upon its menu" (197).
9. For a further discussion of Rousseau's and *The Dream*'s sources and reception, see Christopher Green's "Souvenirs of the Jardin des Plantes: Making the Exotic Strange Again," from which I have quoted here, as well as Frances Morris's "Jungles in Paris" and "Mysterious Meetings," all in the collection *Henri Rousseau: Jungles in Paris*.
10. In 1981 Frank reflected that his "preoccupation" with spatial form "was never abstract or theoretical," focused as it was on an effort rather "to say something helpful and enlightening about" the "particular work" of *Nightwood* (qtd. in Glavey 755). It is not surprising that *Nightwood*'s role in the formulation of Frank's highly influential theory of the modernist aesthetic would be missed since, as Glavey elaborates, its original "lengthy exegesis of *Nightwood* was left on the cutting room floor, an amputation repeated ever since" (755).
11. This is one of many homophobic remarks attributable to Barnes. Though her relationship with Thelma Wood was no secret, Barnes never identified as a lesbian, and she repeatedly took issue with the characterization of *Nightwood* as a lesbian novel.
12. The most significant instance of this error actually comes from Barnes's friend and editor, Emily Coleman, who repeatedly beseeched Barnes to edit down the roles of Felix and O'Connor, feeling that they detracted from the core subject of the novel, the relationship between Robin and Nora (or, for her, between Thelma Wood and Barnes). Coleman's objections to Barnes are paraphrased by Plumb (xvi–xvii); her objections, recorded in her own diary, are paraphrased by Herring (203–204).
13. Barnes was very open about the fact that Robin's character was based on her long-time lover Thelma Wood and Jenny on Henriette Metcalf with whom Wood began an affair in 1928. Wood and Barnes had been living together in Paris since 1922. Wood and Metcalf moved to America where they lived together until at least 1942.

14. Chisholm grounds much of her reading of the "obscene modernism" of *Nightwood* in the doctor's "primary tactic of demystification...his shocking use of obscenity" (177).
15. The similarities between Robin, O'Connor, and Sylvia counter, to my mind, those readings of the novel which interpret *Nightwood* as affirming the narrative of Nora and Robin simply because it returns to them in the final chapter. See AnnKatrin Jonsson's claim, for example, that this ending "suggests resistance" to O'Connor's prediction at the end of "Go Down, Matthew" by giving "Nora and Robin's relation...the final word" (274–275).
16. From J.M. Barrie's *Peter and Wendy*, 148.

CHAPTER 6

The Children of Double Consciousness: From *The Souls of Black Folk* to *The Brownies' Book*

At the turn of the twentieth century, W.E.B. Du Bois famously articulates the problem of internalized racism as an experience of double consciousness. "It is a peculiar sensation," he writes in *The Souls of Black Folk* (1903), "this double-consciousness, this sense of always looking at one's self through the eyes of others, of measuring one's soul by the tape of a world that looks on in amused contempt and pity." What is often overlooked in this moment is that Du Bois is describing the "self," the "soul," and the "sensation" of childhood alongside the experience of being an African American. It is a crucial intersectionality.[1] The experience of double consciousness would not be what it is if it did not "burst upon" the romance of youth; this youth, in turn, is forever distinguished—not just from normative white America but from normative white childhood—by this new feeling of "being a problem." Du Bois locates the emergence of double consciousness in the "early days of rollicking boyhood," and it is a formative convergence that he returns to and importantly revises across the vast body of work that he went on to produce and edit for black children in the teens and twenties (4).

As one of the first modernist texts by an African American, *The Souls of Black Folk* famously juxtaposed music and essay, poetry and sociology, memoir and history. In so doing it not only spoke to the psychological, political, and daily complexities of being black in America but also inscribed that complexity into the form of its telling. After the unparalleled influence of *Souls* on modern African-American literature, it is puzzling that Du Bois's subsequent body of work—a body that grew for another

57 years—has received such minimal attention in literature, teaching, and scholarship. Many locate the waning interest in Du Bois's work in the narrowing aesthetic and political vision of the work itself. According to Arnold Rampersad, Du Bois's "momentous but slow" shift toward "the rhetoric of the militant propagandist" commenced just two years after the publication of *Souls* (94). And as Susan Wells surmises, "After the dazzling performance of *Souls*, Du Bois seldom attempted a form of address so complex" (123). Of course, scholars have recognized some notable exceptions to this perceived trend. Wells herself, following Paul Gilroy, proposes as one of them Du Bois's *Dark Princess: A Romance*. Other scholars have similarly re-evaluated other of Du Bois's later works, including *Darkwater* (1920), *Black Reconstruction* (1935), and *Dusk of Dawn* (1940), as extensions of the experimental paradigm so successful in *Souls*.[2] If there is strength in numbers, then these various exceptions coalesce into a powerful reformulation of Du Bois's career post-*Souls*. Together, they illuminate a trajectory, only begun in *Souls*, that continued to shift and change and grow in the direction of a Pan-African, international, and anti-imperialist political aesthetic.[3]

In this chapter I want both to re-sound the importance of taking a long view of Du Bois's work and to add this heretofore overlooked set of texts: Du Bois's works for children. Du Bois's intervention into the arena of children's literature is historically remarkable; arguably, it laid the groundwork for the field of African-American children's literature.[4] But Du Bois's own early contributions to that field, particularly in the context of the golden age of children's literature, were unconventionally mature. From 1912 to 1919 Du Bois was both the main editor of *The Crisis* as well as the chief architect for that periodical's annual October Children's Number, which placed the journal's usual reports of black Americans' suffering, outrage, and uplift in ironic juxtaposition with dozens of gorgeous photographs of America's black "children of the sun."[5] When, in 1920, Du Bois, Jessie Fauset, and Augustus Dill launched *The Brownies' Book*, a periodical designed explicitly for black children by black Americans, Du Bois created his most enduring editorial persona, the Crow, a figure whose epigraphic flights in "As the Crow Flies" reminded readers of the American promise but whose "caws" also exhaustively recorded the experiences of race-based discrimination the world over.

Although there has been a tendency to read Du Bois's child-centered writings as part of his shift toward propagandist, pedagogical discourses of racial uplift, there is ample evidence to suggest that these texts, like *Souls*, are modernist texts that resist the rigors of classification by inhabiting the uncertain regions between culturally conflicted genres, voices, and experiences.[6] Indeed, the duality rich juxtapositions of readers, voices, experiences, and forms throughout Du Bois's works for children in the decades after the success of *Souls* insist that the color line, double consciousness, and black childhood are analogous, intersecting problems. The color line that Du Bois crossed and re-crossed in *Souls*—by addressing readers, black and white, by musing on Shakespeare and the sorrow songs of slaves, and by arguing that white consciousness is imbedded in the black American's perception of his or her own blackness—finds a dynamic echo in these later works for children.[7] *The Crisis* Children's Numbers and *The Brownies' Book* are not only dramatically cross-written for an audience of adults and children, but they are also employed by Du Bois to stage, theorize, and transgress the duality of youth and age as the center of a new problem for black Americans in the twentieth century: the question of how to responsibly raise black children in the face of inevitable disillusionment and probable despair.[8] And the answer to this question, at first subtle in *Souls*, resounds in this children's literature, which seeks at once to be the source for the black child's entry into double consciousness and to represent double consciousness as a model for a revised and resilient black subjectivity beginning in childhood.

Being Divided and Being Double

In 1897 Du Bois published the essay that would become the conceptual foundation for *The Souls of Black Folk*. In "Strivings of the Negro People," he introduced for the first time his use of the term "double-consciousness." But the term itself was not original to him. Bruce D. Dickson has usefully traced its dual history through psychology and Romanticism to at least the early nineteenth century. While Du Bois was still a student at Harvard, his professor William James published *Principles of Psychology* (1890), which described the concept of double consciousness in a manner consistent with its psychological history as a pathological "mutation of the self" (373), characterized by a "double" or "alternating personality" (379). For both Romantics and psychologists alike, double consciousness marks a particular kind of problem. Indeed, what James's analogy helps to make clear is the extent to which the problem of being double is paradoxically synonymous with the problem of being divided. For the Romantics and transcendentalists in America, the term had a long figurative history as a signifier of man's conflict between his worldly and transcendent, other-worldly, selves. For psychologists, it had a similarly extensive record as a term for diagnosing split personality.

Each of these conceptualizations plays a role in Du Boisian double consciousness which evokes not just the burden of internalized racism but also the potential and the resilience that can come with the "gift of second sight." But Du Bois's use of double consciousness also diverges from these historical formulations in at least one crucial respect. Rather than collapse doubling into division, Du Boisian double consciousness acknowledges the potential for simultaneity in the place of alternation, for the compound in the place of the conflicted, and ultimately for resilience in the place of disorder. Though Du Bois gestures in *Souls* toward a dialectical vision of double consciousness, one in which the black American hopes to achieve "self-conscious manhood" by "merg[ing] his double self into a better and truer self," the vast majority of his working strategies actually reach, not toward the resolution, but toward the democratic suspension of the double. In *Souls*, Du Bois himself helps to clarify this point, for "in this merging," he writes, the black American "wishes neither of the older selves to be lost…He simply wishes to make it possible for a man to be both a Negro and an American" (5). Ross Posnock has elucidated the pragmatism underlying Du Boisian double consciousness, remarking that the real issue for Du Bois is less a problem of identity than it is a question of agency—of how "to be both a Negro and an American" without being "cursed" to turn "hither and thither in hesitant and doubtful striving" (6). From this perspective, Posnock continues, the "explicit question" of double consciousness is actually "how to maintain," not dissolve, "this doubleness" (327). The problem, in short, for Du Bois is not double consciousness so much as it is divided consciousness, or a consciousness that is really best characterized by an absence of "two-ness" (5).

Du Bois's understanding of the problem of a consciousness that is polarized and paralyzed and his pragmatic sense of a more enduring, hybridized course seated in childhood are each echoed by, and perhaps even arise through, the distance he came to perceive between his own Berkshire youth and that of the majority of his race. In *Souls* Du Bois recounts that "It is in the early days of rollicking boyhood that the revelation first bursts upon one, all in a day, as it were" of "being a problem." And to this general claim, Du Bois puts the specifics of his own childhood experience:

> I remember well when the shadow swept across me. I was a little thing, away up in the hills of New England, where the dark Housatonic winds between

Hoosac and Taghkanic to the sea. In a wee wooden schoolhouse, something put it into the boys' and girls' heads to buy gorgeous visiting-cards...and exchange. The exchange was merry, till one girl, a tall newcomer, refused my card,—refused it peremptorily, with a glance. Then it dawned upon me with a certain suddenness that I was different from the others; or like, mayhap, in heart and life and longing, but shut out from their world by a vast veil. I had thereafter no desire to tear down that veil, to creep through; I held all beyond it in common contempt, and lived above it in a region of blue sky and great wandering shadows. (4)

Though Du Bois consistently rebuked the spirit of Romanticism as a child-rearing strategy, he represents his own childhood, from the "days of rollicking boyhood" to his sense of a transcendent "blue sky" and "fiercely sunny" mentality, in precisely those terms. The differences between this experience, which Du Bois offers, in part, as a model of double consciousness, and the more general, realist experience are suggested in the return to third person. "With other black boys," Du Bois writes, "the strife was not so fiercely sunny: their youth shrunk into tasteless sycophancy, or into silent hatred of the pale world about them...or wasted itself in a bitter cry, Why did God make me an outcast and a stranger in mine own house?" (4–5). Du Bois slips uneasily from the general to the specific and then back again. The middle course charted by his own experience seems at last more digression than exemplification for when he resurfaces in broad strokes, it is to find that those "other black boys" have arrived elsewhere, or they have not arrived at all, having "wasted" themselves in despair. In this case, Du Bois's use of a Romantic/transcendentalist discourse emphasizes the distance between his and the childhoods of "other black boys," highlighting the extent to which his childhood, though imperfect, was nonetheless exceptional and the extent to which his experience of double consciousness was similarly thus, for it came not with the curses and closed doors encountered by most.

These differences, subtle in *Souls*, are vastly magnified in Du Bois's later childhood accounts in *Darkwater* and in his 1968 *Autobiography* (where much of what follows reappears with some variation). In *Darkwater* Du Bois begins, "I was born by a golden river and in the shadow of two great hills, five years after the Emancipation Proclamation. The house was quaint, with clapboards running up and down, neatly trimmed, and there were five rooms, a tiny porch, a rosy front yard, and unbelievably delicious strawberries in the rear" (3).[9] Here the boy of Du Bois's memory is given a fitting space for "rollicking," a "paradise" of hills, rivers, roses and strawberries.[10] Indeed, until the age of adolescence, Du Bois professes in these recountings little consciousness of race.[11] More prominent among his memories are the divisions of wealth. He remembers in *Darkwater* "despis[ing] the poor Irish and South Germans, who slaved in the mills" and "annex[ing]" instead "the rich and well-to-do as [his] natural companions" (6). Though he acknowledges that his "brown face and frizzled hair must have seemed strange" to the townsfolk, "yet," he writes, "I was very much one of them." Even the shift to double consciousness is described differently:

> Very gradually,—I cannot now distinguish the steps…but very gradually I found myself assuming quite placidly that I was different from other children. At first I think I connected the difference with a manifest ability to get my lessons rather better than most…Then, slowly, I realized that some folks, a few, even several, actually considered my brown skin a misfortune. (6)

There are a handful of what might be termed minor discrepancies between this and the *Souls'* account. In *Souls*, Du Bois "remember[s] well" the dawning of double consciousness; in *Darkwater*, he "cannot distinguish the steps." In *Souls* the dawning is "sudden"—it happens "all in a day"; in *Darkwater* it is "very gradual"—it occurs in "steps," and it occurs "slowly." At first, even, in *Darkwater*, Du Bois's embryonic sense of double consciousness is not tied to race but to intelligence, and indeed this sense seems to stay with him in both accounts in the manner of his academic defiance, his determination to prove his intellectual worth. But what comes across at first only implicitly in *Souls* and then far more clearly in *Darkwater* is Du Bois's sense of his own childhood experiences as no real model for the lives of other black children. To return to the dual trajectories of double consciousness in the nineteenth century, Du Bois clearly stresses his own experience as part of the Romantic, Emersonian tradition of internal transcendence and spiritual supremacy in the face of earthly strife, but in writing his own experiences in this way, Du Bois also suggests their obsolescence to the present demands and overwhelming experiences of the majority of his race.

Having grown up in something of a sheltered environment, in a small, isolated New England town, with a neighbor who paid for his books, with a principal who encouraged him to pursue a course of higher education, and with a community that helped financially to send him to Fisk, Du Bois's own education was the fruit of much generosity in addition to his own considerable will and innate ability. In returning to America from Europe, a period he called his "Days of Disillusion," he catalogues the accidents of his good fortune:

> *Suppose* my good mother had preferred a steady income from my child labor rather than bank on the precarious dividend of my higher training?...*Suppose* Principal Hosmer had been born with no faith in 'darkies,' and instead of giving me Greek and Latin had taught me carpentry and the making of tin pans? *Suppose* I had missed a Harvard scholarship? *Suppose* the Slater Board had then, as now, distinct ideas as to where the education of Negroes should stop? Suppose *and* suppose! (*Darkwater* 9)

In retrospect, Du Bois imagines his life under ordinary circumstances. If convention had ruled the mentalities and actions of his family and community, would he have achieved the same degree or even the same kind of success? In a moment of confessed humility, Du Bois writes that he "began to realize how much of what [he] had called Will and Ability was sheer Luck!" (9).

The notion of "Luck" brings the individual and her or his circumstance to a crossroads. Regrettably, it reveals and underscores the limits of American self-reliance and self-fashioning, but, more usefully, it highlights the systematic weaknesses in the social support structures available to African Americans in the first part of the twentieth century. "What is the real lesson," Du Bois asks, to be learned from such a life when the fact that he or any African American who has been able to develop her or his genius has done so by "sheer accident?" (120). And he answers:

> It is this....We have a right to assume that hundreds and thousands of boys and girls today are missing the chance of developing unusual talents because the chances have been against them; and that indeed the majority of the children of the world are not being systematically fitted for their life work and for life itself. (120–121)

Though Du Bois was able to rise through the cracks of convention, to be recognized in his "two-ness" as a black American scholar, he argues that his own exemplary life provides no ready model for others because the opportunities he had are not systematically available to the majority of African Americans. On the other hand, the fact of his chance success also underscores the potential for "hundreds and thousands" more like it if such opportunities could become the norm rather than the exception.

The Politics of Race Meets the Politics of Age

Du Bois's increasing concern with the widespread failure of education for black children goes hand-in-hand with his growing interest in what can be systematized in terms of child-rearing and instruction. While in *Souls*, Du Bois argues that "the problem of the Twentieth Century is the problem of the color-line"; by the time he writes *Darkwater* (1920), he proclaims: "All our problems center in the child" (125). But these claims are more contiguous than not, for if double consciousness has a history, an experience or event that necessarily precedes it, for black Americans, Du Bois suggests, that history lies in childhood. Whereas in *Souls* Du Bois strives to articulate the experience of double consciousness, in his writings for children he returns to the scene of double consciousness, as it were, in an effort to systematically transform and repurpose that experience for young black Americans. The concerns that Du Bois expresses in *Souls* (1903) and in *Darkwater* (1920) that the problems of racial discrimination begin in childhood and so must be addressed in childhood are reflected in his writings for children in *The Crisis* Children's Numbers from 1912 to 1919 and in *The Brownies' Book* from 1920 to 1922. In *Darkwater*, Du Bois advises black parents that they "can no longer wholly shield" the child when to do so is to produce "wayward, disappointed children," nor should they, "realizing this, leave their children to sink or swim in this sea of race prejudice," but they must rather chart a middle course, "between extremes," characterized by "frank, free, guiding explanation" alongside "every step of dawning intelligence" (119–120). This sentiment is echoed in Du Bois's nearly contemporaneous *Crisis* introduction to *The Brownies' Book*, an effort which arises, he writes, out of the realization that "To educate [our children] in human hatred is more disastrous to them than to the hated; to seek to raise them in ignorance of their racial identity and peculiar situation is inadvisable—impossible" ("True Brownies" 285). In terms of the child's self and social awareness in each of these instances, Du Bois rejects both its excessive limitation and its excessive exposure, advocating instead an approach which more genuinely embraces the spirit of two-ness through a complicated, compromising program of guided exposure.

Introduced as a problem in *Souls*, the manifestation of double consciousness is at the center of Du Bois's work for and about children. Given the pervasive ontology that reduces black development to the undeveloped, Du Bois's goal of "self-conscious manhood" begins paradoxically with a set of unconventional maxims and materials for the construction of a new and revised black child. As with many modernists, Du Bois confronts a common Edenic vision of childhood, and like them, he perceives a danger in the child's actual, practical internalization of what that ideal espouses in the form of an innocent, transparent, and unsophisticated mentality. But this threat is heightened in Du Bois's case because his concerns are for a race of men and women (but especially men) who have been reduced through the lens of prejudice to a state of perpetual childhood. Lesley Ginsberg has documented the degree to which "justifications of slavery promulgated during the antebellum period were predicated on an increasingly literal analogy between the peculiar institution and the more familiar pattern of subordination upon which the antebellum family was built." Black children were thereby often thought of as "pets" and the black man as a "child by his nature" (90–91). The infantilization of black men and women was nowhere more apparent than in the "selective tradition" of early twentieth-century children's literature, which, as Violet Harris has explicated, routinely "suggested that Blacks were inferior, happy-go-lucky, and childlike" ("Race" 192).[12]

Again and again, Du Bois confronts the problem of racial infantilization. In his chapter on "The Immortal Child" in *Darkwater*, he writes that the very existence of black man is a "'problem'" for white society, that for them "he should never be educated, for he cannot be educated," and that in their eyes he "should never have been born," for his interiority is imagined as incapable of growth (119). Elsewhere in this same text, Du Bois writes that the dehumanized and the infantilized meet in the European justifications for slavery, which posit "Darker people" as "of dark, uncertain, and imperfect descent; of frailer, cheaper stuff" as "fools, illogical idiots,—'half-devil and half-child'" (24). And in a lecture contemporaneous with *Souls* on "The Training of Negroes for Social Power," Du Bois warns that the misperception which equates black Americans with a "child-race,"—thereby seeking to strip black men of responsibility and "to train these millions as a subject caste, as men to be thought for, but not to think; to be led, but not to lead themselves"—must logically back-fire, for "such a subject child-race could never be held accountable for its own misdeeds and shortcomings…above all, its crime would be the legitimate child of that lack of self-respect which caste systems engender" (131).

Du Bois's sense of conventional childhood and manhood as contrasting concepts resonated throughout many of his works, including *Souls*. And his calls for the recognition of a complex subjectivity, one beginning even in childhood, are addressed not only to the other white world but also to black Americans, especially to black men and to black parents. In his 1905 speech addressing the purposes of "The Niagra Movement," Du Bois presents journalistic evidence for the double-standard that while "white men" in America are depicted as having heroically secured their rights as men "only after asserting the right and sometimes fighting for it," for black men there arises the excuse that "A child should use other language." In the face of this, Du Bois asks, "Are we not men enough to protest"? And as a prelude to J. G. Holland's poem "God, Give Us Men," he proclaims, "This is the critical time, black men of America; the staggering days of emancipation, of childhood, are gone" (148).

One of the signature dangers of a romanticized notion of childhood interiority is its actual internalization, for while notions of perpetual childhood may fulfill nostalgic fantasies for white Americans, they construct overwhelming obstacles to progress for a people who seek to write a different future. As Caroline Levander has shown, America from its colonized beginnings identified itself with the liberty-loving qualities presumed of childhood as well as with its emblematic representation of the newly born nation-state. That the child-freedom bond was intimately racialized was revealed in America's own rationalizations for the enslavement of a people and a children of another caste. Levander cites John Woolman who in 1754 argued for the abolition of slavery on precisely these grounds—that it had no innate logic but only a superficial one. To prove his point, Woolman offered a hypothetical case that asked his reader to imagine an orphaned "'white child,'" who "comes under the power 'of a person, who endeavours to keep him a slave.'" So sure is such a case to provoke a "sense of outrage" in readers "otherwise untroubled by the idea of the 'many black [who] are enslaved'" that Woolman readily drew the conclusion "'of slavery being connected with the black colour, and liberty with the white'" (29). Many of America's notions of childhood have excluded black children. Woolman's critique reveals the degree to which the antebellum American majority imagined the ideals of liberty and of democracy as interdependent with the preservation not just of childhood but of whiteness.

For Du Bois, on the other side of "the color line," the perspective is, not surprisingly, quite different. For him, freedom is not symbolized in the child but in the man. And, indeed, in *Souls* Du Bois makes the radical substitution of the "darker ones" as the "true[st] exponents of the pure human spirit of the Declaration of Independence" in the place of the nationally recognized symbol of American liberty, the white child. And yet, though Du Bois calls, in one sense, for an ideological end to childhood, proclaiming that "the staggering days of emancipation, of childhood, are gone," in another, socially realist sense, he models a new and revised attention to the African-American child. In the October 1922 Children's Number of *The Crisis*, Du Bois once more expresses concern for the misapplication and misinternalization of the romantic child ideal with regard to black children. He wonders "how many are being regarded" by their parents "as negligible playthings" and chastises the "new mother" who "dresses...up" her children "like living dolls" ("Infancy" 250; "The Children" 247). Lesley Ginsberg has documented the degree to which slavery was justified using "an increasingly literal analogy" between slavery and the structures of domestic subordination. Black children were thereby often thought of as "'pets in the house,'" and the black man as a "'child in his nature'" (89–90). Robin Bernstein extends this argument into postbellum America and into bourgeois consumer culture where racialized dolls became the special, indestructible targets for a permissible, "innocent," virtual violence against black Americans (187). In this instance, Du Bois may well be drawing upon the loaded historical weight of misconceptions of black people as dolls or "negligible playthings" in order to stress the particular dangers of replicating this dynamic within the African-American community and home. To the "grown-ups" who "think of little children as 'cunning,' 'pretty,' 'cute' and 'amusing,'" Du Bois offers the correction that "our jails are full of children who once were unbelievably cunning" (247). Though the tone is quite different, the terms of the critique, here in *The Crisis* as in *Darkwater*, are the same. The threat of childhood to black children is dehumanization (whether as "subject caste" or as "negligible playthings"), and dehumanization threatens to become its own self-fulfilling prophecy.

On the heels of this scorching rebuke, Du Bois makes a case for the conservation, not of childhood, but of adult rationality and autonomy. In contrast to the "many and singularly different ideas" of childhood, from the child as "bond slave," "automaton," "Item of Expense," or parental "personal adornment," Du Bois offers what "few people think of," that is, "the child as Itself—as an Individual with the right and ability to feel, think and act; a being thirsty to know, curious to investigate, eager to experiment."[13] The child subject Du Bois addresses, far from being even a mirror of her or his parents, is to be more complex, for s/he is to have guidance where they did not. Du Bois's case is not only thusly explicit, but it is conveyed powerfully as well via its performance. In choosing the Children's Number as the space not only to address children but to address their parents about them, Du Bois invites child readers who will be privy to the methods of their own upbringing, who will be doubly conscious in the sense of knowing themselves as children and knowing themselves as their parents see them. Du Bois fosters the construction of a meta-perspective in childhood, a layered interior aware of its own scripted part as well as of the totality of the play in which it figures. For Du Bois such awareness seems vital to the aesthetics and politics of self-fashioning, to casting new and revisionary models of subjectivity. Du Bois extends the point even further because, given his chastisement of the conventional parental position, his child readers are situated at a double remove, being at a vantage to view not only many parents' point of view on childhood but also the magazine's (and its editor's) disapproving perspective of it. In other words, the child readers of *The Crisis* Children's Numbers are envisioned with the potential for knowing, and perhaps then of traveling, a path other than the one they are presently on and other than the one their families have laid for them.

In a move parallel to his treatment in *Souls* of "the problem of the color line," in this 1922 piece on "Childhood," Du Bois writes of the relationship between parent and child as one in need of democratic revision. To the discovery of some parents that they "must teach," "must persuade," and "must direct" the child, Du Bois offers the corrective amendment:

> ...if [parents] are honest they soon learn that in a duel between two human wills even though one is four and the other forty, there is information to be imparted on both sides; and that youth can teach age some things; and that persuasion is a game that two can play; and that Experience, great as it is, is not all. Many people begin with trying to teach and persuade and end by commanding in anger, "instant" obedience, leaving the child with a tremendous and never-to-be-forgotten sense of being wronged and cheated. Only God's Few take this dialogue between Age and Childhood seriously and give to it as much time and money and study and thought as they give to their clothes and houses and horses. (252)

Du Bois's claim here has two parts. The first is to acknowledge the needs of childhood: for patience, for education, for monetary support. The second is to make the more controversial claim for the needs of age. Experience, money, and power are "not all." Youth, too, has something to "teach." The dialogic exchange, what he terms "this dialogue between Age and Childhood," is nearly identical to the argument laid out by Du Bois for the black American's struggles in the Reconstructive Era. The former slave, suddenly free, is triply "handicapped"; he feels "his poverty," feels "the weight of his ignorance," and feels too "the hereditary weight of a mass of corruption from white adulterers, threatening almost the obliteration of the Negro home." As "the child of Emancipation," he needs no less than the actual child: financial footing, education, and equally as important to these, he needs time. "A people thus handicapped," Du Bois writes, ought not to be asked to race with the world, but rather allowed to give all its time and thought to its own social problems" (*Souls* 9). The white world, like the figure of "Age" in *The Crisis* Children's Number, is too quick to criticize, to berate, and to withdraw from a recognition of its own responsibilities and imperfections. In addition to the basic needs of the newly emancipated, stands Du Bois's, again more controversial, claim for the far deeper wants of white culture, wants, painted by Du Bois as "a dusty desert of dollars and smartness," that can be met by the "sole oasis of simple faith and reverence" embodied in the "souls of black folk" (*Souls* 11–12). In both cases Du Bois's aim is to democratize the hierarchical divide—to offer a critique of those on high and to articulate for the low an interiority approaching self-conscious manhood.

Du Bois suggests that the child and the black man possess a shared struggle: to communicate and gain recognition for theirs as sophisticated and valuable subjectivities. And he also posits that the principles of democracy have not only been violated by the enslavement of black men and women and children but that a parallel violation has occurred and occurs in the homes of the most privileged Americans. Far from thinning Du Bois's investment in the color line, the addition of age to the dialogue of race thickens his sense of what can distinguish and lend distinction to black Americans. Attaching the child to the black man is a move that may underscore the gaps in white America's so-called democratic principles while strengthening the new seat of the democratic ideal in the black community and in the black home.

The Crisis Children's Numbers: A Successor to *Souls*

As the author of *Souls*, Du Bois seeks to convey a multitude through the polygeneric form of the essay. As the editor of *The Crisis* Children's Number, he coordinates his often polemical editorials as one voice and one generic approach among many. More than the typical monthly issues, the Children's Number organizes itself around polarized images and content. Beginning in 1912, the child aspects of the Children's Number under Du Bois's editorship were rarely separated within isolate compartments but

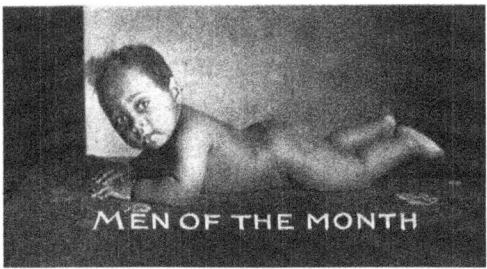

Fig. 6.1 *The Crisis* Children's Number 16.6 (October 1918) 282

instead were interspersed throughout and within the magazine's other compartments. Most popular was the visual interspersal of photographs of black children—usually very young toddlers or infants—submitted by *Crisis* readers. The intertextual layout of these images varies from issue to issue and within the issues themselves. Often there is at least one page entirely devoted to displaying as many baby photos as is possible. Also common is the playful use of photos as departmental headers (Fig. 6.1). No doubt many of the 80 or so photographs that appeared in any single Children's Number were likely selected and positioned somewhat arbitrarily, as Du Bois claimed for the photo selection process as a whole,[14] but there are key moments where the juxtaposition of the Romantic child image alongside the textual violence of *The Crisis*'s reports are ripe with intent.

One particularly striking instance occurs in the 1914 issue (Fig. 6.2). In this case, the image of three children beneath the textual account of the avenged rape of a twelve-year-old black girl (see the second bulleted "crime") confronts readers, child and adult, with a graphic, unsettling reality. Though the image, captioned "Missouri," by itself might have suggested that these children represent America—that they are every child—the manner of their juxtaposition, following a catalogue of crimes including those against black children, belies this sentimentality. Rather, the heading for this page, "Along the Color Line," insists that childhood is not exempt from race prejudice and should not be excluded from race consciousness.

Louisville, Ky., claims that he has positive orders from the Superintendent of Parks to forbid colored children from bathing in the pool in the park.

CRIME

THE following colored men have been lynched since the last report: At Monroe, La., Preston Griffin and Charles Hall, charged with murderous attack upon a white man, were taken from the jail and lynched; twenty-four hours before Henry Holmes was lynched for the same crime. Near Monroe, La., an unidentified man, charged with the murder of a white man, was lynched.

¶ A serious race riot came near resulting

¶ It was reported that a colored mob had lynched a white man in Clarksville, Tenn., for rape upon a 12-year-old colored child. Later reports are that the man was not lynched but killed by the uncle of the outraged child who went with the sheriff to find the man.

¶ Police Patrolman William Fincher of Mobile, Ala., has been dismissed from the service and is being held without bail for the murder of a colored man.

¶ Jailer E. J. Farris of the Paris (Ky.) jail, killed the leader of a mob which was attempting to break into the jail. The purpose of the mob was to lynch Henry Thomas, a colored man accused of assault and attempted robbery.

MISSOURI

Fig. 6.2 *The Crisis* Children's Number 8.6 (October 1914) 273

Another startling example of this kind of juxtaposition occurs in the October 1916 issue, where the image of a child standing on a stool accompanies an NAACP article on the recent Florida lynchings of the adoptive mother, wife, and neighbor of Boisy Long, a black man accused of stealing hogs who, when served with a warrant in the middle of the night, apparently shot the two men who delivered the warrant and then escaped (Fig. 6.3). Katharine Capshaw has written of the use of the child image in this politically charged context that it "requires the reader, both adult and child, to imagine the boy at risk himself for future lynching, particularly because of his sad expression and the fact that, standing on the stool, he

THE LYNCHING FUND

AS we go to press the Ten Thousand Dollar Anti-lynching Fund has reached the sum of $10,177.50 in cash and pledges. We Congratulate America.

ANOTHER LYNCHING
By M. A. H.

GAINESVILLE, a charming town about eighty miles southwest of Jacksonville, Fla., has a population of about 11,000. The town is a desolate place of shanties and small houses, and has the reputation of lawlessness. There is not one good building in the place and many of the houses are vacant. The sun beats down on the roofs and there is almost no shade. The white men live chiefly by small stores. The colored people hire out to farmers, etc. Many of the colored women go out to service in other cities.

The driving road between Gainesville and Newberry is more of the Gainesville character. Most of the land is under cultivation. Four or five large farms lie along the road, but most of them are small farms. Roads branch off from the main road leading to other farms. The chief products are cotton, corn, some sugar cane, peanuts, pecans, melons, cucumbers, and other garden truck. A large number of the farmers are Negroes. They own their own land, to a large extent, and are prosperous.

Jonesville is a blacksmith shop and a store with adjacent farms five miles from Newberry and thirteen miles from Gainesville. The rioting was along the road between Jonesville and Newberry. The white men were all either from Newberry or the neighborhood.

The trouble arose over hogs. In the last few years hog raising has become profitable here. A Gainesville firm buys the farmers' hogs and ships them to a large packing concern in Georgia. Many of the farmers have hogs which roam at large in the road and in the woods. They are sup-

Fig. 6.3 *The Crisis* Children's Number 12.6 (October 1916) 275

is already set suggestively above the ground" (Smith 9). The image also no doubt seeks to connect the child's innocence with the innocent victims of a racist society's unchecked and self-sanctified violent oppression of its black citizens.

But the use of the child image in this case, and throughout *The Crisis* Children's Numbers, does more than underscore the attendant text; it stands in ironic juxtaposition to it. Here the child, standing literally on a pedestal, reified on high, serves as a pure white contrast to the violent reality of lynching for many regions in America, serves on his or her pedestal as a contrast to the adults whose footing has been violently removed, and assumes a counter-stance, as an emblem of humanity, empathy and compassion, to the article's detailed account of society's widespread and astonishing inhumanity to its fellow man. From the image to the article, *The Crisis* presents a set of extreme positions, put in the simplest of terms as innocence and violence, and suggests with its call for the further funding of the anti-lynching campaign that the resolution to the crisis lies between them. Galvanizing as the idyllic image of innocence may be, in reality the article attests to its impotence in the face of indiscriminate hatred and violence. Innocence did not save the mother, wife, and neighbor, not to mention their surviving children and families, from suffering and from death. Violent retaliation similarly fails to preserve the freedom of Boisy Long, later captured and imprisoned, or the friends and family he left behind. In contrast to the tone of either its opening image or of the events it describes, the article's method is one of painstaking, thoughtful detail. Its attention to recreating the context of the crime—before, during, and after—suggests that objective reporting, political involvement, and financial contributions are all more viable and successful measures than the relatively mindless positions of innocence and violence at either end of the spectrum.

The picture/text relationship in the Children's Numbers often serves the politically-charged democratic purposes of the magazine. Sometimes this is a rather straightforward affair, as with the 1914 issue, which labels a significant portion of the children's photos with their state of residence, thereby positioning the children as representatives of a diverse people and readership. Indeed, readers of this issue could identify with one of at least 21 states, plus D.C. and Cuba. More typically, however, the democratic ideals of the Children's Numbers are suggested through the representation of contrary positions, set side-by-side in the partnership of an ironically divided image and text. Later issues, for instance, invite readers, child and adult alike, to linger on the photos, to apply even a more thoughtful interpretive lens to them through the use of literary and biblical captions. These captions, as often as not, speak to the death of childhood or to the injustices suffered by black children and synecdochically, by the entire race. One 1917 caption quotes the Lord's warning in Exodus that his mercy is not all-inclusive; for the unrepentant, he threatens to punish by "visiting the iniquity of the fathers upon the children and the children's children to the third and the fourth generation" (288). This and other 1918 captions, which ask, "Does it show any superiority of mind or soul to believe or pretend to believe in the 'inferiority' of these little ones?" (286) or "Can real Democracy deny to these children when they are grown the right to vote and take part in the government of their country?" (290), are not only directed toward arousing the indignation of black readers but are also, and more directly, addressed to a white audience, one which, practically speaking, was less likely to receive them in a similarly direct fashion.

Several 1916 poetic captions contrast the smiling faces, white bows, and white dresses with reminders of suffering and death (Fig 6.4). One comes from a Francis Turner Palgrave poem, "A Danish Barrow: On the East Devon Coast," that mocks the sentimental treatment of death and ends instead with a *carpe diem* affirmation of life: "Let the children play and sit like flowers upon thy grave and crown with flowers,—that hardly have a briefer blooming-tide than they" (287). Other lyrical captions in this same issue come from William Sharp's (Fiona McLeod, pseud.) "Little Children of the Wind": "I hear the little children of the wind crying solitary in lonely places"—and from William Wordsworth's "We Are Seven":

"LET THE CHILDREN PLAY AND SIT LIKE FLOWERS UPON THY GRAVE AND CROWN WITH FLOWERS,—THAT HARDLY HAVE A BRIEFER BLOOMING-TIDE THAN THEY"

Fig. 6.4 *The Crisis* Children's Number 12.6 (October 1916) 287

"A simple child that lightly draws its breath, and feels its life in every limb, what should it know of death!" Separately and together, these passages encourage an ironic reading of the photographs on display, inviting *Crisis* readers to see, beyond what is visibly present, that which is present but invisible to sight—that which is, as in Palgrave's poem, buried underneath, or that which is, as in Sharp's case, isolate and alone and evidenced not by sight but only by sound, or, finally, that which is realized through undying memory, as with Wordsworth's child subject, whose math refuses to distinguish between the living five and the two lost siblings.

Du Bois's editorial commentaries on the photos of the Children's Number emphasize, as one of their many ironic attributes, their role as representative reminders of the masses of unseen, though equally worthy, beautiful, and able, black bodies and souls. There is always an implicit effort at pluralistic representation in the choice and layout of the photos in the Children's Number. Though nearly all appear to represent the most privileged of the race at that time, Du Bois insists on their democratic qualities. In fact, very few are of a casual, everyday nature; nearly all consist of children posed and in their Sunday best. On one hand, the selection of such photos might speak to Du Bois's interests in depicting a "talented tenth." Early in the century, Du Bois had used photography in much this way when he procured 363 photographs for the American Negro Exhibit at the Paris Exposition of 1900. The majority of these photographs favored images of educated, prosperous, and light-skinned African Americans as representatives of the race.[15] In an era when casual photography was becoming increasingly popular, the children pictured in Du Bois's exhibit were distinguished, as Shawn Michelle Smith argues, from the cultural imagery of white "barefoot boyhood" by their "impeccable grooming, crisp, clean, stylish clothes, and composed faces" (72).

But on the other hand, this earlier example of Du Bois's work with child photography may help to bring the changing aesthetics and politics of the Children's Numbers more sharply into focus. Though it appears that Du Bois may have once requisitioned photographs of perfectly angelic, perfectly poised children, here he solicits not just a more democratic imagery but a more democratic imaginary as well. In 1916, Du Bois persists in the claim that those "who look at you from these pages are but a little and imperfect selection of those who might" (268) and makes a special request in 1923 for photo submissions "of interesting children, not necessarily pretty and dressed-up, but human and real" (103). In a 1917 editorial on "Consecration," he writes, "Look upon these little faces that broider our pages. Think of the millions that are not here—just as lovely and alluring—and remember that it is our present business to write in on the souls that look through these dark eyes wishes, wills, determinations, consecration" (284). Though the pictures spring "mostly from the well-to-do of a large group," as Du Bois himself confesses in 1914, he nonetheless hopes that the partnership of image and text—the combination of the "look" of "these dark eyes" and "our present business to write in on the souls" behind them—will expand the testimonial boundaries and affective outreach of either medium by itself.

Indeed, as with the musical bars in *Souls*, the image of the black child, as so many of the captions reveal, is far more than a literal representation of a "physical type" but is also a sign of the ineffable, a visual testament that surpasses the capabilities of logical, textual argument, providing a kind of tangible proof of the African American's universal humanity and intrinsic equality. The caption which asks the reader "Does it show any superiority of mind or soul to believe or pretend to believe in the 'inferiority' of these little ones?" implies that one look at the nine infant photos above it, or of the nine on the adjacent page, will instantly attest to the fact of racial equality at every level: physical, intellectual, and spiritual. Of the musical notations in *Souls*, Steve Andrews has written that their disruption of Western textual protocols does not simply invert "the terms of binary opposition by overturning the hierarchical inflections—ear *over* eye, black *over* white"—but rather "leaves the reader to ponder instead the problem of synaesthesia, of how to 'feel together,'" to "better facilitate a response on the part of readers toward recognizing simultaneous, omni-sensual cultural interactivity by blacks and whites" (149–150). In the same way that the sorrow songs, of black culture, already an intermixture of African memories and American experiences, are placed in *Souls* alongside Western cultural forms in the manner of a sustained dialectic, or such that each "balance[s]" each (Sundquist 485), the pictures and text of the Children's Numbers speak side-by-side in the counter-languages of feeling and of fact, of youth and of age. In the same way that *Souls* generically suspends the dialectic of race such that neither black nor white is subsumed by the other, even such that the new and exceptional hybridized subjectivity of the African American can be articulated and felt, the Children's Numbers suspend the cultures of childhood and maturity such that their own "synaesthesia" within the black community can commence. The generic hybridity and insistent cross-writing of these *Crisis* issues go beyond troubling the line between child and adult text to suggesting, as Katharine Capshaw argues, that all of the material in *The Crisis*

Children's Numbers—every image, every caption, every article—is equally "applicab[le]...to every reader, regardless of age" (Smith 4).

Like the epigraph, bar, and essay in *Souls*, the picture and text in the Children's Numbers lend themselves to a hermeneutics which is not simply hybrid but multiply and ambiguously so. As part socio-political organ, part literary periodical, and part picture book, there is no one way to interpret the place of the photos in *The Crisis* Children's Number. The issues, with their 80–100 photos of black children can be read from vantages most general and abstract to depths most personal, most specific. For some, particularly for picture contributors, they may have imbued the issue with the intimate status of family album or scrapbook. For others the photos may have been mere propagandist tools to meet a militant political agenda. For some the photos may have provided visual validation of black beauty, health, and future prosperity. And still for others they may have even been seen as representatives of the unseen, of the soul, and of the unrepresented.

For its child audience, the photos interspersed throughout the more traditional compartments of the magazine, from "Opinion" to "The Horizon" to "Along the Color Line," may have been viewed by the magazine as a way to draw the attention of its youngest reader/viewers to a political message they might have otherwise skipped or glossed over, to prepare them for realities beyond their own present personal experience, or to echo and lend communal support to those experiences potentially already encountered. And they may also have operated as a means for mitigating for those young eyes the effects of the perhaps too serious or too violent content of the standard *Crisis* fare. While there is little record of the effects of *The Crisis* Children's Numbers on actual child readers, Horace Mann Bond does offer one retrospective glimpse of his own experiences as an "avid" child reader of *The Crisis* and of its singular and consequently profound impact on shaping his "inner world." In a *Freedomways* tribute to the legacy of Du Bois, he writes:

> I remember the pleasant faces of brown and black children pictured in the magazine…and I remember, also, the horrifying cartoons depicting 'lynch law'…Indeed, I remember a period during which the same frightening nightmare would recur, night after night; I was being pursued by the grisly form of 'lynch law'….
>
> The cartoons were strong stuff for a child, perhaps, as were the factual accounts of the lynchings…Yet I am glad that through Du Bois I had these

vicarious experiences with the real and brutal world of race and color, as with the real world of black men and women clothed in beauty and dignity. (16)

Evident in Mann's memories of reading *The Crisis* is the feeling of twoness. His primary recollection is not only dualistically structured, between the "pleasant" photos of black children and the nightmare-inducing accounts of lynching, but it is also itself doubled in his consequent appreciation for what these divergent readings fostered, the "vicarious" experience of two opposite and equal realities: the one a "brutal world of race and color," the other "the real world of black men and women clothed in beauty and dignity."

All of these, and many more, independent readings of the picture/text placement are possible. The more important point is that by its very variety, and more so by the frequent method of contrasting variety, the Children's Numbers invite each reader to engage with multiple perspectives, similarly intertwined and similarly diverse.[16] Though the Children's Number draws upon a children's picture book tradition, the relationship between picture and text utilized within it, in part because of the dual audience of the magazine and in part because of Du Bois's own ideological stance, is, as with the experimental variety of *Souls*, more modernist than conventional. For the traditional picture book of this era, the collection of images was akin to the twice-told tale, where the picture's chief function was illustrative, promoting and echoing in visual form the message of the text.[17] Indeed, picture book scholars agree that the move toward more complex and even ironic relationships between picture and text did not begin in any widespread sense until the middle of the twentieth century when there was a growing appreciation for child psychology and for developing figurative, on top of literal, avenues for meaning.[18] And while the Children's Number does allow for some such synchronic readings across image and text, more often than not it simultaneously or even preferably juxtaposes picture and text such that, rather than their proximity, it is the gap between the image and the caption or article which is the most striking feature of their partnership. In other words, the selective content and layout of the Children's Numbers asks the child not only to understand the hopes, aspirations, and beauty that others see in him or her but also to see these adults' very different—concerned, discouraged, outraged—perspective of the world at large and to discern, perhaps also, the often enormous distance separating the two. For its adult readers, this same disjunct between image and text visually affirms that it is possible to fill the traditional mold of childhood with the bodies of their own black children, and yet it signals with caution that this substitution may yet nonetheless be undesirable, given the very different set of experiences that await their children just the same.

The selection of child images, replete with pedestals, backdrops, pristine children, and all photography's finest, set alongside poetic lamentations of motherhood, reports of segregation, lynching, and even child rape (to name a few of the subjects "broidered" with the child image in the Children's Numbers) creates a pendulous effect, one that swings widely from the loftiest of romantic heights to the most mournful of reality's lows. Du Bois often warned about the dangers of the extremes of child-rearing, from harboring the child in the enclave of racial and realist ignorance to exposing him or her with abandon to a climate of hostility, hatred, and despair; but in advocating a middle course, he also, in the same breath as it were, presented the very thing which he criticized. To travel the road between, for Du Bois, meant rejecting and ignoring neither side, meant actually holding them each, at once, together. The presentation of the romanticized and the deplorable, side-by-side, is, in the context of the periodical, a striking print rendition of the manifest simultaneity of double consciousness. The dream of double consciousness meant embodying the specificities of one's history and experience as a black person in America with dignity and pride and at the same time claiming patriotic membership to a nationalist spirit of equal rights, responsibilities, and opportunities. Du Bois's dialogue of youth and age seeks similarly to negotiate, in equal measure, a vital heritage of cultural/personal experience alongside a merged early American and transcendentalist idyllic vision.

Beyond the more visually striking shifts in media, Du Bois's textual contributions to the Children's Numbers, and more so later in *The Brownies' Book*, engage in a similar phenomenon across the lines of generic, tropic, and typographic difference. Du Bois's 1914 editorial, for instance, makes continued use of the child photographic heading but contains sufficient ironic division within the story itself and indeed is as much a series of visions in the manner of its telling as are they. I have here used the term story because this editorial, adapted for the child reader, draws upon fiction as well as fact. The subject matter for the article is war, the title "Of the Children of Peace," but like the optometrist's phoropter—Du Bois manipulates the narrative lens to reveal the limitations of veiled awareness. First, he begins in the coterminous manners of legend and fairy tale, beckoning "all my father's children" to come and sit at father Du Bois's knee to hear the "Once upon a time" of war, glittering and great. He describes an army of "Tall, handsome men, all gold and silver and broadcloth" with "little innocent guns" and horses "that curvetted and tossed their shining bits" with "great, sweet eyes and quivering shining softness." But at the point that Du Bois reaches the "great cry of pride and joy and battle from the people," the fairy tale transforms abruptly into a dream sequence. "With that cry," Du Bois writes, "I seemed suddenly to awake. I somehow saw *through*." In a language reminiscent of *Souls*, the romantic vision of war is revealed as a veil of fiction. Du Bois invites the sympathetic cognition of the child reader "(You know sometimes how you seem to see, but are blind until something happens and you really see?)" and in so doing emphasizes, once more, the end of a romanticized childhood for *Crisis* readers (289). In describing the glittering veil of war as fairy tale, as dream, Du Bois also describes the veiled idyllic sight of the ideal child. Indeed, he uses the former to entice the latter, to gather the imagined child audience around him, and to attract actual child readers in turn. As Du Bois descended behind the veil in his journey from North to South in *Souls*, so here too he enters, on a much smaller, briefer scale, the veiled world of childhood. The impetus in both cases is to raise awareness, to rend the veil, to reveal blindness and confer greater sight. In this case, the narrative itself, as with *The Crisis* Children's Numbers at large, seeks to be for the child reader nothing less than the "something" that "happens" to make "you really see."

The remainder, which is the majority of Du Bois's editorial, acts as a mock twice-told tale in which every object from the first fairy tale vision is rewritten and reseen. The story is told a second time, but now every object seems its opposite through the new lens of unsheltered sight. The previously "Tall, handsome" soldiers become men "who trudged and limped, naked and dirty, with sodden, angry, distorted faces." Their previously "little innocent guns" become "little innocent children" carried to their deaths (289). The horses are all killed save one who lives "a gaunt, sweating" thing "with bloody nostrils, great pain-struck eyes, and bowels trailing on the earth" (290). In one sense, this is a striking predecessor to the NAACP article on lynching introduced with the image of the child, posed in white on a stool. In both, Du Bois uses the divided child-adult audience to frame a story between the two extremes of innocence and violence. In both accounts, neither innocence nor violence serves as a means to a profitable or even bearable conclusion. The innocent, once again, die. Violence, once again, breeds only more and vaster violence. But in another sense, Du Bois's editorial is a forerunner to his later work for children in that it is far more global in its reach and is also far more explicit about the new kind of globally and doubly aware child reader it seeks to foster.

Du Bois's editorial on war addresses not one war but all wars, for, as Du Bois writes, "The cause of War is Preparation for War." There is no logical cause that is not expressly circular. The "Hatred and Despising of Men" leads to "Death, Hate, Hunger, and Pain!" (290). But, of course, the essay is written at the start of World War I, and though war in general is its subject, its urgency comes from the present global crisis. Breaking the cycle here, as always for Du Bois, means graduating from single to double vision. As in *Souls*, Du Bois insists on the twoness of the present dilemma and in the binding twoness of its resolution. For him, the "Children of Peace" cannot bring their namesake without first knowing the many truths and lies of war. The conflict must come to reside within before it can ever come to rest without. In the bait and switch method of fairy tale turned horror story, Du Bois reveals his investment in and simultaneously seeks to compel a new kind of childhood, one which is doubly aware, aware of innocence and violence, aware of the fairy tale and the reality, the dream and the nightmare. Rampersad notes of Du Bois's method in *Souls* that, more than a subject of exploratory import, "the notion of duality is central to Du Bois' perception," and it is, in conjuncture with enumeration, among the crucial elements of his stylistic approach (73). Such is also dramatically the case in Du Bois's writings for children, where in addition to the lines of race, gender, and nation there has been added the line of age. And here as there, Du Bois encourages the simultaneous and reciprocal expression of all, which is to say both, sides of each of these preconceived dualities. Americans, in order to see and understand the problems of America, must cross her borders. The child, in order to prepare for the problems of and the resolutions to age, must enter early the territory of adults.

The New Child Is the New Adult: Du Bois and "As the Crow Flies"

So strong is Du Bois's belief in this new hybridized model of childhood, as much a man as a child and as much a child of the world as of the nation, that 1914, the same year that he wrote the editorial in question, saw his own child Yolande, along with his wife, in Britain with the purpose of not only acquiring a formal educational experience still largely unavailable in America, but also of gaining a worldly education in the causes and experiences of war. Nina Du Bois's letters from Brighton to her husband at home in New York attest to the climate of warfare: from the many wounded soldiers she meets, to her visit to a recently opened trench, one of many that "are all around London,"[19] to the need for "zeppelin drills" at Yolande's school because of recent bombing raids on London.[20] Du Bois's November 10th letter to his daughter includes conciliatory responses to her queries about riding lessons and a new watch with postponed promises to take up later the matter of both expenses, but his emphasis steers quickly to the matter of Yolande's education. He writes: "But most and foremost—lessons, lessons, lessons! Learn, learn, learn! Master your books, think and read. Read hard, dry books as well as stories. Read English history and French history and German history and see the reasons of this war."[21] Du Bois closes by sending her an issue of *The Crisis* and encourages her to share it with the other girls at her school. It is not clear which issue he encloses for her, but given the November date of the letter it may very well have been the October 1914 Children's Number. Here Du Bois shows his investment in providing a wide-ranging education for his daughter, one which spans nations and genres (he pushes "dry books as well as stories"). Last, but not least, he seeks to remind her of her own heritage at the same time that he has actively removed her from it. Though she is living an ocean away, he uses *The Crisis* to remind her "about our people—your people and mine, whom we must love and of whom we must be proud."

Du Bois's concerns over the reading and periodical reading practices of his own daughter may have also been a contributing factor in his 1919 decision to expand the appeal of the annual Children's Number into a monthly magazine designed directly for young black readers. That decision may also, however, have been the result of concern on the part of staff and parents over the conflicted content of the Children's Numbers. The year 1919, in fact, saw not only the first advertisements for *The Brownies'*

Book but also the addition of Jessie Redmon Fauset to *The Crisis* staff, as literary editor and as the future editor of its new periodical offspring. Though much work has been done to recuperate the unconventional in Fauset's work as editor and author, her unconventionality often arose from her unpopular application of conventional narratives and ordinary qualities to her black characters—this in a time when many white readers and publishers craved depictions of a "black 'underworld'" and when many black artists were striving in yet another direction, toward the more radical and experimental.[22] In sum, there were a number of voices and perspectives, quite different from Du Bois's own, which contributed, though in uncertain degrees, to the formation of *The Brownies' Book*.

Certainly, there are significant portions of the 1919 announcement of *The Brownies' Book* in that year's Children's Number that sound little like the Du Bois of previous issues. The primary cause, as Du Bois records, for the new, distinctly child venture is "the consternation of the Editors of The Crisis" that they "have had to record some horror in nearly every Children's Number" (285). While accurate, there were also certainly horrors which were not factually necessary under the magazine's role as newspaper informant and which Du Bois chose to record in the Children's Number as part of its principally dual design, as with, for example, "Of the Children of Peace," Du Bois's own fictionalized editorial on war. Then, too, there is little room in the seven listed aims of the *Brownies'* project for what would be Du Bois's own contribution to it: "As the Crow Flies." These aims were to make black children "realize that being 'colored' is a normal, beautiful thing," to teach them "the history and achievements of the Negro race," to make them aware "that other colored children have grown into beautiful, useful and famous persons," "to teach them delicately a code of honor and action in their relations with white children," "to turn their little hurts and resentments into emulation, ambition and love of their homes and companions," "to point out the best amusements and joys and worth-while things in life," and "to inspire them to prepare for definite occupations and duties with a broad spirit of sacrifice" (286–287). In addition and in contrast to this new semi-pragmatic, mostly optimistic program, the Crow is a clear extension of Du Bois's earlier effort, expressed in "Of the Children of Peace," to produce a "cry" (in this case a "caw") capable of lifting the veil of childhood in order to partner the dream of childhood with mature reality and to make them "really see" the "Truth" with a capital "T," "particularly," as Du Bois would write in the later *Crisis* version of "As the Crow Flies," "the unpleasant truth."[23]

Other authors, however, who made the transition from the Children's Numbers to *The Brownies' Book*, took the revised project to heart. Particularly striking is the contrast in Georgia Douglas Johnson's work in these two different periodical contexts. Take, for instance, Johnson's Children's Number contribution (after the dissolution of *The Brownies' Book*) in October 1922, titled "Motherhood," whose closing stanza reads:

> Don't knock at my heart, little one,
>
> I cannot bear the pain
>
> Of turning deaf ears to your call,
>
> Time and time again.
>
> You do not know the monster men
>
> Inhabiting the earth.
>
> Be still, be still, my precious child,
>
> I cannot give you birth. (265)

And compare it to the opening of her *Brownies' Book* poem, titled "Brown Eyes," published two years prior:

> Little maid with troubled hair,
>
> Nothing blows than you, more fair,
>
> Sweeter far than breath of morn
>
> In its cradle, newly born.
>
> All the world was made for you,
>
> Beauties rare and mother, too.... (158)[24]

While each of these poems is openly addressed to a child or child audience, in the first, tonal preference is given to the mother-speaker rather than to the child recipient. Where the world of the first poem is not for children, full of "monster men" and mothers who despair at their inability to mother, the world and mother of the second poem are "made for" the child. Each poem speaks to the rigid definition of motherhood as one's absolute devotion to her children, but where the burdened and embattled mother of the first poem, unable to embody this role, attempts to abort her child, everything, from the world, to the mother, to the poem itself, seamlessly conforms to the child center in the latter *Brownies' Book* verse.

Most fundamentally and most divergently from the cross-written Children's Numbers of *The Crisis*, the goal of *The Brownies' Book* is to occupy much more fully, much more consistently the space of children's literature. Though short-lived, *The Brownies' Book* marks an important milestone, becoming the first substantial periodical for children created by and for African Americans. As such it would have offered black children a singular and substantial alternative to the plethora of periodicals circulating for white audiences. The title itself would have had unmistakable resonances for child readers of the time with Palmer Cox's widely popular *Brownies'* series—the first of which was even similarly titled *The Brownies: Their Book* (1887). But unlike Cox's mystical Brownies, who invisibly and under the cover of night playfully imitate man's daytime activities and also correct his daily mistakes by performing neglected good deeds, Du Bois's periodical is addressed to the "True Brownies," just as playful, just as good, but visible and real.[25] Dianne Johnson-Feelings and Elinor Sinnette, who have described the history of *The Brownies' Book* in more detail, have also described it as an important alternative for black children to what was far and away the most successful children's periodical of the time, *St. Nicholas Magazine*, edited by Mary Mapes Dodge (where, perhaps incidentally, Cox's "Brownies" made their first appearance in print).[26] The September 1919 advertisement for *The Brownies' Book* promises all that *St. Nicholas* and its competitors have to offer, including "pictures, puzzles, stories, letters from little ones, clubs, games and oh—everything!" The goal in every case is to imitate and to revise. *The Brownies' Book* seeks to occupy the space of the traditional children's periodical, but it has to adapt everything that such texts routinely provide for the experiences, needs, and desires of black children, and it also has to confront and reject a number of black stereotypes not altogether uncommon in such white children's fare.

Certainly, Du Bois was aware of *St. Nicholas* and its draw for young readers. Yolande Du Bois herself was an avid subscriber to the periodical, as her 1916 letters home from England attest. There she politely persists in reminding her father that the time to renew her subscription has in fact already come and gone.[27] But the most striking evidence for positing *The Brownies' Book* as a conscious alternative to *St. Nicholas* comes in the form of Du Bois's own running contribution to it in "As the Crow Flies." *St. Nicholas* was probably original in its use of a hybrid editorial persona, in the form of the part plant, part preacher named Jack-in-the-Pulpit, to address the child reader and to deliver custom-fit news and information to him or her as it has been delivered to him, through his "chicks."[28] In "As the Crow Flies," Du Bois likewise makes use of a hybrid persona who shares world events as seen through the eyes and means of feathered-flight. As *St. Nicholas* wrote of the knowledgeable but implanted Jack, that the magazine itself will be the celebrated means for his communication to children the world over, having "laid the paragraphic wires" for him,[29] so too does Du Bois characterize the Crow in the first issue as a figure full of knowledge, who "*must see and hear*" "*a lot of things*," but who, given his linguistic limitations, needs *The Brownies' Book* to "*ma[k]e him talk for you.*"[30]

But unlike *St. Nicholas*, and indeed unlike much of *The Brownies' Book*, there is a prominent difference between Dodge's Jack, the naturally-interested bearer of odd and amusing facts, and the two-toned voice of hope and despair embodied in Du Bois's Crow persona. Indeed, Du Bois's new venture not only extends the juxtapositions of the Children's Numbers but it systematically solidifies, upholds, and encourages double consciousness as a method and model for black youth. This implicit aim is made manifest most strikingly in the figure of the Crow, a figure of transcendent blackness whose flights steer pendulously between hope and despair and who, as such, recollects Du Bois's own boyhood response to double consciousness: to live "above [the veil] in a region of blue sky and great wandering shadows" (*Souls* 4). But where Du Bois served up his own transcendent experience of double consciousness as an accident of fortune, here he reimagines it, through the double-voice and double-methods of the irritatingly ordinary Crow, as a model of resilient self-awareness for the new black child reader.

For the two years that *The Brownies' Book* circulated, "As the Crow Flies," all 24 entries, follows a remarkably consistent formula, opening with an embellished literary passage of hopeful tone and intimate address, starkly set apart from a main journalistic body which highlights cases of political turmoil and socio-economic distress on a global scale. In the first issue, the introduction is distinguished first by the ornate, floral styling of its premier letter, a line break, and a pair of centered swastikas; the news portion is demarcated in turn by its bullet-marked, no-nonsense delivery of the news. By the second issue, the opening is even further set apart typographically. In addition to the elaborate lettering, the section is off-set in italics. A short line now divides the opening from the news, which remains matter-of-factly bulleted. In some ways, this is clearly an extension of the ironic aspects of the picture/text relationship in the earlier Children's Numbers of *The Crisis*, but the consistency of the media in this case renders the contrasting styles and methods far more apparent. Du Bois has removed many of the variables that made the Children's Numbers so open to diverse interpretation. At the heart of these changes are precisely the formulaic aspects of this new set piece. Where the ironic partnerships of picture and text in the Children's Numbers shared the stage with the synchronous and with the haphazard, Du Bois, as the sole creator and producer of "As the Crow Flies," constructs it as a far more systematically double method and model.

Beginning with the latter, the subjectivity of the Crow is insistently proposed as an alternative model to the errors and even the atrocities of humanity. As much as Du Bois called for photo-submissions of less than perfect children which could better represent the masses of ordinary black Americans, he himself acknowledged failure in this (acknowledged it even in the need for the request). The figure of the Crow is in many respects Du Bois's unlikely solution. In the place of the picture perfect baby, Du Bois invites child readers of "As the Crow Flies" to imagine themselves as "crowlets" or "crowlings" and to imagine the Crow himself as their periodical parent. The September 1920 entry begins (Fig. 6.5):

THE *world squirms and rattles beneath my flying wings. I hear the laughter of little folk, the growl of men and the sweet sleep of the dead. I see the trees and waters and the great wild winds come down and up and swing me to and fro. But on and up I fly and fly to find the bits of news for my sweet babies—my dark Children of the Sun.*

❡ The world is still at war and thousands are suffering and dying. In western Asia the English population, millions are homeless and other millions crowded. Such are the costs of war.

❡ The Treaties of Peace between the Allies and Hungary and between the Allies and Turkey have finally been signed. The city of Budapest put on mourning and tolled the bells because the peace was so humiliating. Many of the Turks refuse to accept the peace and are still fighting.

❡ Conference has been held at the Hague, Holland, at the invitation of the League of Nations to organize a permanent International Court of

Fig. 6.5 *The Brownies' Book* 1.9 (September 1920) 272

The Crow is a surprisingly sensitive figure. Though he flies above the child-world that "*squirms and rattles,*" he senses its discomfort as if by touch; he hears its individual sounds; his eyesight, for which he is most celebrated, is keen enough to see even "*the great wild winds.*" And, too, though he flies above the world's sufferings, his journeys are not without obstacles, swung as he is "*to and fro,*" and they are not without purpose. Where Du Bois is able to send his own daughter to Europe to learn first-hand the lessons of war, for the homebound readers of *The Brownies' Book* he sends the Crow in their stead. The Crow travels the world in search of a new kind of sustenance for a new kind of child. The "*bits of news*" he finds and redistributes among the "*children of the sun*" are largely summed up by the first issue's first fact, that "The world is still at war and thousands are suffering and dying," followed by a double-digit catalog of battles presently underway, from Asia Minor to Syria, from Siberia to Ireland. As with his editorial, "Of the Children of Peace," printed six years prior in *The Crisis* Children's Number, Du Bois makes a now repeated and systematic effort in "As the Crow Flies" to instruct African-American children in the awareness of war and to lend them strength through an awareness of global suffering.

The Crow, thus, not only makes for a most unconventional parent, as devoted to exposing his "*sweet babies*" as he is to protecting them, but he repeatedly serves as a revisionary foil to the ideals of race representation. It would be difficult to imagine a persona more removed from Du Bois's earlier "talented tenth" imaginary. Yet while the latter has continued to represent an important part of the way Du Bois is read—as prudish, as elitist, as a lifelong Victorian—the figure of the Crow, irritatingly common, is Du Bois's most enduring persona.[31] Conceived for *The Brownies' Book*, "As the Crow Flies" became Du Bois's signature editorial title for the next 30 years. With the *Pittsburgh Courier* at least, Du Bois encountered some resistance over the matter. Publisher Robert Vann explained that the Crow was too reminiscent of Jim Crow, the minstrel figure who gave institutional segregation its name in nineteenth- through twentieth-century America.[32] But this may have been part of the proverbial point. The problem of imperialism, including American imperialism, while an important concern for Du Bois when he wrote *Souls*, becomes pervasive to his politics, aesthetics, and thought with the onset of the First World War. Du Bois comes to see European imperialism, especially in Africa, as the "root" cause for the First World War and also as integral to the failure of American democracy (as yet) to cross the lines of inequality separating races, nations, genders, and (we may now add) generations as well.[33]

That Du Bois feels powerfully that children need to "see the reasons of this war" is made clear in his letter to his daughter as well as in his 1914 Children's Number contribution on the subject. "As the Crow Flies," despite the other aims of *The Brownies' Book*, is a clear and persistent extension of this project. It is no coincidence that the anti-imperial Crow is conceived for the pages of *The Brownies' Book* at the same time that Du Bois is composing *Darkwater*, viewed by many as Du Bois's Pan-African revision of *Souls*. In fact the presence of the Crow persona may be visible in the voice and structure of *Darkwater*, which Du Bois describes as a compilation on the wing as it were, oscillating between "the sterner flights of logic" and "little alightings of what may be poetry" (ix). The Crow's is likewise a traveling method, one characterized by a "*swing[ing] to and fro*" not just between the lyrical and the cacophonous but between home and abroad. Even by the second issue, the format of "As the Crow Flies" begins to double itself around these international and national foci. By the eighth issue, the same elaborate, italicized font that opens the Crow's journalistic view onto the world now routinely returns, midway through his journey, to introduce a second look at America (Figs. 6.6 and 6.7).

The obvious parallels between these twice-told openings in the Christmas issue serve the larger purpose of highlighting their more distinct polarities. The slippery inversion that opens the issue, leading the reader from the anticipation of a celebration to starvation, is echoed in the second which moves once more from American visions of feasting and fun to a reminder of its global, physical, and emotional counterpart on the other side of the ocean. The subtle differences between the two openings (from "see[ing]" in the first to "hear[ing]" in the second) and

Fig. 6.6 *The Brownies' Book* 1.12 (Dec 1920) 378

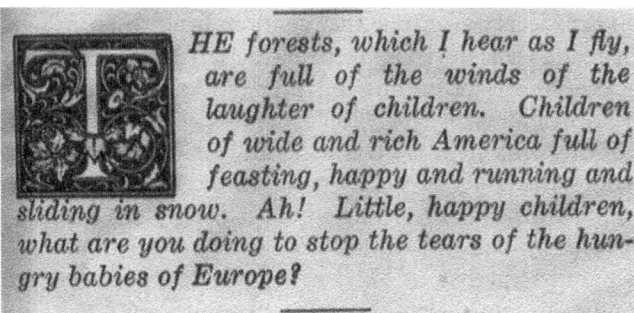

Fig. 6.7 *The Brownies' Book* 1.12 (Dec 1920) 379

between the endings (exclamatory in one "I hear their sobs!" and interrogatory "what are you doing?" in the other) enacts in yet another way the "synaesthesia" of double consciousness, but the direction is less toward enhancing "the cultural interactivity of blacks and whites" than it is now toward encouraging the interactivity of African Americans with subalterns of other nations and circumstance.

Additionally, the Crow swings here not only between extremities of feeling, of rhetoric, and of geography but also between two polarized notions of childhood: between "hungry children" and "happy children," between certain realities and ideations of childhood. In the context of the Crow's international perspective, neither the romanticized child of America nor the impoverished child of Europe appears acceptable or sustainable. In one of the most crucial paradoxes of "As the Crow Flies," happiness may well be its own kind of hunger. From the outset, the Crow has positioned himself as feeding the *Brownies'* readers with these "bits of news." Flying between these polarized experiences of childhood may be one way of remediating the differences between them. One of the truest facts of the Crow, no less than of the conventional child, is that he is always "*happy*," always "*free*." But, of course, the other truest fact about him, one not typically extended to ideas of childhood, is that he is also always devotedly attendant to turmoil and sorrow. He flies above but never out of sight of human suffering. He sees the worst that human beings can do to one another, but he never succumbs to despair. The Crow advises his July 1921 readers that "*Happiness is not something to seek, it is something in us. I am happy, yet as I fly and fly, I cannot find happiness*" (206) and conversely that "*Sorrow is not in us, but about us. I find sorrow everywhere, but there lies no sorrow in my light and flying heart*" (207). In this important instance, the Crow succeeds in presenting a simultaneous consciousness of happiness and sorrow and yet the doubleness of this awareness is far from debilitating. Maintaining the doubleness of double consciousness without falling into despair is among the signature concerns of *Souls*. Though Du Bois has succeeded personally in negotiating this tightrope, he nonetheless repeatedly expresses the feeling that his life cannot be held out as a model for other "black folk."

The addition of these American introductions also makes clear the Crow's interest in folding the child reader into the process of its dualistic method and concerns. These second introductions become spaces to directly address this readership, but the contrary styles and subjects of the two-toned "As the Crow Flies" have indirectly invited child readers to mimic the oscillations of the Crow all along. From one perspective, the shifts between these flying introductions and the more weighty factual catalogs that follow encourage an oscillation back and forth between different kinds of reading practices, between the familiar and unknown, and between the pleasing and the difficult. From another, the shifts invite child readers to see themselves through a different set of eyes, not the eyes of the condescending white world—as was the problem in *Souls*—but through the eyes of the transnational Crow. The Crow's subjectivity signifies chiefly the rejection of so many extant role models for the black child. He refuses romanticized models of childhood for his "children of the sun" and rejects, perhaps more surprisingly, most all adult models as well. In the June 1920 issue, the Crow interrupts the onslaught of news to observe that *"Humans the world over are much worse than Crows and, goodness me! But Crows are no angels—specially in summer times when planted seeds are sweet"* (184). And in a manner most akin to signifying, the Crow asks (Fig. 6.8):

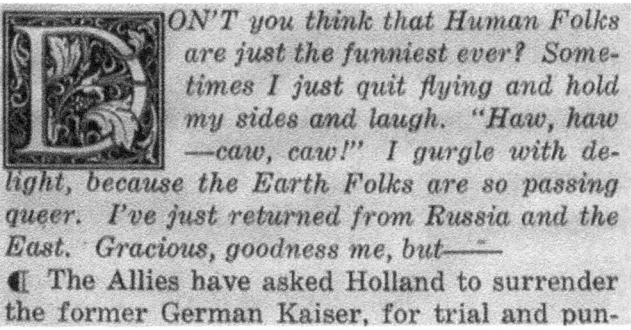

Fig. 6.8 *The Brownies' Book* 1.3 (March 1920) 76

It goes without saying that the aftermath of World War I is far from the stuff of entertainment. The transitioning of the Crow's human-sounding laugh, "*Haw, haw,*" to his own cacophonous cry, "*caw, caw,*" underscores his sarcasm and implies that the celebrations, following on the heels of the war, are not only vastly premature but several notes off-key. The twice-appearing and very versatile long dash invites the child audience to mentally fill the gaps that the dashes so conveniently provide—first between the uneven tones of human and crow and then between the Crow's own pendulous perception.

Most importantly this passage and the Crow's earlier "human" chastisements suggest a realignment of the parent-child relationship, with the Crow making a case not only for black children as the new adults but also for himself as their new parent. There is in "As the Crow Flies" a note of fantasy and of science fiction. Through the Crow's eyes, black children become crowlets, and adults become by turns members of an alien species of "Earth Folks" or they become children. Just as Du Bois reverses the presumed roles of child and adult in *Darkwater* when he describes imperialist Europe as a "precocious, self-centered, forward-striving child" (97), the Crow offers a widespread critique of adults in the terms of childishness: "*O the naughty men and women who will not learn of Little Children and behave! Wherever the Crow flies he brings the glad message of little children—caw, caw, caw!*" (November 1920, 333). The Crow's reprimand in this case serves to diminish the stature of the adult. Meanwhile, the subjectivity of the child becomes nearly indistinguishable from that of the Crow. This is not only because the child's "glad message" is unconventionally, even ironically disciplinary (the Crow translates it as a lesson to "behave!") but also because the child's "glad message" elides with and may even literally be the "caw, caw, caw!" of the Crow.

Given national contrast, the child of divided consciousness in *Souls* feels inferior in relation to a more privileged white America. But given international contrast, the Crow suggests that there is enormous responsibility in being a black child in America. In "As the Crow Flies" there is ample evidence for Amy Kaplan's thesis that Du Bois effectively "turns the white man's burden into the black man's burden" by elevating the

African-American's American status (177–178). But rather than emphasize the metaphors of exceptionalism inflected in the idea of American imperialism, Du Bois's ideology of the black man's burden emphasizes the weight of a double burden. The emblematic black man shoulders the burden of race oppression because he is imagined to be so burdened. The quality of this difference is magnified as it is funneled through Du Bois's sometimes lyrical, often cacophonous works for children. Elsewhere, most notably in Du Bois's international romance, *Dark Princess*, the figure of the child has been read as an "exceptional heir" who "signifies the heroic synthesis of double consciousness among African Americans and the liberation of all peoples of color" (Tate xxi). But Du Bois's works for children posit the child not as exceptional but, perhaps more radically, as equal. Beyond the white or black man's burden, the Crow conveys not only that black childhood comes with its own burdens but that black children themselves must be prepared to carry them. To this end, the consciousness of the Du Boisian child is ideally modeled along trans-generic, transatlantic, and trans-generational lines. From the politics and aesthetics of juxtaposition showcased in the epigraphs of *Souls* through the picture/text cross-writing of *The Crisis* Children's Numbers to the double-voiced Crow, Du Bois has moved from a double consciousness that begins in childhood to posit a reimagined model of twoness as a uniquely resilient subjectivity for the black child in America.

While in *Souls*, Du Bois famously proclaimed that "the problem of the twentieth century is the problem of the color line," by the time he writes *Darkwater*, some two decades later, his emphasis has shifted. Now, he writes that "All our problems center in the child" (125). I have, in part, been attempting to trace the evolution of double consciousness from *Souls* to its new seat in Du Bois's works for and about children, but the more focused attention to the problems of black childhood, in the place of or in addition to those of race, brings important differences, particularly between "As the Crow Flies" and *Souls*, into view as well. There is, in comparison to *Souls* and even in comparison to *The Crisis* Children's Numbers, an important geographical and social widening in "As the Crow Flies" that is consistent with Du Bois's emerging transnational democratic philosophy[34]; but there is also—in the formulaic patterns and heavily articulated twoness of Du Bois's *Brownies' Book* contribution—a tapering off of the heterogeneity that many would identify as a hallmark of *Souls* and which I have argued carries over into the multimedia, multi-contributory layout of the Children's Numbers as well.

From a practical point of view, one reason for this latter shift is the, already remarked, divergence in aims of *The Brownies' Book*. Though founded in part by Du Bois, *The Brownies' Book* represents in practice a compromise to the position Du Bois had long held on black childhood as importantly in need of dialogic exchange with "Age" and concomitantly as necessarily and principally distinct from the conventions governing childhood for white, mainstream America. Without the cross-written features so evident and ironic in the Children's Numbers, *The Brownies' Book*, wonder that it was, treats its child audience to a far more consistent and far more conventional reading experience, one which enacts the principle that childhood and adulthood are distinct, separate entities, who should read distinct, separate texts. Where Du Bois had created contrast, as the editor of the Children's Numbers, out of various different media and too out of the stylistically and substantively divergent submissions he received, as an independent contributor to *The Brownies' Book*, it was for him and him alone to create the double-method and model he sought. While other contributors to *The Brownies' Book* who had also contributed to the Children's Numbers dramatically changed their approach to align it with more conventional children's fare, Du Bois's own work is consistently inconsistent, which is to say that it remains attuned in either context to the complexities of contrast and to the dual awareness that Du Bois felt necessary in times of struggle and, indeed, of violence.

The other, and to my mind more significant, reason for the formulaic shift in "As the Crow Flies," for the de-muddying of the literary and interpretive waters so beloved in *Souls*, arises from the distance between the elder text's attempt "in vague and uncertain outline" to represent a complex people and the newer venture's efforts to create out of that representation a specific type of person, to take the polarities of the historically divided consciousness and craft a revisionary and resilient double awareness out of their simultaneous suspension. The cross-written Children's Numbers were to a large extent both a polemic for this revised subjectivity, implicitly directed at a more conventionally-minded adult body, and an attempt to systematize that subjectivity through the replication and repetition of the periodical format. "As the Crow Flies" signals in one sense a heightening of this agenda, for it follows a vastly more explicit double course and appears and reappears in that form much more frequently than had been theretofore possible, but in another sense it abandons the other aspect of that agenda, over-writing the biological providers of the Brownies to bring them directly, as it were, a new, figurative, and actual kind of food. In crafting the Crow as parent, Du Bois creatively bypasses a group for whom he has had much criticism and takes his case for a revised, de-Romanticized childhood directly to the child reader. In contrast to "cooped up" Human Folk the world over, and as the new bird parent of the Brownie, the Crow's subjectivity emblematizes theirs as a two-toned, resilient, and sustainable alternative to the segmented divisions of race, of nation, and of age.

Notes

1. The term "intersectionality" was coined by Kimberlé Crenshaw to highlight the ways that racism and sexism converge in the experiences of discrimination faced by black women, but the term gestures more broadly toward the limits of identity politics to account for the ways that race, gender, and class intersect in the experiences of many who live at the crossroads of multiple identity categories.
2. Alys Eve Weinbaum argues that the form of the interracial romance, of which *Dark Princess* is the strongest model, is a crucial internationalist and anti-imperialist expression of "the politics of juxtaposition" made famous in *Souls*. Lawrie Balfour makes a case for Du Bois's essays, *Black Reconstruction* (1935) and *Dusk of Dawn* (1940), as extensions of the "trial and revision" paradigm so successful in *Souls* (18). And Eric Sundquist and Amy Kaplan both argue that Du Bois's vision of a global color line, subtle in *Souls*, reaches "full flower" (Sundquist's phrase) in the period after the First World War when Du Bois wrote *Darkwater*.
3. Sundquist, 551. Du Bois himself aids in this reassessment. Even before *Souls*, Du Bois had already begun to imagine the color-line in a global light. He titled an essay "The Color Line Belts the World" in 1906 but used that expression as early as 1898 (Kaplan 176–178).
4. Rudine Sims Bishop asserts that African-American children's literature "begins to bloom" with Du Bois's publication of *The Brownies' Book*, and she likewise provides a thorough account of the circumstances, including the "dearth of suitable materials connected to the lives of Black children," that drove Du Bois's intervention into the field (24).
5. The caption "Souls made of fire, and children of the sun, with whom revenge is a virtue" appears beneath a set of child photographs in the 1916 Children's Number (285). The quote is from the eighteenth-century English tragedy, *Revenge* by Edward Young, about a slave who seeks revenge

against his Spanish master. And in 1919, when Du Bois announces *The Brownies' Book* in that year's Children's Number, he dedicates it to "all children, but especially for *ours*, 'the Children of Sun'" (286).

6. Elinor Sinnette's 1965 study of *The Brownies' Book* focuses on the magazine's efforts to counter racial stereotypes and provide black child readers with emulative images and stories of black history and life that could not be found in popular American children's literature. Violet J. Harris agrees with Sinnette that replacing stereotypes with "authentic representations of African American life" is a central goal of *The Brownies' Book* as part of its editors' "explicit appeals for racial solidarity, pride, and uplift" (547). Dianne Johnson-Feelings likewise describes the creation of *The Brownies' Book* as "in essence, an experiment in pedagogy and propaganda aimed at African-American youth" (336).

7. The color line is a living line whose meaning Du Bois persists in re-evaluating long after the publication of *Souls*. After the First World War, Du Bois increasingly reflects on that proclamation made "once upon a time in my younger years" to ask "how far was it prophecy and how far speculation?" ("Worlds of Color" 423). In addition to extending the global reach of the color line, in *Darkwater* Du Bois also expands its meaning by placing the problem of women's uplift "next to" the color line as "our greatest cause" (105).

8. "Cross-writing" is a crucial concept in childhood studies. It was first theorized by U.C. Knoepflmacher and Mitzi Myers as "any text that activates a traffic between phases of life we persist in regarding as opposites" (viii). Often, cross-written texts address a dual audience of adults and children, but more important than the double audience is the implicit double-voice of the cross-written text, which contains "a dialogic mix of older and younger voices" (vii).

9. In *The Autobiography of W.E.B. Du Bois: A Soliloquy on Viewing My Life from the Last Decade of Its First Century* this passage is interrupted by a description of the town and with a more historical account of the year of Du Bois's birth, but the wording is the same (61).

10. This description appears both in Du Bois's *Autobiography*, 93 and in Du Bois's 1938 speech (later published as a pamphlet) "A Pageant in Seven Decades: 1878–1938," in *W.E.B. Du Bois Speaks: Speeches and Addresses, 1890–1919*, 22.

11. In "A Pageant of Seven Decades," Du Bois describes the sheltered "provincialism" of life in Great Barrington and writes of the various historical happenings of racial import, such as the passing of the Fifteenth Amendment, the death of Charles Sumner, and the closing of the Freedmen's Bank, that "of these things my little village said nothing" (23).

12. Given this, it is not surprising that Du Bois would direct a substantial part of his revisionist efforts toward black children. Dianne Johnson-Feelings,

Elinor Sinnette, and Fern Kory have all described *The Brownies' Book* as a consciously-constructed alternative, for example, to *St. Nicholas Magazine*, the most popular American children's periodical of the era. For Kory, *The Brownies' Book* can be read as "self-consciously 'signifying'" on *St. Nicholas*'s patron figure with its tribute to the trickster Brownie as well as on an entire "unself-conscious" Eurocentric fairy tale tradition (92–93).

13. W.E.B. Du Bois, "Opinion of W.E.B. Du Bois: Childhood," *The Crisis* 24.6 (October 1922) 250. Though Du Bois's conception of the child as "little man" is, as his own assessment attests, unconventional, it is hardly new. Over two centuries prior, John Locke's *Some Thoughts Concerning Education* (1693) sought to make a similar case. It was Locke's argument that the qualities so cherished in the modern man, namely reason and liberty, were likewise to be valued in childhood, for "children," Locke argued, "have as much a mind to show that they are free, that their own good actions come from themselves, that they are absolute and independent, as any of the proudest of you grown men, think of them as you please" (51).

14. Du Bois writes in "Our Baby Pictures" that "At first we tried to make our selections with some system and according to certain rules of human interest, beauty and physical type. All this, however, was quickly given up and we frankly confess that there is no reason in the world why most of the pictures which we have not used should not have been printed instead of these" (298).

15. David Levering Lewis (30–33) and Shawn Michelle Smith (100) each read Du Bois's exhibit in these terms.

16. In what is an important turn from the method of *Souls*, Du Bois does not leave the interpretative variety of the Children's Numbers unremarked. In October 1914, he writes, "The pictures which we have published may be considered from many points of view." And he proceeds with his own explication of some of these. For the students "of a great social problem," he writes that they will first be seen "as physical types" (298). By another "prejudiced jury," they will, "notwithstanding" all of their many attributes, be "looked upon as 'problems'" (299). And last, but certainly not least, Du Bois describes the child images as "argument[s] against war" and "against the greatest modern cause of war,—race prejudice" (300).

17. Denise E. Agosto refers to the traditional picture book in the terms of the "twice-told tale" and distinguishes from this form of "parallel storytelling" the more modern "interdependent tale," where the images bear much more of a burden in the meaning-making process (267).

18. Maurice Sendak's 1963 *Where the Wild Things Are* is often cited as a highly influential forerunner to this new trend in modern American picture books. On the mid-century shift to the "internal child" see Barbara Bader's "American Picture Books: From Max's Metaphorical Monsters to Lilly's

Purple Plastic Purse," 142, and for the shift in value to the figurative and intangible see William Moebius's "Introduction to Picturebook Codes," 137.
19. Nina Du Bois, letter to W.E.B. Du Bois, 8–15 August 1914, General Correspondence Part 1, Reel 4:680, Special Collections and University Archives, W.E.B. Du Bois Library, University of Massachusetts Amherst.
20. Ibid., 31 October–15 November 1914.
21. W.E.B. Du Bois, letter to Yolande Du Bois, 10 November 1914, General Correspondence Part 1, Reel 4:681, Special Collections and University Archives, W.E.B. Du Bois Library, University of Massachusetts Amherst.
22. Deborah McDowell describes these dual disadvantages during Fauset's publishing career, from white and black communities alike, in her introduction to Fauset's novel, *Plum Bun*.
23. W.E.B. Du Bois, "As the Crow Flies," *The Crisis* 36.6 (June 1929) 187. While it is significant that Du Bois continues for adults what began as a children's editorial series, it is worth noting that the later adult versions of "As the Crow Flies" lack the dualistic qualities of the earlier *Brownies' Book* numbers, exhibiting to a far greater extent the Crow's as not only a truthful but a peculiarly sardonic voice.
24. These excerpts from Georgia Douglas Johnson's poems, "Motherhood" and "Brown Eyes," are used here with the permission of the Moorland-Spingarn Research Center.
25. W.E.B. Du Bois, "The True Brownies," 285. For a more thorough explication both of the history of the Brownie figure in children's literature and of how that figure is revised in *The Brownies' Book* see Fern Kory's "Once upon a Time in Aframerica: The 'Peculiar' Significance of Fairies in the *Brownies' Book*."
26. According to Johnson-Feelings, it was "the estimation of W.E.B. Du Bois" that "young black readers needed information that was interpreted and reported from a radically different perspective than that offered in *St. Nicholas*," which was not immune from the "preponderance of negative black images in the American mass media" (336). And Elinor Desverney Sinnette argues that *St. Nicholas* was, by turns, guilty of presenting child readers with gross caricatures of the black race or (as was more often the case) altogether remise in the representation of black childhood. And too Sinnette argues that *The Brownies' Book*'s manner of presenting the news (a clear reference to "As the Crow Flies") was "more mature" than was *St. Nicholas*'s journalistic counterpart, "The WatchTower" (134–135).
27. Yolande Du Bois, letters to W.E.B. Du Bois, 12 January 1916 and February 1916, W.E.B. Du Bois Papers, University of Massachusetts Amherst Libraries.

28. Suzanne Rahn writes that Dodge's "non-human editorial persona" is, as far as she knows, "the first of his kind" (110).
29. Mary Mapes Dodge, "Jack-in-the-Pulpit," 46.
30. W.E.B. Du Bois, "As the Crow Flies," *The Brownies' Book* 1.1 (January 1920) 23.
31. The perception of Du Bois as a modern Victorian is common. Vanessa D. Dickerson may take this argument the furthest in her thesis that Du Bois affirms the benefits of a "Victorian soul" throughout his career, even into his late Pan-African politics.
32. See Robert L. Vann's January 21, 1936 letter to Du Bois (in Aptheker 124).
33. I draw here from Du Bois's 1915 essay, "The African Roots of War," which traces the First World War to the battle for profits that white cultures have waged along the color line. Yet Du Bois remains hopeful that "our democratic ideals" may yet be "extended" to "yellow, brown, and black peoples" (712).
34. I would agree with Vilashini Cooppan that the philosophy of double consciousness in *Souls* is consistent with and foundational to Du Bois's nationally and globally dialectical politics of later years, but this latter investment, while nascent in *Souls*, seems to me far more of a foreground issue in later works such as, in this case, "As the Crow Flies."

CHAPTER 7

Drowning in Childhood: Gertrude Stein's Late Modernism

Like W.E.B. Du Bois and Djuna Barnes, Gertrude Stein becomes progressively concerned with the hypocrisies of narratives that invest children with a utopian mindset despite the violently prejudicial and oppressive realities that the majority of American adults (women, African Americans, the poor, and the queer) habitually endure. Gertrude Stein's war-time literature also clearly shares in the larger modernist project forwarded by American writers like James, Barnes, Du Bois, and Hughes of introducing a critical consciousness into the stream of children's narratives, notions of childhood, and child life. Still, Stein's literature of the 1930s and 1940s is at the farthest and most radical end of this spectrum for a number of reasons. For one, there is a destructive violence in Stein's late modernist treatment of childhood that is antithetical to Du Bois's interests in imparting a sustainable and upwardly mobile psychology to African-American children through a literature written chiefly for an African-American audience. And too, Stein pursues the problem of America's youth-centered culture in ways that are not only attentively repetitious but relentlessly so.

After the long-awaited popular success of Stein's 1933 *The Autobiography of Alice B. Toklas*, Stein entered an unprecedented (for her) period of writer's block that she personally linked to a profound identity crisis. When she resurfaced in 1934, her writing was noticeably altered by a new investment in children's narratives. In addition to her works "for children": *The World is Round* (1939), *To Do: A Book of Alphabets and Birthdays* (1940), and *The Gertrude Stein First Reader* (1941), nearly every work from 1934 through the end of her career in 1946 incorporates children's narratives in one form or other. But overwhelmingly this is a parodic turn. It is the preoccupation of a skeptic. Often, children's narratives are the objects for Stein of a Socratic-style inquest into the role these narratives, like the shadows in Plato's cave, play in identity formation. In some the target is Mother Goose where Stein questions the validity of identity by recognition—the validity as she puts it in Mother Goose terms of "I am I because my little dog knows me." In others, it is a question about personal evolution. Stein often asks, "what is the use of being a little boy if you are growing up to be a man." In others still, Stein uses that quintessential scientific discovery of childhood education—"the world was all round and you could go on it around and around"—to explore the conflicts between identity and sociopolitical organization.[1]

Children die or nearly die in Stein's children's narratives in numbers and in ways that are as disturbing as they are familiar. In *The World is Round*, Stein's two protagonists Rose and her cousin, Willie, nearly drown on multiple occasions. In *The Gertrude Stein First Reader* the make-believe drama of "Three Sisters Who Were Not Sisters" is comprised entirely by a series of exercises in children killing children. In *To Do: A Book of Alphabets and Birthdays*, five children die by drowning, two are eaten, and one is starved. Children who are drowned (or nearly drowned) or who are eaten (or nearly eaten) are favored subjects of much children's literature. Stories of babes lost in the wood, like "Hansel and Gretel" and "Little Red Riding Hood," caution readers that predators—from witches to wolves—are ubiquitously, so it seems, on the prowl for the unchaperoned (abandoned, lost, or pseudo-autonomous) child.[2] Like the child-dinner, the child-drowned trope also serves to reinforce as vital the relationship between children and their adult protectors. Stein herself recalls reading Mary Mapes Dodge's story of "Donald and Dorothy," twins rescued at sea by the heroic actions of such caretakers. Donald and Dorothy do not drown but their parents do, exemplifying to the extreme the counterbalance between child survival and adult sacrifice.

U.C. Knoepflmacher describes the phenomenon of the child nearly-drowned as a literary device that locks children into roles of vulnerability while also demanding that adults play their parts as the responsible saviors thereof. All told, Knoepflmacher assesses the death-by-drowning trope as a powerful nineteenth-century device for compartmentalizing and preserving childhood as a world apart from the demands and disappointments of adult reality. Even if worldly rescue fails in this literature—death by drowning could still mean the spiritual salvation of children for childhood. The hero of Kingsley's *Water Babies* (1863) is rescued and restored to childhood in precisely this way. Here a poor, young chimney sweep receives a moral education and finds redemption in the alternate, fairy tale reality under water. Knoepflmacher concludes that "the nineteenth-century imagination frequently associated childhood spaces with the oblivion of a death-by-drowning" ("Spaces Within" 299). This particular kind of oblivion underscores the already strong connection between post-Romantic notions of childhood and other-worldly spaces. Drowning can mean a kind of worldly escape. Near-drowning can sound an alarm, ringing in the rescue and refortification of the child. The drowning trope in nineteenth-century fiction can thus be a vehicle for keeping children in their idyllic separate sphere or of returning them to it.

Stein's deployment of these common childhood death tropes calls upon this history while challenging its symbolic end-game. One of Stein's signature epiphanies in *Wars I Have Seen* (1945) is that "there is a mingling" of "children's lives and grown up lives" in times of war (7). Stein's children's narratives are wartime narratives not just in their timing but in their manifestation of this principle of mingling. The violence in these narratives is both cloaked and heightened by an ordinary everydayness that collapses the separate spheres of child and adult representation.[3] They offer no after-the-violence narrative catharsis, no parental rescue, sometimes no rescue at all, and no afterlife. Clearly, these are texts which also pay little heed to the bulwarks separating children's literature from its elder relative. Few could envision the works that Stein designated for children—*The World is Round, To Do: A Book of Alphabets and Birthdays*, and *The Gertrude Stein First Reader*—as children's literature. But few could envision them as modernist either. Tyrus Miller, in theorizing late modernism, has emphasized the literary violence that imbues the work of this period. It is a violence which is not just thematic—though it is that—but which is also structural. "[L]ate modernist works," he writes, "dramatized the comic fragility of modernist attempts to contain contingency and violence aesthetically, through literary form." "Within the late modernist novel," he continues, "the formal 'lapses' bound to laughter allowed expression of those negative forces of the age that could not be coaxed into any admirable design of words: its violence, madness, absurd contingencies, and sudden deaths" (20). Though Miller does not treat Stein's work directly, this description clearly brings her wartime writing into the field of late modernism. In fact, in addition to her plays, this description suits her children's literature best of all, where violence and absurd contingencies and sudden deaths prosper with the abundance of the everyday. Stein doesn't just venture into children's literature, she invades it, producing deconstructed, sardonic versions of the alphabet book, the first reader, the nursery rhyme, and the fairy tale forms. At the same time, she explodes the formal, innovative reifications of much of "high modernism" by embracing popular forms and even more importantly by challenging, like Barnes before her, the youth-centered spirit of newness at modernism's innovative core. In other words, Stein's late modernism is arguably centered around her experiments in children's narrative.

Stein hypothesizes a new "mingled" subject for wartime, and she produces a new genre of mingled children's and modernist narrative. Her use of the child-drowning trope clearly derives from children's literature, but the terms in which she challenges that trope also come from modernism. Marianne DeKoven has usefully offered the metaphor of "sea-change" to describe modernism's attraction to water imagery and also to describe its particular, ambivalent relationship to that imagery's symbolic and pre-symbolic significations. Drowning in modernism signifies "death," "suffering," and "horror" as well as "redemptive transformation," "resurrection," and "rebirth" (3). In Kate Chopin's *The Awakening*, Edna Pontellier's drowning is at once a suicide and a feminist rebellion against the strictures of "True Womanhood." In T.S. Eliot's *The Waste Land*, "Fear death by water" is a terrifying but also captivating prophesy. The image of the drowned Phoenician Sailor captures the threat of a death-by-drowning but also suggests the potential for a "positive sea-change, 'those are pearls that were his eyes'" (DeKoven 192). For DeKoven the ambivalence of these images symbolizes modernism's intensely conflicted relationship to the feminine, to the womb of the mother that suffocates and entraps, on the one hand, and produces pearls and rebirth, on the other. But in addition to wrangling with the birth-mother, these images also evoke a tandem ambivalence to childhood. When Edna swims irretrievably out into the ocean, she feels "new-born," like a "little child," but she abandons her own children in order to effect this return to childhood (Chopin 152).

The turn from child forms to children's narratives marks a subtle shift from the aesthetic to the political, from representing the child subject to engaging that subject. And in Stein's case the terms of this engagement are distinctly modernist: deconstructive, ambivalent, ironic, and violent. And yet the turn to the new genre and new audience represented by children's literature—a turn in which Stein was joined by Langston Hughes, T.S. Eliot, Djuna Barnes, and W.E.B. Du Bois among others—must be acknowledged as part of a late modernist push against and away from the formal and cultural structures of high modernist innovation. Edna Pontellier affirms, like so many emergent and canonical modernist protagonists, the youth discourse at the heart of modernism's "make it new" mantra. But Stein's children's narratives of this era are preoccupied with representing and with killing children, with writing and with destroying children's narratives, and with engaging child (and adult) readers and attacking childhood. Together, these paradoxical aims suggest that Stein's real target is not just the image of childhood but is the living, breathing mentality of that image. Stein's late modernism targets the child within so many concentric circles of the self, American culture, and modernism. She takes aim at precisely what Virginia Woolf contemporaneously identifies as the "impediment in the centre of…being," but by structuring this project across the genres of modernism and children's literature, it must be said that Stein raises the aesthetic, political, and cultural stakes in ways that few others did and perhaps dared to do ("Lewis Carroll" 82).

Death-by-Disappearance in *To Do*

In "The Winner Loses, A Picture of Occupied France" (1940), Stein reflects on her efforts to assuage the anxiety she felt at the onset of World War II, an anxiety inflicted most sharply by the urgings of friends that she leave what was in many ways her dream home in Bilgnin in her chosen nation of France. In the interim, between these urgings and her ultimate decision to stay among friends rather than to "'risk'" herself elsewhere "'among strangers'" (121), Stein writes *To Do: A Book of Alphabets and Birthdays.* In her words:

> I had begun the beginning of May [1940] to write a book for children, a book of alphabets with stories for each letter, and a book of birthdays,— each story had to have a birthday in it,—and I did get so that I could not think about the war but just about the stories I was making up for this book. I would walk in the daytime and make up stories, and I walked up and down on the terrace in the evening and made up stories, and I went to sleep making up stories, and I pretty well did succeed in keeping my mind off the war except for the three times a day when there was the French communiqué, and that always gave me a sinking feeling in my stomach. (117)

As Stein relates it, *To Do* represents an absorbing and remarkably successful distraction from the anxieties of wartime.[4] Yet, Stein's description of *To*

Do in this instance is largely misleading. The language of evasion does not apply thematically to *To Do*, which substantially represents the emotional and physical violences of wartime. Likewise, the language of absorption and distraction understates the esteemed position that *To Do* held for Stein among her own works. While *To Do* clearly served a pragmatic purpose for its author, Stein's correspondence testifies to the value that she came to place on this particular children's narrative. Almost every letter from 1940 through 1941 that Stein writes to longtime friend and professional liaison Carl Van Vechten, or "Papa Woojums" as she likes to call him, seeks to advance the publication of *To Do*. At times Stein nearly pleads with Van Vechten that he like the book as much as she does. In August of 1940, she writes, "most and foremost I want to know how you feel about it, send me by cable or air-mail, a word, we are suffering for a word from you, and tell me if you like it, I myself am attached to it" (678). Stein apparently failed to receive Van Vechten's responses, for she writes again in October to "Papa Woojums" from "Baby Woojums": "You do like the book don't you because if you didn't I would know it was no good but you do, and I can't help being sure that the stories are very Frank Stocktonish, and that you know I think awfully high praise to Baby Woojums, please like the book..." (685).[5] Frank Stockton was a wildly successful writer of modern fairy tales for children in the late nineteenth century whose work went on to be reprinted and illustrated by the likes of Maurice Sendak (of *Where the Wild Things Are* fame) and whose "The Lady, or the Tiger?" has become a school-anthology mainstay. Stein would have likely become familiar with Stockton's work as a child reader herself of *St. Nicholas Magazine*, for which Stockton was an assistant editor and longtime contributor. Thus, Stein's comparison of her own work and style to Stockton's speaks not only to her growing personal fondness for *To Do* but also to the high literary-esteem she has come to place upon it.

    Remarkable as it may seem to readers of *To Do* then and still, Stein appears sincere in her belief in this narrative's popular potential. In the same letter where Stein compares herself to Stockton, she relates to Van Vechten the rejection she has received from John McCullough of William R. Scott Publishers, who had just the year prior published Stein's *The World is Round*. Stein's disappointment comes with a healthy dose of sarcasm: "he has not yet tried it on the children and he seems to think that even if the children like it, they would not want to try it" (685). Perhaps most telling, one of Stein's first post-war communications to Van Vechten picks up, nearly four years later, from where these letters leave off: "was

To Do ever done..." (765). It was not done. All along the news of *To Do*'s reception, even as filtered through the doting Van Vechten, had truly provided little basis for Stein's persistent optimism about the work. Everyone, from Scott Publishers to Stein's contracted Random House publisher to Harcourt, had felt that *To Do* was not for children. This was a sentiment that Van Vechten too, in a rare moment of qualified sycophancy, expressed to Stein: "I'm MAD about [*To Do*] but I hardly think it is for les enfants" (679), "especially as you say letters M and N are unlucky and half the children who read it will be named Nathan and Mary" (680). While Van Vechten is turned off by the darkness of *To Do*, others are numbed by the coldness of its prose. Cerf from Random House wrote to Van Vechten that everyone at Random House was "as cold as a slab of alabaster" about the book (697N), suggesting that the reality of the responses to *To Do* may have been much harsher than even Van Vechten, who so often shielded Stein from criticism, let on.

To Do is both cold and dark. Though it may have been conceived as an escape from war, *To Do* holds more fear and violence than it deflects. Throughout its pages children and animals die with deadpan insistence. In this modernist alphabet book, Stein pairs each letter with the names of four children and the stories about their birthdays, but unlike its namesakes, *To Do* is not a narrative of creation. Instead of projecting alphabets and birthdays as building blocks of language and of self, *To Do* places these elements at the center of various narratives of violent disintegration, loss, and death-by-disappearance.

Brave, for B, is the first of many children to drown in *To Do*. The picture Stein paints of Brave has many of the markings of a cautionary tale. Brave lacks humility. He is self-professedly "rich and strong." He is white "with delight." The world is his oyster, or, as Stein puts it, "any day might be his birthday" (15). Brave is also bold. Upon meeting A is for Annie he quickly decides both that she is like honey and that he will give her all of his money, a move that speaks both to his patriarchal privilege and to his impending death. Showing that Brave is not so much courageous as cocksure, Stein hones in on his character's ill-fated habit of fishing at night with a light:

> Brave always fished at night with a light. Nobody should because that dazzles the fish and they cannot see where for the glare so it is not fair. But Brave did he fished at night with a light. And tonight, yes tonight, he was drowned at night, drowned dead at night, and Never Sleeps barked all night

and Was Asleep was asleep and Annie had all his money and she spent it on honey and Brave was never any more white with delight. And the fish could rest every night.

This is what happens when you are not born on your birthday, that is what everybody does say.... (15)

Brave's death appears the net effect of so many causes. The offspring of patriarchal wealth and power, Brave both has too much and risks too much. His patronage of Annie is absolute as is his unconscionable lack of sportsmanship. It would be easy for readers, particularly those familiar with Stein's longstanding critique of patriarchy, to pinpoint Brave's power, his arrogance, his wealth, his bad-faith hunting methods, or his whiteness, each separately or all together, as his fatal flaw. Yet *To Do* undermines each of these more obviously just causes in favor of the most morally and rationally opaque: Brave was not born on his birthday. At one end of the life-spectrum, not being born on your birthday might mean a refusal of origins or, at the other, it could signal a false claim to immortality. It could suggest an inability to recognize one's own human limitations. Or it could indicate an excess of celebratory zeal.

Or it could be nonsense. The text's efforts to pass the expression off as a centuries' old saying seems disingenuous at best and suggests some narrative comedy is underfoot. Though framed as a cautionary tale, Brave's story arouses none of the sentimental pathos that such tales traditionally inspire. Brave dies without ceremony, without agony, pity, or even clear cause. Far from a cautionary tale about the dangers of drowning, this may well be a story about the dangers of such cautionary tales. While the story of Brave seems to insist upon his death as a lesson to readers, at last the text appears to diffuse any possibility for deciphering or perhaps more importantly for caring what that lesson is. The text goes some distance to make Brave and all he may or may not stand for as forgettable as possible. Following his death, Brave's two dogs Never Sleeps and Was Asleep continue their routine: "Never Sleeps barked all night and Was Asleep was asleep." And Annie, who now "had all [Brave's] money...spent it all on honey." Like this sing-song rhyme, the rhythms of life go on without missing a beat. Brave's drowning has produced, it seems, not so much as a ripple on the lives of those who survive him.

Even though it comes so early in the book, Brave's death doesn't seem like much. The narrator, the reader, and the text barely register his loss. As a mock cautionary tale, Brave's is a childhood that is wholly lost. There is no suggestion that it lives on in the sphere of spiritual symbolism, a space haunted by so many of literature's children. Brave disappears in the darkness, and he disappears underwater. And his drowning is an emblem of the kind of child death that permeates *To Do*. Brave's is only the first of many deaths in *To Do*. All of the J's—James, Jonas, Jewel and Jenny die a similar death to his. These siblings lose or damage their birthdays in the process of playing with them or fighting over them. They all, like Brave, drown, and they do so for far less cause and without much narrative *to-do*. These child characters disappear not just from view, from life, and from memory, they also disappear quite unceremoniously from the text. In these moments, *To Do* is not just a story about how children drown; it is a story that participates in their submergence.

Easily the saddest story in *To Do* is the story of George. George technically has a birthday—it's April Fools' Day—but this timing is so unfortunate that it represents more of a false start to life than the sure footing of a true birthday. Like his birthday, George lacks substance. Literally. He is "so thin," Stein writes, that he is "next to nothing." On the verge of invisibility—or death, George goes away, taking nothing but "five rich American cookies" and a camera (30). Stein writes:

> ...he could take one photograph a day but that was not enough to pay his way, he had no way to pay, poor George poor dear thin George poor dear thin grey-haired George poor George he was away there is nothing more to say poor dear thin grey-haired George he was a thin grey-haired boy and he had no toy and he had no joy and the lightning and thunder were brighter and louder and the big tree was bigger and he was thinner... and pretty soon and in every way George dear George began to fade away, fade fade away.... (30)

There are strong parallels between George's story and the story of youth that Stein tells elsewhere in her wartime writing. In *Paris France*, what epitomizes the wartime experience of the child, Helen Button, is the loss of her best friend Emil and his dog, both of whom vanish suddenly and without explanation. Whether they went away "to the war or not Helen never knew" (92). Stein captures the feeling of impermanence: "There are so many people who go away in wartime and there are always so many everywhere in war-time here there and everywhere" (92). Estranged from so many familiars and surrounded by so many strangers, modern communities and homes that have for so long organized themselves around the children in their midst find themselves in wartime facing an empty center. In *Wars I Have Seen* Stein analogizes the communal anxiety that young men will suddenly be "carried off from them in their midst" to a kind of cultural kidnapping which she likens to a return to "the middle ages" (86). What Helen Button perceives and what Stein then turns into an emblematic realization is that there can be neither any protection for the children and youth of war nor any adult identification with the role of being their protectors. Both are vulnerable. It is easy, she writes elsewhere in *Wars I Have Seen,* in times of war "to know more about what children feel"—not just to "remember about [the] feeling" of childhood but to "just feel the feeling" (7).

For there to be a "mingling" of "children's lives and grown up lives" means that the opposing walls of this social structure have failed, collapsing inward upon one another (*Wars* 7). The mingling is in the rubble. Stein paints this mingling into George who with his rich American cookies and his gray hair makes for a strange mosaic. Stein's multiple depictions of the child in wartime converge most in her insistence that George "fade[s] away" "in every way." George goes away, inexplicably and unprepared, like so many of the young men during war time. But the fading of George is much more graphically a wartime image that points from so many angles to the problem of hunger. Fading in George's case is a lot like starving. And, it must be said, it is also much like being consumed. The strength of the storm grows and the big tree gets bigger while George gets progressively thinner. Stein's way of accumulating descriptors to and around George—"poor dear thin grey-haired George"—helps to suggest the weight of the circumstances that finally engulf him.

But George does not simply fade in body, he also fades away as an image. With his camera in tow, George's vocation is both to convert experience into image and to preserve it as such. Reduced to black and white, to stillness, and to two-dimensional form, the photograph is an externalized analog of the mind, seeking to capture and preserve the past, however selectively, however unreliably. Frozen beneath the tall tree (and George is literally freezing from the cold), with his graying hair and his increasingly frail physique, George seems like an old photograph—being drained of color and motion, as of life. Like his vocation which cannot sustain his life, this image of George fails to do what most images are designed to do: preserve the subject. As a subject George is under erasure. Stein's insistence that George fades away "in every way" points at last to the final stage of his disappearance. As with Brave, this happens at the level of the narrative. It would seem no coincidence that the words "faded away" serve also as the final terms of Stein's narrative about George (31). After that, George is again reduced (or erased) back to "G" only. "After G is H for Henry" captures the strange alphabetical momentum of *To Do*. Rather than moving through object lessons of the "A is for apple" variety, *To Do*'s alphabet moves through children's lives. The signifier alone is the engine that drives the traditional alphabet forward—from A to Z. Stein's alphabet book insists on the inseparability of signifiers and what they signify—the end of G it would seem also means the end of George.

The sense of *To Do* as a distinctly wartime alphabet book intensifies as the narrative approaches Z. Like the many child disappearances in *To Do*, Xantippe and Xenophon also appear in the roll-call of *To Do* only to vanish pages later. They are swallowed whole. Xantippe and Xenophon spend their narrative trying to outmaneuver the five men and ten women who are following them. They try exchanging the X's that begin their names and they try exchanging birthdays, but they cannot shake their pursuers.

> All of a sudden, the five men and ten women they walked so quickly they walked right into Xenophon and Xantippe and as they walked into them all five of them the men and all ten of them the women opened their mouths as if they were yawning and just then Xenophon and Xantippe disappeared down the mouths of them and no one ever saw Xantippe and Xenophon again and the ten women and five men went away.
>
> And now we have Xylophone and Xmas. (111)

As with the story of George, the story of Xantippe and Xenophon seems a thinly veiled wartime narrative. These are the relatives-in-kind of the children suddenly "carried off from them in their midst" that Stein describes years later in *Wars I Have Seen* (86). Xantippe and Xenophon are marked by the X's that begin their names. The "X" is, of course, a notorious symbol of death, but it may also gesture toward the Star of David that was used to identify and to mark so many Jews during World War II. And though the ten women and the five men bear a remarkable Gestapo-likeness, they are in some ways more ominous because they seem more ordinary, everyday—an affect largely achieved by having women outnumber men two to one.

Stein's use of these well-worn childhood-death tropes is radical because it does nothing to save children for childhood. Everything about these scenes of child death and disappearance suggests how commonplace these occurrences are—at least in the world of Stein's narrative which it seems more and more likely is also the world of World War II. Xantippe and

Xenophon are marked by the X's that begin their names, and they are swallowed without ceremony. Brave doesn't just drown. He "drowns dead" (15). The adverb seems unnecessarily gratuitous, like an extra nail in the coffin for good measure. George's death is the most alive on the page but is also absolute. Stein's insistence that he faded away in "every way" leaves nothing of George to be saved.

And Stein's choice of the alphabet book genre is equally striking and ironic. In what Patricia Crain has described as the "Alphabetization of America," the alphabet—as the cornerstone of literacy—had become by the nineteenth century the cornerstone as well of a standardized, progressive subjectivity. "[A]lphabetization," Crain writes, "becomes more than a rite of initiation. It is now the primary means of socialization, the lack of which renders one not just déclassé...but subhuman" (103). *To Do* clearly projects the alphabet book in this vein: as a genre of identity. Stein recognizes the formative power of the genre by the way she associates each letter in her text, not with an object, animal, or action, but with a set of names. But in her hands, the alphabet book becomes a Trojan Horse.[6] With it, she takes a trusted form of children's narrative and uses it to target notions of childhood explicitly for a child audience. As with the death-by-drowning trope, Stein breaks with the customs of birthdays and alphabets, depicting them as traditions with artificial value. By emphasizing how Xantippe and Xenophon are marked for annihilation just because their names begin with an unpopular first letter, by emphasizing how not having the right birthday can lead to certain death, Stein suggests that there is something truly ridiculous about these structures of identity formation. And she also suggests that there is something inherently destructive in them as well. What Crain refers to as initiation and socialization, Stein might well call dying.

Despite the problems with *To Do*, John McCullough of Scott Publishers suggested yet another child-project to Stein: a first reader, a request that highlights an imbedded assumption about Stein's work as inherently childlike and which also grossly misunderstands her late sardonic style. Unsurprisingly, the first reader that Stein produced was not the first reader that McCullough had in mind. "Lesson Number One" begins:

> A dog said that he was going to learn to read. The other dogs said he could learn to bark but he could not learn to read. They did not know that dog, if he said he was going to learn to read, he would learn to read. He might be drowned dead in water but if he said that he was going to learn to read he was going to learn to read.

He never was drowned in water not dead drowned and he never did learn to read. Are there any children like that. One two three. Are there any children like that. Four five six. Are there any children like that. Seven eight nine are there any children like that. Ten. Yes there are ten children like that. (7–8)

From the outset, Stein sets up several layers of unreliability. The dog who says he is going to learn to read but doesn't may not even be a dog. He hasn't yet learned to bark and yet he "says" he is going to learn to read. More importantly, the narrator is equally unreliable because she vouches for this dog against all of his canine nay-sayers—"they did not know that dog," the narrator propounds with authority.

Far more implicit is the unreliability of the first reader as a whole. There is a strange relationship here at the very beginning of this first reader between learning to read and learning to swim. One could perhaps chock up the initial swear that "He might be drowned dead in water but…he was going to learn to read" to dramatic effect, but the next line insists eerily on some actual correlation. For one, the second statement no longer hinges on the conditional "if" and is no longer qualified by the word "might." Now the logic seems surer—"he was not drowned and he did not learn to read." And too, the one qualification that is present—that he was not "drowned dead"—only makes the correlation more disturbing. It invites the comparison between struggling to read and struggling to swim and raises the question: Was the dog nearly drowned in the process of trying to learn to read? And finally, if all of this could be dismissed as nonsense—under the heading of dogs learning to read—Stein counts out for us how many children there are "like that."

Perhaps most interesting, Stein's first lesson is metacognitive. It's less useful *for* learning to read than it is for learning *about* learning to read. In the same way that *To Do* is something of a meta-alphabet book that enlists the alphabet form in its own undoing; this first reader offers a parody of first readers. Stein's first lesson, which (if sincere) should be the simplest and easiest to read, rings in at a whopping 1250 words. Focusing again on reading, Stein writes, "Just think of read if red is read, and read is read, you see when all is said, just now read just then read, do you see even if a little boy or a little girl is very well fed if they do not read how can they know whether red is read and read is red. How can they know, oh no how can they know" (11). Stein is, of course, being melodramatic—particularly in the last line—and she's being ironic. On the surface, she proclaims that reading is of vital importance, but the suggestion between the lines is that it is of little use. What are the implications after all of confusing "read" with its homophone "red"? Even so, knowing how to read doesn't help terribly much with reading this passage. When is "read" pronounced [reed] and when is it pronounced [red]? Stein's *First Reader* has a way of making all readers feel like first readers, and this is perhaps the proverbial point.

When McCullough tried *The First Reader* out at two schools, with third graders, the lessons received mixed reviews. One child commented, "Hey, this is crazy. I think it should be more of one story—you don't get much meaning out of the short little ones. I think it is too old for the First Graders to read—they should have something they can understand. I like her style." Another observed: "It is sort of dizzy—it doesn't make sense—it doesn't have much point to it. It repeats things. It is hard to catch on. I can't think for what age group it would be good. There is one thing: it stops right in the middle of things I don't enjoy reading it—it makes me dizzy" ("Comments on 'The Reader'" 3).

The lessons in American first readers traditionally taught far more than literacy. They also provided character lessons in patriotism, integrity, industry, patience, and politeness for an audience that was deemed particularly impressionable. By contrast, lessons in Stein's *First Reader* rely on superstition, false fairy tales, and absurd who-done-its. "Lesson Eight" tells the story of a boy and a hen who drown because each fails to heed the warning that "the thirteenth of March was a day when it was dangerous to play" (29). The hen decides to play at being a duck and swims out over the water to eat a trout. But she is "drowned dead" not only because it is the 13th of March but because she in fact was not "a duck in a theatre but a hen in the water" (30). The boy observing this tragedy tries to return home, but it is too late. He has already made the fatal error of playing outside on the 13th of March, and he, like the hen, drowns. Lessons like this one mock the rational progressive laws that guide the first reader's formal and thematic intentions to build a more literate and more civilized child. But this lesson also undermines a core attribute of Romantic childhood. Imagination, the ability to play, and to make-believe are for many adults idyllic features of childhood, yet for Stein they can seem like mythologies of ominous proportions. In both *To Do* and in *The First Reader*, there are certain circumstances, not governed by reason, when make-believe violence turns into actual violence and when play becomes dangerous, indeed deadly.

Stein's choices of the alphabet book and first reader are ripe with significance, for these are genres not only almost exclusively associated with childhood and child readers but they are also imagined almost universally as formative of childhood interiority. Early readers are written for children to make children. Stein commits a violence toward these school books by integrating stories of violence and death into her versions but also by suggesting that such violence is latent within the genre's lessons and progressive structures for being. In *To Do*, Xantippe and Xenophon are marked by the X's that begin their names. In the *First Reader* learning to read is too much like giving one's self up to the currents to be drowned.

Drowning in Children's Narratives

The drowning that is delivered with such literalized force in Stein's children's literature is more of a conceptual splinter, underlying and inflaming Stein's adult meditations on identity formation following the 1933 success of *The Autobiography of Alice B. Toklas*. And in this way the child characters who are actually swallowed up and drowned in Stein's parodic children's narratives lift the veil, so to speak, on what has long been an embedded problem for Stein: that is the drowning power of these narratives of education and growth. While many critics and admirers alike have noted a childlike or childish quality in Stein's work, very little scholarship has focused on the connections between Stein's preoccupation with narratives from childhood and her actual literature for children.[7] But for Stein, who often embraced the view of her poetry as "children's poetry," these lines are unsurprisingly blurred.[8] Reviews—like Laura Riding's 1928 assessment that "None of the words Miss Stein uses have ever had an experience. They are no older than her use of them"; or the Robert S. Warshow's 1946 memorial essay that opens with the tribute: "The chief thing Gertrude Stein tried to do was write as if she had kept her innocence"; or even Dr. Schmalhausen's 1929 no-holds-barred insult that "Gertrude's mental age is 12, her emotional age is 14, her artistic age is 7"—are drawn to (or repulsed by) an essentialized type of child language associated with Stein's portraits and poems of the teens and twenties.[9]

By contrast, late Stein not only develops a serious politics of childhood (Stein shared the radical view that children should have the right to vote)[10] but also proves more interested in and troubled by children's narratives—that is, not the supposed language of children but the language arranged and packaged for children by adults. In her children's literature these narratives take on the parodic shape of the alphabet book, the fairy tale, and the first reader. In her adult work, Stein condenses her focus on singular sentences which nonetheless represent canonic children's narrative forms. Stein meditates on the problem of identity anchored by an external subject through the nursery rhyme ("I am I because my little dog knows me"), repeatedly questions the coming-of-age narrative of organic growth and cultural assimilation ("what is the use of being a little boy if you are growing up to be a man"), and challenges the quasi-imperialism of narratives of scientific discovery ("the world is round it goes around and around"). Each of these narratives traditionally offers both a soothing and a smoothing representation of life-history, normativizing the subject and naturalizing a whole set of uneven relationships of power across species, ages, and peoples the world over.

Jacqueline Rose has provocatively argued that there are no children in children's literature; rather children's fiction is populated by adults' romantic fantasies of childhood. Devoid of children yet directed at children, children's literature for Rose is part of a colonizing enterprise that "sets up a world in which the adult comes first (author, maker, giver) and the child comes after (reader, product, receiver)" (1–2). Roses's interest in imperializing narratives, in psychoanalysis, and in J.M. Barrie's *Peter Pan* as a case study are all choices that are steeped in the culture and concerns of modernism. But far from acknowledging this connection, Rose actually laments the absence of a modernist children's literature, even as she immerses herself in a text which was arguably seminal to that very enterprise (142). It is possible, I wish to suggest, that Rose's dystopic view of children's narratives might have something to do with the modernist literature she studies. Her pessimism is most certainly predated by J.M. Barrie's. Years after *Peter Pan*'s runaway success, Barrie continued to insist that there is something sinister about Peter that cultural adaptations missed.[11] The division between the narrator of *Peter and Wendy* (1911) and the child protagonist, Peter Pan, is quintessentially modernist in its ironic distance. In fact, in *Peter and Wendy* it is Peter and not the narrator who most embodies the "heartless" ideologies of masculine imperialism. By the end of *Peter and Wendy*, readers may note the narrator's explicit move to represent him/herself as a "servant" to the text and to the Darling family, a choice that aligns the narrator with another character in the novel—not Peter but rather—the children's St. Bernard, Nana (135). Peter Pan remains a boy imperialist at the end. In fact, his empire and authority have grown. After defeating Hook, Peter alone carries the title of "Captain" (134).

Though Jacqueline Rose was right that the field of modernist children's literature has been remarkably dry, at least in the sense of academic recognition, it is possible that reconceptualizations of children's literature like hers, framed by postcolonialism and poststructuralism to question the social constructedness of the child in children's literature, may find modernism's children's literature among their literary ancestors. Stein's work most clearly raises the issue of modernism's potential role in the changing landscape of children's literary criticism because, for her, the violence of the post-Romantic child-ideal is concentrated most, as it is for scholars like Rose, in children's narratives. Stein precedes postmodern critics of children's literature in her assessment that narratives, particularly children's narratives, do not just shape identity, they occupy it.

From the beginning, Stein's use of the nursery rhyme theme, "I am I because my little dog knows me," is as much about writing as it is about identity. The expression makes its first appearance in 1931 in *How to Write* as part of the question: "What is a sentence for if I am I then my little dog knows me" (19). Stein was rarely a fan of such sentences. For her, the only prosaic evil that surpassed the sentence was the paragraph. In "Poetry and Grammar" Stein expresses the problem as two-fold. Not only do sentences and paragraphs subordinate the diversity of the individual word to the meaning of the whole but each also creates, perhaps strives to create, a state of "balance" (322) as between various parts of speech, between subject and predicate, or between sentences. "One and one make two," Stein writes of natural prose, but the trick is to "go on counting by one and one" (324). In the world of grammar, as with most everything else, Stein has favorites. She prefers nouns because nouns can stand alone, and Stein prefers that they do. The independent linguistic and subjective complexities of the "I am I" and the "little dog" are overwritten by the relationship that the sentence imposes between them.

But that quintessential sentence about sentences makes a more pronounced and enduring debut in "And Now." Written some two years after *The Autobiography of Alice B. Toklas*, "And Now" reflects on Stein's struggle with writer's block following the astonishing success of *The Autobiography*:

> What happened to me was this. When the success began and it was a success I got lost completely lost. You know the nursery rhyme, I am I because my

little dog knows me. Well you see I did not know myself, I lost my personality. It has always been completely included in myself my personality as any personality naturally is, and here all of a sudden, I was not just I because so many people did know me. It was just the opposite of I am I because my little dog knows me. So many people knowing me I was I no longer and for the first time since I had begun to write I could not write. (63)

To capture the dysfunctional relationship between identity and creative expression, Stein returns to a lesson from childhood. And at first, she appears to affirm the logic of the Mother Goose. "You know the nursery rhyme," she writes, and in so writing she confers upon the poem, "The Old Woman and the Pedlar," the weight of common knowledge. She likewise compliments her reader with the expression of assumed intelligence. Stein assumes that her readers will know, as by heart, the poem from childhood, and she makes the further assessment that, knowing this, they will also understand her predicament. Stein imagines herself in this passage as sharing much with her readers: of sharing this common memory (and memorization) from childhood, first and foremost, but the mode of the essay is also confessional. In affirming her audience to the extent that she does—by addressing them informally and sincerely twice—and also by affirming what they share, Stein deepens the sense of their connection, a connection that would seem to echo the dynamic between woman and dog in the poem.

On the other hand, the content of what Stein confesses stands in opposition to each of these formal, rhetorical gestures: "all of a sudden," she writes, "I was not just I because so many people did know me." What Stein is confessing to her readers is nothing less than the problem that they themselves pose to her. What Stein assumes her audience will understand is the role they have played in her identity crisis. Stein "no longer knew [her] self" because her audience, in some senses, got inside her. Like the poem, Stein imagines that she too has become common knowledge, that she has been internalized by others, and worries that this process has and must have repercussions for her and anyone who is a person and not a poem. Stein's abrupt turn from affirming the poem as common knowledge to questioning its truth-value may serve as a means of distancing herself from it. Stein discovers that the "opposite" of the Mother Goose might actually be true, that being known might not secure one's identity but might actually cause it to be "lost completely lost."

Others have interpreted this tension in "And Now" between embracing and resisting a common audience as both rhetorical for Stein and as intrinsic to the paradoxical mode of high modernism. Of the ongoing historical reassessment of canonical modernism's relationship to the marketplace, Timothy Galow summarizes that "the last three decades have seen an explosion of volumes examining the various ways in which canonical authors, despite their occasionally dismissive rhetoric, have engaged with and been implicated in the marketplace" (315). Addressing "And Now" specifically, Galow argues that its "trope of writer's-block-overcome allows Stein to emphasize her status as an elite artist who has strong reservations about the literary marketplace while she is simultaneously writing pieces that will be marketed to a broad reading public" (325). Undergirding Galow's argument are two crucial assumptions. The first is that to "overcome" writer's block is to restore a former style of writing, in this case Stein's and modernism's pre-1930s high or "elite" aesthetic. The second is that content is secondary to form, an assumption that clearly supports high modernist affiliations. Thus, Stein's deployment of rhetorical devices is perceived as outweighing any substantive expression of anxiety on her part.

But there is room in "And Now," for another interpretation, one that, taking its first cue from the title, perceives sequential change in the place of contradiction. Before Stein concludes that her experience has been "just the opposite of I am I because my little dog knows me," she describes a transformation: "It has always been completely included in myself my personality as any personality naturally is, and here all of a sudden, I was not just I because so many people did know me" (63). The phrase "all of a sudden" points to a dramatic change in Stein's relationship to identity. While that relationship might have been natural and common before, it is as such no longer. While it might be tempting—because Stein writes "And Now" in the past tense and because she has so obviously overcome her battle with writer's block—to read Stein's loss of identity as a struggle that has also been overcome, the title's insistence on the unfinished present alongside this language of change suggests otherwise.

Another sign that a change has taken place in Stein's thinking about identity comes in *Everybody's Autobiography* (1937). Whereas Stein writes in "And Now" that "any personality naturally" is "completely included" within that person, here she again cites the Mother Goose, expresses her anxiety, but then asks "who has to be themselves inside them, not any one" (300). What seemed like a personal experience in "And Now"—the loss of identity—now seems like a more generic possibility for "any one." When Stein returns to the nursery rhyme expression at the end of *Everybody's Autobiography,* it is to conclude the train of her thought as well as the text. I am I because my little dog knows me makes its final and most cited appearance in Stein's closing sentiment: "…perhaps I am not I even if my little dog knows me but anyway I like what I have and now it is today" (328). Far from recovering her sense of identity after the success of *Alice B. Toklas*, Stein indicates here an effort to come to terms with the loss.

In between "And Now" and these two reflective assessments of latter years stands Stein's *A Geographical History of America, or the Relation of Human Nature to the Human Mind* (1936), her most thorough meditation on the formative aspects of children's narratives and "the question of identity" (401). The role of children's narratives in *Geographical History* cannot be overstated because overstatement is so precisely the mode that Stein applies to them. Stein references the Mother Goose no fewer than 11 times. But this is only part of the children's narrative story in *Geographical History*. Though the problem of identity-as-recognition, as expressed in Mother Goose terms, has occupied Stein's writing since her lecture tour in 1934, in *Geographical History* that narrative comes to share the stage with the new narrative problem of boys evolving into men. The question "What is the use of being a little boy if one is growing up to be a man?" likewise appears no fewer than 14 times in the text. In the mode of overstatement, Stein proclaims in one of these instances that "One cannot say it too often and it need not bring tears to your eyes what is the use of being a little boy if you are going to grow up to be a man what is the use" (372). James R. Mellow, who characterizes the nursery rhyme and the boys-to-men leitmotifs as "maddeningly repeated and rephrased" in *Geographical History*, may not be alone in disagreeing with Stein on this point (418). The problems of an identity fixed by recognition, on the one hand, or changing according to developmental norms, on the other, seem in the final version of *Geographical History* like two distinct, maybe even contrasting (maybe even "maddening"), pieces of the elusive Steinian puzzle.[12]

In contrast, the draft manuscript of *Geographical History* may offer some clarity. Here these two identity problems appear to be not only far more prominent but also appear to be far more interrelated and entangled. One of the clearest expressions of the potential relationship between them was cut from the final version. In it Stein suggested that the problem of development had actually succeeded, in her mind, the problem of the Mother Goose: "I am I because my little dog knows me is not true. What is the use of being a little boy if you are growing to be a man. That is the secret of identity."[13] What's more, while the final version of *Geographical History* displays itself first and foremost as a treatise on the differences between human nature and the human mind, the manuscript version displays a more primary interest in the identities of dogs and children and the interaction between them.

The final published version of *Geographical History* begins with a series of observations. The first is that February is the month in which "were born Washington Lincoln and I." The second is that everyone has to die in order to make "room" for those who have not lived. The third brings in the text's subtitled theme, "or The Relation of Human Nature to the Human Mind," by stating the first in a long line of distinctions that "Human nature cannot know" about the necessity of making room, "But the human mind can" (367). In other words, in its final version *Geographical History* begins with one of Stein's favorite subjects: genius. George Washington, Abraham Lincoln, and Gertrude Stein are all geniuses. The category of the human mind will become the category of genius *sine qua non* in *Geographical History*, in contrast to the ordinary, herd-like qualities of human nature. The first use of the phrase "What is the use of being a little boy if you are growing up to be a man" does not appear until a few pages in, in the first of many Chapter IIs. The first mention of little dogs comes a few pages still further in at the beginning of the second Chapter IV.

But in the original manuscript of *Geographical History*, the narratives of "little boy[s]" and "little dog[s]" actually precede even the first reference to human nature and the human mind. The earlier version reads:

> What is the use of being a little boy if you are going to grow up to be a man.
>
> Use is here used in the sense of purpose.
>
> But to begin with what man is man was man will be.
>
> When children play tag they tag each other that is they touch each other to start, well dogs do that, a big dog with a little dog a white dog with a black dog a dog to a dog. That is what they do to begin to play. Any child does that.[14]

Collectively there is little in this version that does not also end up in the final. Technically, all of the lines are used, but they are not used together, and they are not given the same pride of place. Reorganizing the manuscript such that the subtitled distinction between human nature and the human mind takes precedence over that between boys and dogs makes perfect rhetorical sense, akin to one of the most common revisions in the writing process: that is, framing the thesis after the fact. What this change generally conceals (is designed to conceal) are the mental meanderings through which the thesis was first thought. And this is true even for Stein whose meditations seem (are designed to seem) like mental meanderings of the most unadulterated kind. In addition to acting as a textual precursor, it is possible that Stein's thinking about boys and dogs also served as a theoretical precursor to the main claim about the relationship between human nature and the human mind that would come to take its place.

Then too, the separation of "What is the use of being a little boy" from the game of children and dogs playing tag, ultimately five chapters apart, disguises the work that has been done to achieve that separation. The problem of identity vis-à-vis dogs and children is much messier in the original version. An excerpt from Stein's original manuscript illustrates the point (Fig. 7.1):

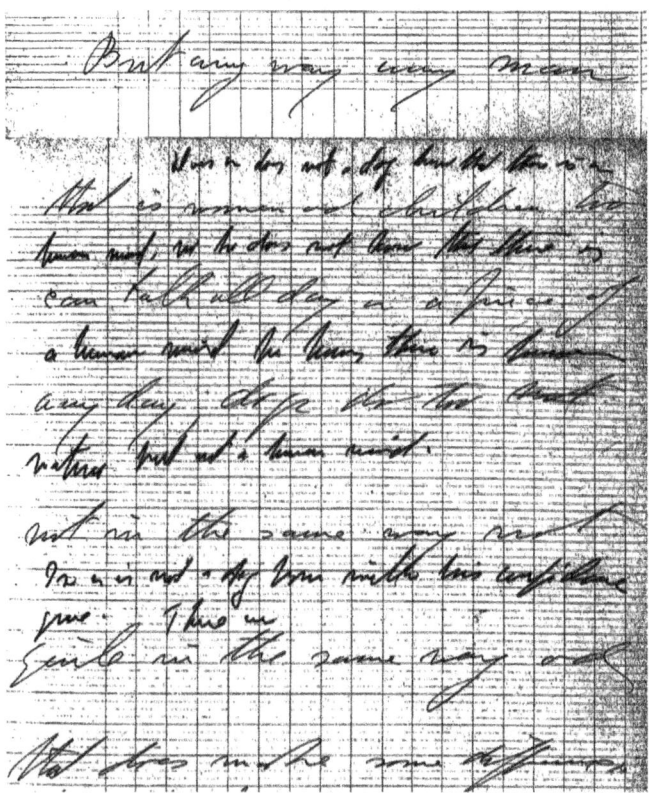

Fig. 7.1 Facsimile from Gertrude Stein's manuscript, *Geographical History of America*, Beinecke Rare Book and Manuscript Library, Yale University, used here with permission by the Estate of Gertrude Stein

Many who have studied Stein will recognize that such moments of intense revision are rare. First drafts were all too often also final copy. Such moments of narrative difficulty or doubt are consequently in Stein's case all the more meaningful. Here, because I cannot immediately read the page, I am impressed first by what the excerpt looks like as an image. This is probably the first and only time that I have been grateful for Stein's notoriously bad hand-writing. As an image, the taking-turns quality of the lines is striking. I am reminded of William James's definition of double consciousness as an alternation between first one and then another state of mind.[15] This page looks most distinctly as though it were of two minds. Even if this is an image of revision, it is of a particular kind. Even if the lighter set of lines were written first, as it seems likely they were, they have not been crossed out (and Stein did cross lines out) in order to be rewritten or replaced. Rather, they have been juxtaposed line-by-line. There is a choice to be made, it seems, but that choice has not yet been made. Here is an image of indecisiveness, ambivalence even. Here is an image of a text unable to move forward, a page unable to be turned. The bold, erratic text appears to do a kind of battle with the lighter, more regular penmanship with which it alternates its way down the page. Though it does not make its way into the final version, I am reminded when I see this image of Stein's own description of the "roughness and violence" of the work of art that refuses to be narrative ("Transatlantic Interview" 19).

Reading the text reveals that dog, child, human nature, and human mind have all been crowded onto this page. The text between the lines, in darker ink, reads, "Does or does not a dog know that there is a human mind, no he does not know that there is a human mind he knows there is human nature but not a human mind. Is or is not a dog born with his confidence gone...." The other set of lines records, "But any way any man that is women and children too can talk all day or any piece of any day dogs do too not in the same way not quite in the same way and that does make some difference...." In this moment the notions of human nature and the human mind do-si-do in such a way as to belie Stein's unequivocal claims that they have no relation to one another. Likewise, the concept of continuity between men, women, and children overlaps with the new marriage of human nature and dog in such a way as to underscore, for the second time, that Stein's thinking about these two concepts—of development and identity—was more integrated than the printed text lets on.

In *A Geographical History of America*, dogs are not just dogs and boys are not just boys. To resolve the problem of essential identity—of "I am I if my little dog knows me"—Stein shifts and dislocates that identity onto the dog. Basket, a figure in *Geographical History* and also the name of Stein's own standard poodle, exemplifies for Stein more than just the complexity of canine consciousness; he also proves the possibility that identity might be insignificant after all and indeed that its loss may even be desirable. Stein writes:

> Identity is very curious.
>
> Not even the dogs can worry any further about identity.
>
> They would like to get lost and if they are lost what is there of identity.
>
> …They would like to get lost and so they would then be there where there is no identity, but a dog cannot get lost, therefore he does not have a human mind, he is never without time and identity. (464)

The first assertion of this sequence "Identity is very curious" is, on the one hand, disproven by nearly every line that follows. There is nothing about identity to incite the curiosity of anyone or any dog. It is so not curious, so uninteresting, that "even the dogs" would like to "be there where there is no identity." On the other hand, what is perhaps "curious" about this delineation of identity is Stein's insistence on relegating it to the dog. The dog is both the reluctant and compulsory heir to this hand-me-down of humanity. By displacing identity from herself on to the dog, Stein manages to equivocate the loss of identity, allowing it to be something that can at once be "completely lost" and yet which also "cannot get lost." In this way, it might be accurate to say that Stein gets to have her human nature and leave it too. She is distinct from her dog—as the human mind is distinct from human nature—and yet he is also her former self.

The problem of the nursery rhyme "I am I because my little dog knows me" increasingly comes into clarity in Stein's writings of the thirties as more than just a problem of identity, but much more precisely as the problem of a past identity internally contained and preserved. The little dog represents a past conception of identity that Stein would personally and culturally very much like to leave behind, and in fact by identifying identity with the little dog, Stein also and at once begins to negotiate this leave-taking. But the trajectory of Stein's identity-critique is thickened by the introduction in *Geographical History* of another narrative from childhood, one whose center is the child. Stein has relied on the Mother Goose to do a great deal of heavy lifting for at least two years in her writing. The addition of the evolutionary question "What is the use of being a little boy if you are growing up to be a man" signals that one of the central concerns and critiques of Stein's work of this period is not merely the idea of identity but the idea specifically of a former, historical self: the self of childhood.

Though Stein once believed in the idea of an internally "settle[d]" identity, what she termed in *The Making of Americans* "bottom nature," the 1930s see her rejecting all of the dominant notions of identity available to her (qtd. in Ashton 295). In examining Stein's experimental 1938 play, *Doctor Faustus Lights the Lights*, Sarah Bay-Cheng shows that the categories of boy and dog have become interchangeable as representatives of identity. Faustus wonders, "if a boy is to grow up to be a man am I a boy am I a dog is a dog a boy is a boy a dog and what am I I cannot cry what am I oh what am I" (qtd. in Bay-Cheng 98). In the place of identity as "integrated" and "developing," Bay-Cheng contends that Stein offers an image of humanity's inability "either to comprehend itself or to evolve." In the place of the "psycho-scientific certainty" about the principles of identity formation, Stein's uncertainty about these principles are melodramatically bound toward deconstruction (Bay-Cheng 89). There are many moments in the printed version of *Geographical History* where Stein's meditations on Mother Goose and evolutionary narratives also read like melodramatic farce. Indeed among the genres embedded within it is a modernist melodramatic restaging of Stein's identity crisis called "The question of identity: A Play." The statement, repeated throughout *Geographical History*, that "human nature is no longer interesting" has a declarative appeal. And Stein's "play" seems so playful with its disordered and repeated acts and scenes and with its self-referential absurdisms (the first of many "Scene II"s tells us that "Any scene may be scene two" [404]) that *Geographical History* can certainly be seen as quite literally performing the break between human nature and the human mind.

Likewise, Stein's repetitions of the nursery rhyme and the boys-to-men question can have a desensitizing effect. Stein emphasizes both that one apparently "cannot say" either of these expressions "too often" and also that doing so "need not bring tears to your eyes" (372). On the one hand, there is a glibness to Stein's discourse on human nature; there is a sense in which its repeated dismissals come to seem nonchalant, easy, even fun. On the other, there is the emotionally-loaded suggestion, represented by tears, that the repetitions may not signal ease as much as they may underscore the struggle and the difficulty of this particular letting-go. In my view, taking the draft version into account goes a long way to suggest the latter of these readings. The threat of nearly drowning, psychologically speaking, in the narratives of human nature and of childhood may take on a performative quality in the final version of *Geographical History* akin in many ways to melodramatic farce, but the weight of this revisionary moment suggests that the "play" of *Geographical History* is far from an empty performance.

Saying that human nature is no longer interesting inevitably brings tears to the eyes of the one saying it, or is necessarily said by "Tears." In realizing that talking, for instance, is not a part of the human mind (because any person can talk and even any dog can talk), Stein writes, "I wish I could say that talking had to do with the human mind, I wish I could say so and not cry I wish I could" (375). Tears act as a sort of touchstone in *Geographical History*; they are what Stein gauges many of her conclusions by—even those which are apparently joyful. When, for instance, Stein experiences the "pleasure" of the "the human mind when it is altogether the human mind," this too is measured in relation to tears or, in this case, to the absence thereof: "No this does not bring tears to anybody's eyes not even to mine and I might I might cry easily oh so very easily" (374). Similarly, saying that there is no connection between the "little dog" and "I am I" requires an insistence on the way that it is said—"without tears" (405). Whether through this "thou doth protest too much" model of dry-eyed insistence or the alternative confessional of "as I say so tears come into my eyes" (373), the division of human nature from the human mind, of the little dog from its human companion, comes to seem like a visceral *tearing* of one from the other. The problem of Stein's identity crisis in the face of mass recognition is one which she has resolved to answer by letting her lost identity be lost, but this resolution is neither cognitively nor emotionally simple.

The tears in *Geographical History* anticipate the tears of Rose, the child protagonist in Stein's first published work for children, *The World is Round*.[16] Rose is factually based on Rose d'Aiguy, the daughter of Robert and Dianne d'Aiguy, neighbors to Stein and Toklas in Bilignin, but her story, including the climactic moment when she inscribes "*Rose is a Rose is a Rose*" around the trunk of a tree, is largely that of Gertrude Stein (52).[17] Rose, like Stein, finds herself in recurrent thought. She "thinks" and then she "thinks again." And at the center of her thoughts is none other than the question of identity. Rose sings:

Why am I a little girl

Where am I a little girl

When am I a little girl

Which little girl am I. (4)

Rose wonders if there is anything essential to her that makes her like no other; she wonders if this is a function of her size; she wonders if it is a function of her gender. Through the interrogative catalog—"Why," "Where," "When," and "Which"—she in effect answers her own questions, rhetorically demonstrating her conviction that both size/age and gender are products of circumstance. But the singing and the questions, as much as they challenge human nature, also illicit the response of human nature; Rose, like Stein, begins to cry, and when she cries, her dog cries too, and they both "cried and cried and cried" until "at last [Rose's] eyes were dried" (4).

The connections between *Geographical History* and *The World is Round* are striking. Both, obviously, take geography as their central theme. Both feature children and dogs, and both are driven by the question of identity. Most importantly, Rose's journey in *The World is Round* to break through the naturalistic narratives that threaten to encircle and ensnare her—by climbing a linear mountain and sitting upon its peak triumphantly in her blue chair—is Stein's journey to leave the identifications of human nature behind for the fuller, more detached genius of the human mind.[18] Both even achieve this break in the same way—by writing in circles: "A Rose is a Rose is a Rose." Archival evidence also suggests that Stein may have begun drafting *The World is Round* at least in part as a response to readings of *Geographical History* if not also as a rethinking of that earlier text. In August 1938, Stein received a long essay by Julian Sawyer on "What The Geographical History of America Means to Me." Some of the lines that make it into *The World is Round* are written in the white space around Sawyer's letter.[19]

The World is Round tells the story first and foremost of Rose, trying to overcome or interrupt the knowledge of roundness that threatens to consume her, but it also tells the story of Willie. Willie is Rose's cousin (at least in the beginning) and her double in the sense that he has already accomplished the feat for which she is preparing. Willie, we are told, has nearly drowned twice in his life, and the result is that he no longer fears death. In the first instance, Willie gets tangled up in the "pretty" water lilies of a lake. The adults, all remarkably unheroic in *The World is Round*, having "just finished eating," know that "you must never go into the water right after eating," so the rescue of Willie is left to a fellow child (6). That Willie should have drowned, that drowning is, in fact, the norm in a round world is illustrated in Stein's conclusion to the event that "Willie was not drowned although the lake and the world were both all around." Survival is something of an anomaly in this scenario. And after the world's second failed attempt to drown Willie, this time with Rose in a car traveling up a hill, Willie is able to sing with confidence "*My name is Willie I am not like Rose/ I would be Willie whatever arose*" (7). Even more important, Willie is able to sing of the world being round in the past tense: "*Once upon a time the world was round the moon was round/The lake was round/And I I was almost drowned*" (8). That the roundness of the world is no longer a reality for Willie is emphasized by his ability to relegate it to the land of fairy tale and is seconded by his dream, not of himself drowning, but of "Round drowned" in his place (8).

Rose, on the other hand, is plagued by the recent knowledge that not only the world, but everything, the sun, the moon, even the stars, is round and "that they [are] all going around and around" (11). Rose begins to drown in roundness. She is taken over by a "dreadful" memory of having sung once in front of a mirror, and in her memory she too becomes round. Rose remembers that "as she sang her mouth was round and was going around and around." And, "of course," Rose cries (12). The remainder of *The World is Round* tells the story of Rose's battle with roundness. Rose's weapons in this queer adventure are her voice, a blue chair, and most importantly her penknife. The holy grail of Rose's journey is the top of a nearby mountain. By following the mountain's linear ascension above the earth, Rose believes she can surmount the drowning effect of the round world. Rose's trek up the mountain is remarkably like the drowning swimmer's experience of struggling to break, to capture, and then to hold the water's surface.

In what is arguably the darkest section of Rose's story, she faces an interminable night upon this mountain. Stein is not subtle about this point. She titles four chapters in the middle of Rose's journey "Night." As each chapter ends, the reader, like Rose, no doubt hopes that this "Night" is over. But "Night" surrounds Rose, or Rose is unable to break through the darkness into day. In the middle of these interminable nights there is trauma, near-death, and there is water. In the chapter, "Rose Saw It Close," which falls between two "Night[s]," Stein writes, "What did Rose see close, that is what she never can tell and perhaps it is just as well, suppose she did tell oh dear oh dear what she saw when she fell. Poor dear Rose. She saw it close" (45). And in the following "Night," Rose experiences yet another terror. She discovers a waterfall and is mistaken to think that she can take some shelter behind it, can escape within its even greater darkness the anxieties and also the unspeakable trauma of preceding nights. But on the wall behind the water, written in triplicate Rose reads the words "*Devil, Devil, Devil*" (47).

The effect of this encounter on Rose has the repetitive ring of trauma. Stein writes:

> She decided she did not like water to fall, water fall water fall…So Rose and the blue chair went away from there she never could go down not there not ever again there, she could never go anywhere where water is falling and water does fall even out of a faucet, poor Rose dear Rose sweet Rose only Rose…So she went on climbing higher and higher and higher…If she did not she would think of seeing that, was the Devil round, was he around, around round, round around. (47-48)

The elements of drowning are all present in this scene—water, darkness, depth, and a near-death encounter. It is also worth remembering that this is not Rose's first terrifying experience with a wall of water on a mountain. One of Willie's and Rose's earlier near-drowning experiences takes place while they are riding up a mountain in a car with Willie's parents. Suddenly, Stein writes, "the rain came down with a will, you know how it comes when it comes so heavy and fast it is not wet it is a wall that is all" (6). Before somebody manages to open a door, the car fills with water, enough "to drown Willie certainly to drown Willie and perhaps to drown

Rose" (7). What is different about this subsequent near-drowning experience for Rose is its psychological quality. Rose is alone, and the feeling of drowning described here seems as much the product of remembering that earlier almost-drowning as of experiencing it again in the flesh. Here the elements of that prior sequence are repeated, but they appear in a dissociated, fragmented way. The darkness, the depth, the water, and the fear of death are spatially disentangled. Each is physically distinct such that their congruence for Rose presents a powerful allegorical experience of drowning felt on a number of physical and psychological levels. Most powerfully, the repeating pattern of Rose's memories as of her encounter of several nights without a day renders this experience of drowning not just traumatic but post-traumatic, as another experience of drowning in a life, a childhood, defined by such experiences.

Rose's ascent, Dante-esque, out of the crucible of childhood requires the shedding of one skin for another. That the "conclusion" to *The World is Round* is one of the most atypical typical endings in a children's book is attested to by the diverse critical responses to it. Many scholars would have preferred, it seems, for Rose's tree poetry climax (where she cuts "*Rose is a Rose is a Rose*" all around the trunk of a tree) to double as the story's ending. Many use the positive climatic effect of this scene as a lens through which to read the far more ambiguous last chapter, which relates the marriage of Rose and Willie. Aptly titled "The End," Stein writes: "Willie and Rose turned out not to be cousins, just how nobody knows, and so they married and had children...and they lived happily ever after and the world just went on being round" (67). Edith Thacher Hurd argues that "the young reader," "skipping over the awkwardness" of Willie and Rose's courtship, manages to arrive at "the desired conclusion" that Rose has found her fairy tale "Prince" (161). Jan Susina too follows the optimistic tone of Rose's writing accomplishment along with its repetitive structure as a guide to reading the whole of *World*, arguing that continuity is a positive quality in the story and that the repetitions of the story and the marriage at the end are attempts to provide child readers with a sense of stability and security (118–119).

Barbara Will's more recent reading of *The World is Round* likewise evinces a strong preference for the early Rose of the story but differs sharply in that it rejects Stein's own declaration for a happy ending in the marriage of Rose and Willie. Rather, Will reads the ending of *The World is Round* as a betrayal of Rose and of Stein's earlier, anti-patriarchal experimental writing. Will's condemnation of this ending is as sweeping as it is harsh. She compares Rose's submission to the patriarch, Willie (with his "phallic searchlight"), to Stein's (alleged) allegiance to Pétain ("'And Then'" 345).[20] And she links the representations of children (as "submissive, masochistic victims") in *The World is Round* and in all Stein's children's literature (345) to Stein's own child identifications and (alleged) masochistic relationship with Alice Toklas (342). Barbara Will's work is important because it is one of the few that reads across Stein's children's and adult literature during the World War II era, but it is also the most troubling to me not only because it assumes much about Stein's personal life and politics and then assumes a congruence between that life and her work but also because it relies heavily on a binary hermeneutic frame in which children must be either heroic agents or masochistic victims and in which Stein must either be a feminist or a collaborationist.

Linda Watts surmises one of the pitfalls of these types of readings of *The World is Round* when she observes that many critics' purported summaries of the story "betray conventional (rather than experimental) readings" (n. pag.). Each of these readings seem inclined to take Stein's "happily ever after" at face-value as a representation of Stein's narrative intent. This is despite the fact that the story is filled with meta-narrative gestures that point to itself not as a fairy tale but as a mock fairy tale.[21] From start to finish, *The World is Round* is too conspicuously framed as a fairy tale for children. The happy-ever-after ending falls in a chapter parodically titled "The End." And the "Once upon a time" beginning actually runs like a loop throughout the story. In fact the frame, which is itself broken, is the most that this story has in common with the utopian expectations of the fairy or wonder tale of Stein's era.[22] Reaching this "happily ever after" has required some pretty dramatic genre and plot changes not only because Rose's story has been anything but happy but also because this is most clearly not the conventional ending of a children's story, but rather the very conventional ending of another genre altogether—the nineteenth-century domestic novel. In a matter of pages, the narrative of *The World is Round* ages up and so does Rose. Not only is the blood bond between Rose and Willie inexplicably severed, but Rose appears by the time she reaches the top of the mountain to have added years, not days to her life.

The actual last words of *The World is Round* are "they lived happily ever after and the world just went on being round" (67). Indeed, the world is probably the only thing that has not changed in this ending. Rose and Willie are different people. This is a different genre. As readers we might be tempted at this point to pass the book to a different reader since the intended audience may too have changed. In contrast to Willie who can imagine early on in *The World is Round* surviving the drowning experience by drowning "round" in his place, Stein does not entertain this possibility. Drowning is the norm in Stein's round world. And what drowns in this case is childhood. *The World is Round* is an experimental, subversive children's narrative, but many critics have crucially overlooked that among the conventions Stein is most set on subverting in this text are the heroic fantasies and fairy tales about childhood. There is an interesting intentional Freudian slip early in *The World is Round* that has greater meaning in hindsight. Willie, like Rose, feels as though he is drowning in a round world. Stein writes: "The world got rounder and rounder./The stars got rounder and rounder/The moon got rounder and rounder/The sun got rounder and rounder/And Willie oh Willie was ready to drown her, not Rose dear me not Rose but his sorrows" (15). Willie does not drown Rose, presumably does not intend to drown her, but by letting the suggestion of that intention stand (and Stein does more than this by making sure the reader does in fact catch that the "her" could be, and naturally would be, read as Rose), Stein perhaps foreshadows the real and metaphorical drownings to come. By the time Rose reaches the top of the mountain she is a child no more, and in that sense some part of her may have been drowned after all. Perhaps – as Stein's quasi-Freudian slip suggests – thankfully so.

Politics In and Out of Stein's Late Modernism

In describing identity (and most everything else) as "funny," Stein utilizes a childlike language to illustrate her concerns about childhood, memory, and children's narratives, but this language should not be mistaken for anything like a lack of seriousness about these issues. When Stein travels from America to France for the second and last time in her life, she "worrie[s]" about her relationship to identity, to "the Mother Goose," and to country:

> To get this trouble out of my system I began to write the Geographical History of America or the Relation of Human Nature To The Human Mind and I meditated as I had not done for a very long time not since I was a little one about the contradiction of being on this earth with the space limiting and knowing about the stars in an unlimited space that is that nobody could find out if it was limiting or limited, and now these meditations did

not frighten me as they did when I was young, so that was that much done. (*EA* 306–307)

For some, the subjects of politics and childhood may make for strange bedfellows, but for Stein they are importantly intertwined. She slips seamlessly from questions about identity to questions about the national landscape. *Geographical History*'s proper, long title says as much by positing as its initial subject the "Geographical History of America" and then offering to rename it (with the crucial conjunctive "or") "the Relation of Human Nature to The Human Mind." National interiors become psychological interiors and vice versa. The goal of *Geographical History*, Stein writes, is "to get this trouble out of my system." The movement she emphasizes is from the inside out. The "trouble" goes by a variety of names including identity, and Mother Goose, and America, but altogether these are the lessons and the homes (local and national) internalized in childhood. National and personal identity, geography and psychology, meet for Stein in this vision of her former, American-child self. The realization that she is no longer, now that she is an American grown-up in France, "frighten[ed]" as she was when she "was a little one" marks a point of accomplishment for Stein. She remarks, "so that was that much done."

Beyond *Geographical History*, this passage strongly anticipates *The World is Round* of the following year, a book that takes up the childhood meditation on the problem of the round world far more centrally. In fact *The World is Round* does much more work on the national anti-nostalgic front than does *Geographical History*. Though *The World is Round* has received little treatment as a political text, Stein, it seems, was intent on marketing it as such. In the fall of 1939, Scott Publishers proposed a second American lecture tour to Stein in order to promote the release of the children's book.[23] The second lecture tour never materialized, but Stein was enthusiastic about its prospects and began to think about a new series of lectures befitting the task. In an undated draft letter to John McCullough Stein proposes a series of titles for this new lecture series. The very first title on this list is especially intriguing, "The World as a Novel or Meditations About Government."[24] Here Stein reproduces the double-title structure of *A Geographical History of America or the Relation of Human Nature to the Human Mind* in order to insist on another equally strange, equally ironic analogy. In this case, the lecture title implicitly rejects the place of *The World is Round* as mere children's book and claims shelf space for that title among the works of public policy, history, and political science. The second title on this proposed list,

"The World is Round for Children and Grown-ups, two different lectures depending upon the audience," underscores the generic complexity that Stein imagined for this text. Indeed, a further proposed lecture title, "An American in France," contributes to the overall sense that Stein hoped to promote *The World is Round* as a children's text with a substantial national, political, and grown-up subtext.[25]

In addition to being semi-autobiographical, Rose's journey up the mountain in *The World is Round* may also be more than a little allegorical. The text's numerous allusions to Dante—from Rose's Devil-encounter to her mountain pilgrimage—certainly invite this comparison. When considered a part of the sequence of texts (I won't call it a trilogy) beginning with *Geographical History* and continuing through *Paris France*, the journey of Rose in *The World is Round* is suggestively framed as the center of a journey undertaken by Stein away from the geographies, memories, and ideologies of America toward those embraced and personified, from Stein's point of view, by France. Set in France, based in large measure on Stein's 10-year-old French neighbor Rose D'Aiguy, with a nod as well to Francis Rose, the French painter and friend Stein first chose to illustrate *World* before choosing Clement Hurd, *The World is Round* was crafted as a very French book.[26] Even more to the point, it was crafted as a very French book for an American audience since *World* was solicited by an American publisher for publication in America.

World's French bias is more understated in the actual content of the story, but Rose's decision to recognize and to work with, not against the round world, by writing cyclically and in full circle "*Rose is a Rose is a Rose*" around the trunk of a tree, aligns her, however subtly, with Stein's vision of France and distances her even more importantly from the American point of view. In *Paris France*, which Stein wrote in the year after *The World is Round* and which also began as a children's narrative (and may have remained one in Stein's view), the French, Stein writes, know that the world is round.[27] They know that the world is round, and they are attached to the earth, a set of claims which Stein uses to emphasize French realism. "[T]he French do not make much lyrical poetry," Stein writes; "they do not get away from the earth enough to look at it, they paint it, but they do not poeticize it" (62). In contrast to the French, in contrast to Rose in *World*, Stein wonders in *Paris France*: "Is it possible that America does not know that the world is round" (44). In *Geographical History* Stein praised America for the flatness of its geography: "only flat land a great deal of flat land is connected with the human mind and so America is connected with the human mind" (388). And in *Everybody's Autobiography* of the following year she likewise compared the Midwestern landscape, as seen from her airplane window, to a cubist painting (198). In each of these instances Stein linked the geographical flatness of America's landscape to the human mind and to the genius of modernist art. Stein's attitude toward American flatness changes radically and in short order through *World* and into *Paris France*. The phony war intervenes, and now Stein wonders critically if America does not know that the world is round "because there is no threat of war" in America as there is in Europe (44–45). Wars for Stein are important temporal forces that have the effect of catching societies up to the present moment. Stein observes that wars "only make anybody know what has already happened it has happened already the war only makes it public makes those who like illustrations of anything see that it has been happening" (*EA* 76). Reading between the lines, it is evident that the threat of war has affected Stein deeply. Her claim that it has not affected her home nation, whether true or not, speaks to her sense of a widening gap between them.

For Stein, who has always prided herself on living in the present moment, it is possible that America, without the threat of war, belongs to a past century. But this new antiquated image of America is, in another sense, a logical extension of her work in *Everybody's Autobiography* and in *Geographical History* "to get this trouble out of [her] system." Stein has been working for some time to align America with her past—autobiographically and cognitively. Now America belongs to the past atavistically as well. And in this way America has become even more analogously linked in Stein's writing and thinking to childhood; neither has learned that the world is round; both embody the past. If Stein's second American lecture tour had materialized, it is not very difficult to imagine just how different it might have been from the first. Stein's disenchantment with America, which had only begun near the end of her first tour, had reached its peak by the time she had finished *The World is Round*, was beginning *Paris France*, and was planning the second tour in the fall of 1939. If Stein indeed felt that America needed a closer proximity to war in order to be brought out of a lyrical, Mother-Goose past, it is possible that she viewed the second lecture tour and the wartime children's narratives it was designed to promote as vehicles to bring the war to America and to American children.

This is an argument that calls upon a synthesized, intertextual reading of children's narrativity throughout Stein's wartime writings—regardless of shelf genre—and it is an argument that can only surface by taking the violence in these narratives seriously. By and large when post-modernist scholars have noted the childlike language in Stein's late modernist writings these observations have lent support to the view that Stein failed to take the atrocities of the Second World War seriously, that her literature evinces a tendency toward escapism and fantasy, and worse that it highlights hers as a politics of collaboration. To write about Stein's Second World War literature is to respond to a paradox: that Stein, herself a Jew and a lesbian, stayed in France (despite ample opportunity to leave for America), lived in the midst of the German occupation, and nonetheless survived and apparently survived without great or even terribly minor suffering. Stein and Toklas we now know owed their lives and livelihoods to Bernard Faÿ, a long-time friend who negotiated their safety with the Vichy leader, Maréchal Pétain. In the absence of strong evidence to the contrary, Stein's lasting friendship with Bernard Faÿ has had the effect of confounding Stein's wartime views, which are mostly ambiguous, with Faÿ's unquestionable sympathies with the German Nazi movement.[28]

Even writers who seem to want to read Stein's World War II writings the way others of Stein's works are read, without the need for moral judgment, nonetheless cave at some point in the process and acknowledge somewhere along the line that Stein's politics, if not her writing, were irresponsible and worse. What I find especially problematic in many of these arguments is the degree to which the children's narrativity of Stein's wartime texts seems to become the clear and obvious target for this kind of moral qualification. Stein's lack of seriousness about the war goes hand-in-hand in too many of these accounts with the seemingly obvious lack of seriousness of narratives for children.

Early on, Stein's fellow modernists and modernist critics may have helped to set the definitive tone about her work of this period. When asked to review two children's books of 1939—Gertrude Stein's *The World is Round* and T.S. Eliot's *Old Possum's Book of Practical Cats*—Edmund Wilson passed on the task but not before publishing a prefatory piece to express his "baffle[ment]" at the assignment and not before publishing his non-review view that he "had difficulty getting through Stein's book." Worse, Wilson goes on to disparage and dismiss the larger modernist trend of writing for children. Observing that many modernists have published recent children's books, including Stein, Eliot, Kay Boyle and E.E. Cummings, Wilson expresses his dismay: "I don't know what this means—except that they evidently do not feel at the moment that they have anything better to do" (qtd. in Curnutt, *Critical Response* 115).

Despite being the editor for this collection of critical responses to Stein's work, Kirk Curnutt suggests a more muted, but still kindred reaction to the overflow of childhood narratives and language into Stein's adult literature of the thirties. To bolster his argument that Stein's expressions of writer's block and of her "anxieties toward celebrity" (296), following the success of *The Autobiography of Alice B. Toklas*, are more rhetorical than serious, Curnutt opens his essay by citing the "nursery doggerel" in *Geographical History* ("Inside and Outside" 291). Though references to this child language and even to *Geographical History* are almost nonexistent elsewhere in the essay, beginning with them sets Curnutt's case before the reader in the manner of a seemingly obvious case-in-point. To express anxiety in the terms of a nursery rhyme apparently proves, full stop, that that anxiety is not to be taken seriously.

In line with scholars like Curnutt and Galow, who have argued that Stein's 1930s anxiety was a mere rhetorical flourish, or with the critic, Wilson, who assessed that she must have had nothing better to do, readers of Stein's wartime writing have used the features of childhood and children's narrative embedded within them as evidence of Stein's immoral lack of seriousness in the face of an imminent or ongoing catastrophic violence. Even many of those critics who set out to be less moralizing and less judgmental about Stein's wartime emphasis on "daily living" apparently cannot find a way to excuse the interjections of childhood into these texts. As an example, Zofia Lesinska's assessment of the child-adult hybrid *Paris France* (1940), a text which has received remarkably little critical attention, is worth discussing at length. "At first glance," she writes, the text "seems to be offensively trivial" (324). And Lesinska quotes the opening paragraph which reads as follows:

> PARIS, FRANCE is exciting and peaceful.
>
> I was only four years old when I was first in Paris and talked French there and was photographed there and went to school there, and ate soup for early breakfast, and had leg of mutton and spinach for lunch, I always liked spinach, and a black cat jumped on my mother's back. That was more exciting than peaceful. I do not mind cats but I do not like them to jump on my back. (1)

Lesinska's set up to this passage, that "at first glance" the text "seems to be offensively trivial," leads the reader to expect a second, deeper, and alternative look. But for Lesinska, and others, the deeper conclusion to be drawn is not that the passage is not trivial but that such "political escapism" was common in "those days" (325). Similarly, Liesl Olson, who seeks to rehabilitate Stein's wartime habits as a more radical representation of pleasure during war, hits a wall when it comes to the child elements of Stein's wartime novel, *Mrs. Reynolds*. In this case, Olson argues that "the nursery rhyming of Stein's style works against the acknowledgement of any real threat" (109) and concludes that "Stein's celebration of the Reynoldses' habits identifies a dangerous kind of self-absorption." Ultimately, Olson's assessment echoes Lesinska and others that Stein's wartime writing "illuminates an extremely problematic escapism" (113).

Part of what sets readers off in Stein's wartime writings, as John Whittier-Ferguson has observed, is their way of vacillating between two voices, two different registers of writing. Whereas in one moment Stein can seem to be writing in a "referential" mode that is engaged with the concrete circumstances of the occupation and the war, in the next her writing can take an "anti-referential" turn that makes her seem detached from these same material realities. Though Whittier-Ferguson does not stress the point, implicitly it is not just any anti-referential voice but Stein's particular "infantile narrative voice," as Lesinska terms it, that piques readers' frustration (324). Take, for example, another passage from *Paris France* where Stein introduces a description of the French order for mobilization by noting just how much she "like[s] words of one syllable." The order, referencing "the army de terre, de mer et de l'air," she comments "works out well" and "is very impressive when you read it in every village" (65). As Whittier-Ferguson rightly points out, this reading "'works out well' if one reads this proclamation of nationwide conscription purely as a collection of words on a government notice…Here, as is so often the case, Stein courts furious accusations from readers who are more directly caught up either in the machinery of war itself or who will resent as unpatriotic this aesthetic attention to words instead of a more direct embrace of their stirring reference to battle" (409–410). Similarly, for Lesinska "the dissonance between the gravity of the political situation during the phony war of 1939–1940…and the rather lighthearted tone of the narrative voice" is understandably unsettling to readers for whom the latter voice must seem "intolerably superficial" despite Lesinska's own correction that the narrator of *Paris France* may not be Stein herself and may even be an unreliable narrator (324).

Where I differ with both of these important revisionary readings of Stein is in the presumption that Stein's language in these moments is either "lighthearted" or "anti-referential." To be sure, in the conscription passage cited above Stein's language is child-inflected in its appreciation for words of one syllable as well as in its appreciation for rhyme—"terre" "mer" and "air," but in what immediately follows this description Stein suggests that she has grasped something, through this seemingly simplistic and superficial observation, that is in fact profound. What Stein notes is that these orders will be effective because they are posted in a nation and in a time that longs for organization to such a degree that ordinary individuals, adults no less, are quite willing to take the place of the conventional child and let the government take authority out of their hands—to order and to organize them. The very next paragraph reads, "It could be a puzzle why the intellectuals in every country are always wanting a form of government which would inevitably treat them badly" (65). In other words, it is possible to read the role of children's narratives—brought to the fore so conspicuously by Stein herself—as a challenge to uncritical thinking. Stein may appreciate, like the child of convention, words of one syllable, but she is not taken in, like this same child construct, by their propagandist, patriotic, and reductively simple display.

Where so much of the scholarly criticism around Stein's thirties expressions of anxiety have sought to minimize them as the rhetorical tropes of modernist celebrity culture, so much of the scholarly criticism around Stein's forties wartime literature has worried about the lack of such expressions, has wondered about the moral implications of a wartime literature, particularly during the Second World War, that does not display as outwardly as possible the tragic sympathies required for such a tragic time in our global history. Thus, where readers of Stein's thirties literature, following *Alice B. Toklas*, seem to feel that Stein's anxiety is over expressed, to the point of insincerity, readers of her forties literature feel that there is hardly enough anxiety to go around. But there may not be as wide a gulf between these two sets of readings as might at first seem to be the case. Rather, each appears to be reacting, in part, to the same sorts of child identifications, narratives, and expressions within Stein's work. Where in the former decade such expressions lend themselves to interpretations of superficial play, in the latter they produce a far deeper sensation of insult. In both cases, the language of children's narratives suggests a lack of seriousness—ranging, respectively, from the rhetorical to the immoral.

What many of these arguments miss is that the lack of serious maturity is precisely the mentality that Stein is working, through children's narrations, to parody. Though many scholars have noted Stein's affinities for childhood, few have noted her serious political view that children should have the right to vote ("Transatlantic Interview" 16–17). Few likewise have noted that her late criticism of America and her condemnation of Germany rest alike on her perception of these nations as embodying the very childhood mentality that she had come to reject as a fiction of Mother Goose proportions. Stein describes how her meditations on the problem of feeling and remembering the past (which is also the inner) self lead her to question the role and purpose of childhood—"what is the use of being a little boy if you are to be a man"—and moreover lead her "to meditate more...on the subject of history and newspapers and politics" (306–307). On the heels of *Geographical History* and *The World is Round*, Stein concludes that the question "what is the use of being a boy if you are growing up to be a man" is a national problem for countries like America that continue to place enormous cultural stock into ideologies of youth. The French have resolved the question and the problem, Stein writes, by collapsing the boy into the man. Just two years after *Geographical History*, Stein reflects in *Paris France*, "I once wrote and said what is the use of being a boy if you are to grow up to be a man what is the use and what is the use" as if these questions have been placed utterly behind her. And they have been placed there by her subsequent realization that "in France a boy is a man of his age the age he is and so there is no question of a boy growing up to be a man and what is the use" because "a Frenchman is always a man" (26–27).

Stein expands upon this dichotomy between America and France in her wartime essays where she contrasts America's "facile optimism" with France's phoenix-like mentality. With more than a hint of disparagement, Stein hones in on the American industrial era "between Roosevelt and Roosevelt" and characterizes it as a period and a people forebodingly shaped by "easy wars, easy victories, easy success, easy money, easy eating and easy drinking and easy madly running around and easy publicity, easy everything" ("The New Hope" 142–143). In this essay, which Stein calls, "The New Hope in Our 'Sad Young Men,'" the young men of the First World War era are "sad" because for them "life began early" and "success was great." After 30, Stein asks, "what was there to do"? Then answers, "nothing." For these young men, for this "lost generation" as Stein also calls them in this essay, "life had ended by 30" (142). The French, in clear contrast, are distinguished for Stein because they do not "like that life is too easy." Rather, "they like, like the phoenix, to rise from the ashes. They really do believe that those that win lose" ("The Winner Loses" 129).

This last reference to "those that win" clearly alludes to America whose "easy success[es]," Stein believes, have set the stage for an entire "lost generation" ("New Hope" 142–143). But it also points the finger at Germany. In fact the essay "The Winner Loses" is explicitly about the German occupation of France. This essay never pronounces outright that the "winner" who will "lose" is Germany, a fact that is understandable given its 1940 publication date. Rather, Stein focuses on France as Germany's alter-ego, as the loser who will win. In talking with the young men around Bilgnin, Stein finds that they are "very pleased" with the armistice, choosing to view the occupation as an interim of suffering, a period of oppression necessary to endure, in a long battle for French liberty. The young Frenchmen seem to have embraced the Nietzschean sentiment, "that which does not kill us makes us stronger." Stein paraphrases their sentiment that "if they had had an easy victory," the vices of weakness these youth feel they had begun to indulge in peacetime "would have been weaker." The war, they actually feel, has intervened in their and France's potential degeneration. "[A]nd now," Stein says, speaking for these youth, "—well, now there is really something to do—they have to make France itself again and there is a future" (131).[29] In contrast to the French who Stein imagines as understanding the necessity and value of "setbacks," Stein writes in *Wars I Have Seen* that "people like the Germans never understand that, they dream fairy tales where everything is as it was or was not, and they make music which makes them feel like that but the French know that you must not succeed you must rise from the ashes and how could you rise from the ashes if there were no ashes" (105).

Many have argued that Stein's politics leaned increasingly conservative in the World War II era, but Stein's broader sense that America and Germany share more in common than not during the wartime era is and was a controversial position of the left. Certainly, Stein opposed what we might now call "big government." She was a staunch antagonist to the Roosevelt administration and was at best ambivalent about Pétain's collaboration with Germany during the war. In *Wars I Have Seen* Stein confessed that she, like France, had "so many points of view" about Pétain (93) but felt on the whole that the Vichy leader deserved credit for "saving France" and "defeating Germany" (92). But Stein's politics are complicated. Not only does she make the far-left argument that children should have the right to vote but the tenor of her Rooseveltian disdain can be radically feminist as when she compares Roosevelt to Hitler, Stalin, and Mussolini in an argument against the spread of patriarchy (implicitly linked to tyranny, empire, and oppression). "There is too much fathering going on just now," Stein writes in *Everybody's Autobiography*. "Everybody nowadays is a father, there is father Mussolini and father Hitler and father Roosevelt and father Stalin and father Lewis and father Blum and father Franco is just commencing now and there are ever so many more ready to be one. Fathers are depressing" (137).[30] Though Stein never places America and Germany side-by-side in her writings, she makes nearly identical remarks about each nation, albeit in separate texts, and likewise contrasts each nation in similar terms, but again in separate texts, with France. In *Paris France*, it is America that lives in the past. In *Wars I Have Seen*, it is Germany. In *Wars I Have Seen*, Germany is the "boy" nation, stuck in a "fairy tale" imaginary.[31] In *Everybody's Autobiography* and *Paris France*, America (and Stein herself) is the child, who does not yet know that the world is round, still trying to make sense of the self in Mother Goose terms. In *Wars I Have Seen*, Germany is the nation that continues to believe in empire and Esperanto and the "white man's burden." But in "The New Hope in Our 'Sad Young Men,'" relinquishing "the white man's burden" is an American problem (145).

Late modernism, exemplified in part by Stein's wartime writing, dramatically shifts course from the fields of innovation and resistance that so marked modernism at its height. Though interest in late modernism has grown substantially, many scholars have noted the appearance, at least, of a favoritism in modernist studies toward modernism's emergence—when aesthetic resistance was highlighted as an integral part of the modernist paradigm. As Rebecca Walkowitz and Douglas Mao have eloquently observed: for many there is nothing quite so "good" as "bad" modernism. In contrast to the experimental anarchist energies of early and high modernism, late modernism can seem radically conservative. In the same way that readers confront T.S. Eliot's late religious conversion or Ezra Pound's fascist ideologies, many confront Stein's late modernist life and work with dismay. It is nearly inconceivable that this avant-garde, feminist, lesbian, Jewish woman could develop and indeed use to her advantage a friendship like the one Stein maintained with Bernard Faÿ, a known anti-Semite and collaborationist. But if Stein's wartime life strains understanding, her writing is at least as taxing for most. Stein's children's narrativity is disorienting if not also offensive, particularly when it is intermingled and interspersed throughout her writings on the German occupation of France. With the exception of *The World is Round*, Stein's children's books are almost universally unconscionable as such. In fact, Stein's children's literature and her wartime writings are unconscionable for the same reason. In the same way that the children's literature assaults the nostalgic ideals of childhood,

Stein's wartime writing may too represent an assault on the nostalgic ideals of modernism. The broad academic oversight of Stein's children's literature and the criticism of her late wartime writings may be two pieces of a nostalgic whole. The first upholds the ideals of childhood as the assuredly unserious counterpart to the serious atrocities of war. The second upholds a past literary tradition of modernist resistance, particularly in the face of war.

Where childhood represents one kind of nostalgic home; early modernism represents another. Stein, I have endeavored to show, violently dismantles both. As Marina MacKay has argued "the soldier poets of the Great War set the standard by which the literature of the second war was judged wanting" (5). But if there is a child of modernism more unpreferred than late modernism, it is, as expressed most explicitly by Edmund Wilson, late modernism's writing for children. Here writers like Stein appear to commit a double-effrontery: they seem to exchange their earlier efforts at avant-garde resistance for another, apparently ordinary set of clothes, and they appear to change in their trademark difficulty for the generic equivalent of easy reading. And yet to really read Stein's children's books and children's narratives (as few actually have) is to discover that there is nothing easy about them. In fact, in an ironic turn of logic, what's quintessentially "easy" for Stein is high modernism. It is an odd turn of events, but Stein's late work may prove more radical than many have been willing to consider. Stein's wartime writings not only challenge American imperialism, not only question the "difficulty" of early modernism, but they also question the value of childhood and youth as an epicenter for American and modernist consciousness in the twentieth century.

Notes

1. These phrases recur in various forms in Stein's writings. The precise wording used here for the Mother Goose line can be found in *Geographical History* (401); the line questioning the use of boyhood can also be found in *Geographical History* (370); and the world is round line can be found in *The World is Round* (2).
2. In *Voracious Children*, Carolyn Daniel describes two important cultural narratives that lay behind the cannibalism of children in children's fairy tales. Citing Marianne Rumpf, she describes one of these as a caution to children against strangers, cast in the roles of witches, werewolves, and ogres. Another, according to Daniel was to represent the problems of widespread famine in which the cannibalism of the child is sometimes (though not always) a euphemism for the abandonment of children by their parents ("Hairy on the Inside" 145–146).

3. Lisi Schoenbach has illuminated the experimental, "shock[ing]" deployment of habits and habitual writing in Stein's "pragmatic" modernism. Schoenbach argues that "Stein takes as one of her most serious engagements the duty of rendering habit visible: from the minutiae of daily life, to textual 'habits' such as punctuation and cliché, to the habits that constitute national identity, to the collective habits of thought that create institutions and literary canons. Even Stein's most radically experimental works famously achieve their difficulty through repetitions. Her readers face not shocks *per se* but habit made visible through sheer exaggeration" (245).
4. Barbara Will, for one, takes this description by Stein at face value as evidence for the "escapist" quality of Stein's children's literature ("'And Then'" 343). Nor is Will alone. Escapism is a term that often comes up in accounts of Stein's wartime writing of this period. Many would agree with Liesl Olson that "Stein's response to World War II was to keep her life as consistent and as pleasurable as possible" (91). And Gill Plain points out that escapist literature grew in general during the second world war (14–15).
5. Many of Van Vechten and Stein's letters were apparently lost to each other in the heightened atmosphere of surveillance and hampered transatlantic communications of this wartime period. Van Vechten frequently complains in his letters to Stein of this period that he "write[s] and write[s] and cable[s] and cable[s]" Stein "but nothing seems to get through" (11 September 1940, printed in *The Letters of Gertrude Stein and Carl Van Vechten*). Stein herself responds to Van Vechten about the publication of *To Do* by mailing out multiple versions of the same letter to him on the same day. Edward Burns notes that "one possible explanation for this is that Stein was deeply concerned about the publication of this book and she wanted to make sure that at least one message got through to Van Vechten" (685).
6. This method is not unique to Stein's children's narratives. As Marianne DeKoven has shown, Stein's experimental writing, at every stage of her career, frequently staged itself as the very thing that it sought to subvert. She "titles 'Patriarchal Poetry,'" for example, "with the name of what its writing demolishes: sense, coherence, lucidity, hierarchical order…" (*A Different Language* 129).
7. Barbara Will's work on Stein is a notable exception.
8. In "A Transatlantic Interview" Stein links her work in *Tender Buttons* with her current work in writing children's books as some her best poetic work (23).
9. The passages by Laura Riding (132) and Dr. Schmalhausen (133) are quoted in Karen Leick's article on "Gertrude Stein and the Making of Celebrity." Robert Warshow's tribute (140) can be found in full in Kirk Curnutt's *The Critical Response to Gertrude Stein*.

10. In "A Transatlantic Interview," Stein expresses her belief that "Just as everybody has the vote, including the women, I think children should, because as soon as a child is conscious of itself, then it has to me an existence and has a stake in what happens" (17).
11. Asked to respond, for example, to Sir George Frampton's statue of Peter Pan in Kensington Gardens (commissioned and paid for by Barrie), Barrie nonetheless expressed his dissatisfaction that "It doesn't show the Devil in Peter" (qtd. in Birkin 202).
12. Thomas Cooley argues that Stein's little dog and little boy discourses concern two different periods in the psychological history of identity. Pre-1865, Cooley explains that American psychology largely viewed the child mind as an adult in embryo. The characteristics of the adult are already present in the child but require cultivation. Identity in this model is predominantly fixed. Modern psychology, by contrast, begins to embrace the notion of development. In this model, the self is evolving and cumulative. Cooley rightly concludes that Stein rejects both of these narratives of education, but his rationale, that Stein rejects them because she prefers a model of youth, uncultivated and undeveloped, rests, I think, on some of Stein's earlier philosophies of youth, views which have changed rather sharply by the time she comes to deconstruct these two particular narratives from/of childhood.
13. This statement appears 23 pages into the original manuscript held in the Beinecke Rare Book and Manuscript Library at Yale University and is used here with permission by the Estate of Gertrude Stein.
14. The original manuscript of *A Geographical History of America* is held in the Beinecke Rare Book and Manuscript Library at Yale University and is used here with permission by the Estate of Gertrude Stein.
15. William James's *Principles of Psychology* (1890) described the concept of double consciousness in a manner consistent with its psychological history as a pathological "mutation of the self," characterized by a "double" or "alternating personality" (379).
16. The first version of *The World is Round* was "The Autobiography of Rose," composed in 1937. By the time Margaret Wise Brown, through Scott Publishers, wrote to Stein asking her if she would be interested in writing a book for children, Stein was fortuitously well underway on her manuscript of *World*. Though Scott Publishers sent similar requests to Hemingway and Steinbeck, only Stein wrote back with an enthusiastic yes. For a fuller account of this history see Leonard Marcus's biography of Margaret Wise Brown.
17. Stein first wrote "Rose is a rose is a rose is a rose" in "Sacred Emily" in 1913, but the expression is popularized and indeed becomes emblematic of Stein and her style as the circular seal on the cover of *The Autobiography of Alice B. Toklas.*

18. Stein describes her passion for mountain hikes with some regularity throughout her career. It is also a common, heroic, genius, and saintly goal in her writings—as most famously expressed in *Four Saints in Three Acts*—to "be seated and not surrounded."
19. These are draft lines that ultimately end up in chapter 3, "Eyes a Surprise." Stein writes in a circle around the white space of Sawyer's letter: "Rose sang as the rabbit ran/And her song that began/My/What a sky/And then the glass pen (Rose did have a glass pen)/When oh say when/Little glass pen/ say when will there not/ be that little rabbit/ When then pen/ And Rose burst into tears."
20. Will has written a book length study of Stein's relationship with Bernard Faÿ and her wartime politics in which she argues, in part, that "there is little doubt that Stein's support for Pétain was authentic" (*Unlikely Collaboration* 143). But Stein herself introduces doubt on this subject in *Wars I Have Seen* when she writes: "And then there was Pétain. So many points of view about him, so very many. I had lots of them, I was almost French in having so many" (82). To support these many views Stein later gives Pétain credit for saving France (92), but she also compares his desire for an ordered state to "the point of view of a crazy man at the end of the last war in 1918…" (81).
21. We may even call *World* a revisionist fairy tale in the feminist sense. In conflating the conventional ending of a children's fairy tale with the conventional ending of the domestic novel, it is not only possible, but likely, that Stein is enacting a double parody of each of these genres. Though I have focused on the children's narrative aspect of *World*'s parodic efforts, there is more to be said about *World*'s subversive potential. Linda Watts's reading of *World*, in fact, marks one of the first significant efforts to identify the gender-transgressive aspects of Stein's children's literature.
22. Jack Zipes writes that a nearly universal purpose of the modern fairy tale is "to provide hope in a world seemingly on the brink of catastrophe" (1). The "once upon a time" of the fairy tale, he goes on to say, "keeps alive our utopian longings for a better world that can be created out of our dreams and actions" (79).
23. On October 9, 1939 John McCullough, editor for Scott Publishers, sent Stein a letter in which he reports that he has consulted with Carl Van Vechten about a second tour, and he offers a list of ideas that he has for such a venture.
24. Stein's letter to McCullough is held in the Beinecke Rare Book and Manuscript Library at Yale University and is used here with permission by the Estate of Gertrude Stein.
25. This letter may have been written in response to John McCullough's October 9, 1939 letter cited above. Specifically, it may have been intended

as a response to number eight on McCullough's list of ideas and questions regarding the tour. Number eight read: "I have asked various people on what subjects they would like to hear you lecture, and enclose the list, which might help you with your ideas: a. Children and children's books. b. Picasso and art…c. Writing. d. Several thought that your views on Shakespeare or critical lectures on other writers classic and modern would be very exciting. e. Many people would like to hear you comment on the European situation. f. If I could work out a lecture for the Metropolitan Opera Guild or in music schools on words and music, would it interest you?…" Stein's lecture ideas, including others titled "Music and large and small countries and civil wars" and "Why I still like painting," appear to address specific items from this earlier request. Both letters are found in YCAL MSS 76, Box 131, Folder 2861.
26. It did not take long for Stein to become fond of Hurd's illustrations as well. She was especially excited by the possibility that some of his illustrations were to be used on rugs and wallpaper to promote the book. For an excellent, behind-the-scenes account of *World* publication see Edith Thacher Hurd's Afterword, "The World is Not Flat," which can be found where it first appeared in the North Point Press printing of *The World is Round* as well as in the newer, 2013 Harper Design edition.
27. Stein appears to compare much of her late wartime writing to children's narratives and children's poetry in "A Transatlantic Interview." Sometimes these comparisons are ambiguous as when she says that "I became more and more interested in the subject of narration…and the bulk of my work since then, has been largely narration, and I had done children's stories. I think *Paris, France* and *Wars I have Seen* are the most successful of this" (19). Here it is unclear if Stein is referencing "narration" or "children's stories," but it is tempting to read into even the confusion between the two. Later, she makes a clearer comparison when she says that most of her recent poetry has been children's poetry and then remarks that "in *Paris, France* there is quite a bit of it, but that is mainly dealing with children" (23).
28. Barbara Will's *Unlikely Collaboration* is the most extensive effort correlating Stein's politics with Faÿ's. Janet Malcolm's *Two Lives* offers a slightly different perspective. While Malcolm uncovers even more abundant evidence for Faÿ's crimes during the war, she appears to agree with Edward Burns that it was unlikely that Stein or Toklas knew about Faÿ's role (99–100). Malcolm also provides a key example of just how easy it is to misread Stein's ambiguous intentions in the wartime context. The case involves an orphan Jewish child, whose adoption—it was initially reported—Stein opposed. But more evidence has uncovered not only that the safety of this child was not in danger but that what Stein opposed was the particular adults who wished to adopt the child. She felt that a Jewish child needed to be adopted by a Jewish family (185–190).

29. The reason I am hesitant to cite Stein's quotations of these youth without qualification is because the syntax and style is so completely Steinian. "And now" is an expression so favored that it titles an earlier essay by Stein; likewise, Stein is so fond of illuminating things "to do" that that expression also serves as the main title for her children's book: *To Do: A Book of Alphabets and Birthdays*. Stein may be paraphrasing the reflections of French youth, but the words are hers which opens the possibility that the ideas may be as well.
30. It's also worth remembering that there were significant reasons for members of the gay community to oppose F.D.R. who spear-headed the witch-hunt for homosexual civilians and sailors in Newport, Rhode Island in 1919–1921, a scandal that led to the Senate's (ironic) recommendation that F.D.R. should never again hold public office.
31. Stein associates the Germans with a fairy tale mentality on page 105. Several pages later, she refers to Germany as "small boyish." In context, Stein is describing a German radio speaker she has heard who has the audacity to call England a subhuman cruel nation because it permits the use of birth control. Stein assesses this speaker and his country flatly: "And so he goes on and so they go on...and in the midst of all the misery it is not childish but very small boyish. It is strange the world to-day is not adult it has the mental development of a seven year old boy just about that. Dear me" (121).

Works Cited

Adorno, Theodor. *Minima Moralia: Reflections from Damaged Life*. Trans. E.F.N. Jephcott. New York: Verso, 1951. Print.

Agosto, Denise E. "One and Inseparable: Interdependent Storytelling in Picture Storybooks." *Children's Literature in Education* 30.4 (1999): 267–280. *Academic Search Premier*. Web. 25 Mar. 2012.

Alridge, Derrick P. *The Educational Thought of W.E.B. Du Bois: An Intellectual History*. New York: Teachers College, 2008. Print.

Andrews, Steve. "Toward a Synaesthetics of Soul: W.E.B. Du Bois and the Teleology of Race." *Re-Cognizing W.E.B. Du Bois in the Twenty-First Century*. Eds. Mary Keller and Chester J. Fontenot, Jr. Macon: Mercer UP, 2007. 142–185. Print.

Ariès, Philippe. *Centuries of Childhood: A Social History of Family Life*. Trans. Robert Baldick. New York: Vintage-Random, 1962. Print.

Ashton, Jennifer. "Gertrude Stein for Anyone." *ELH*. 64.1 (1997): 289–331. *JSTOR*. Web. 24 Mar. 2012.

Bader, Barbara. "American Picture Books: From Max's Metaphorical Monsters to Lilly's Purple Plastic Purse." *Horn Book Magazine* 74.2 (1998): 141–156. *Academic Search Premier*. Web. 25 Mar. 2012.

Baldwin, James. "My Dungeon Shook: Letter to My Nephew." *James Baldwin: Collected Essays*. New York: Library of America, 1998. 291–295. Print.

Balfour, Lawrie. *Democracy's Reconstruction: Thinking Politically with W.E.B. Du Bois*. New York: Oxford UP, 2011. Print.

Barnes, Djuna. "Djuna Barnes Probes the Souls of Jungle Folk at the Hippodrome Circus." *New York*. Ed. Alyce Barry. Los Angeles: Sun & Moon P, 1989. 190–197. Print.

---. *Nightwood: The Original Version and Related Drafts*. Ed. Cheryl J. Plumb. Normal: Dalkey Archive P, 1995. Print.

Barrie, J.M. *Peter Pan: Peter and Wendy and Peter Pan in Kensington Gardens*. New York: Penguin, 2004. Print.

Baudelaire, Charles. "The Painter of Modern Life." *The Painter of Modern Life and Other Essays*. Ed and Trans. Jonathan Mayne. New York: Phaidon, 1995. 1–41. Print.

Bay-Cheng, Sarah. *Mama Dada: Gertrude Stein's Avant-Garde Theater*. New York: Routledge, 2004. Print.

Bell, Michael. "The metaphysics of Modernism." *The Cambridge Companion to Modernism*. Ed. Michael Levenson. New York: Cambridge UP, 1999. 9–32. Print.

Bengels, Barbara. "The Term of the 'Screw': Key to Imagery in Henry James's *The Turn of the Screw*." *Studies in Short Fiction*. 15.3 (1978): 323–327. *Academic Search Premier*. 27 Mar. 2012.

Benjamin, Walter. *The Arcades Project*. Trans. Howard Eiland and Kevin McLaughlin. Cambridge: Belknap, 1999. Print.

---. "Art in the Age of Mechanical Reproduction." *The Nineteenth-Century Visual Culture Reader*. Eds. Vanessa R. Schwartz and Jeannene M. Przyblyski. New York: Routledge, 2004. 63–70. Print.

---. *Berlin Childhood around 1900*. trans. Howard Eiland. Cambridge: Harvard UP, 2006. Print.

Benstock, Shari. "Djuna Barnes: Rue St.-Romain." *Women of the Left Bank: Paris, 1900–1940*. Austin: U of Texas P, 1986. 230–267. Print.

Bernstein, Robin. *Racial Innocence: Performing American Childhood from Slavery to Civil Rights*. New York: New York UP, 2011. Print.

Birkin, Andrew. *J.M. Barrie and the Lost Boys*. New Haven, Yale UP, 2003. Print.

Bishop, Rudine Sims. "For the Children of the Sun: African American Children's Literature Begins to Bloom." *Free Within Ourselves: The Development of African American Children's Literature*. Portsmouth: Heinemann, 2007. 21–43. Web. 7 Jul. 2012.

Blackall, Jean Frantz "Moral Geography in *What Maisie Knew*." *University of Toronto Quarterly: A Canadian Journal of the Humanities*. 48.2 (1978): 130–148. *Academic Search Premier*. Web. 27 Mar. 2012.

Blanchot, Maurice. "The Turn of the Screw." *The Siren's Song: Selected Essays by Maurice Blanchot*. Ed. Gabriel Josipovici. Trans. Sacha Rabinovitch. Bloomington: Indiana UP, 1982. Print.

Blyn, Robin. "*Nightwood*'s Freak Dandies: Decadence in the 1930s." *Modernism/modernity*. 15.3 (2008): 503–526. *Project Muse*. Web. 27 Mar. 2012.

Boas, George. *The Cult of Childhood*. Dallas: Spring, 1966. Print.

Bond, Horace Mann. *Freedomways: A Quarterly Review of the Negro Freedom Movement* 5.1 (1965): 16. Print.

"Books and Authors: Books of the Week." *Outlook* 13 Nov. 1897: 670. *American Periodicals Series Online.* Web. 24 Oct. 2009.
Boym, Svetlana. *The Future of Nostalgia.* New York: Basic Books, 2001. Print.
Bridgman, Richard. *Gertrude Stein in Pieces.* New York: Oxford UP, 1970. Print.
Britzolakis, Christina. "Technologies of Vision in Henry James's *What Maisie Knew.*" *Novel: A Forum on Fiction* 34.3 (2001): 369–390. *Academic Search Premier.* Web. 27 Mar. 2012.
Brooker, Peter. "Early Modernism." *The Cambridge Companion to the Modernist Novel.* Ed. Morag Shiach. New York: Cambridge UP, 2007. 32–47. Print.
Brown, Gillian. "Child's Play." *The American Child: A Cultural Studies Reader.* Eds. Caroline F. Levander and Carol J. Singley. New Brunswick: Rutgers UP, 2003. 13–39. Print.
The Brownies' Book. Advertisement. *The Crisis* Sep. 1919: 275. Print.
Burke, Carolyn. "'Accidental Aloofness': Barnes, Loy, and Modernism." *Silence and Power: A Reevaluation of Djuna Barnes.* Ed. Mary Lynn Broe. Carbondale: Southern Illinois UP, 1991. 67–79. Print.
Caselli, Daniella. "'Elementary, my dear Djuna': Unreadable Simplicity in Barnes's *Creatures in an Alphabet.*" *Critical Survey.* 13.3 (2001): 89–112. *Academic Search Premier.* Web. 27 Mar. 2012.
---. *Improper Modernism: Djuna Barnes's Bewildering Corpus.* Burlington: Ashgate, 2009. Print.
Chisholm, Dianne. "Obscene Modernism: Eros Noir and the Profane Illumination of Djuna Barnes." *American Literature.* 69.1 (1997): 167–206. *Academic Search Premier.* Web. 27 Mar. 2012.
Chopin, Kate. *The Awakening.* 1899. New York, Bantam Books, 1988. Print.
Coats, Karen. "Child-Hating: *Peter Pan* in the Context of Victorian Hatred." *J.M. Barrie's* Peter Pan *In and Out of Time: A Children's Classic at 100.* Eds. Donna R. White and C. Anita Tarr. Lanham: Scarecrow P, 2006. 3–22. Print.
Cole, Merrill. "Backwards Ventriloquy: The Historical Uncanny in Barnes's *Nightwood.*" *Twentieth-Century Literature.* 52.4 (2006): 391–412. *Academic Search Premier.* Web. 27 Mar. 2012.
"Comments on 'The Reader' by Gertrude Stein." 11 June 1941. MSS 76, Box 131, Folder 2861. Gertrude Stein and Alice B. Toklas Papers. Yale Collection of American Literature, Beinecke Rare Book and Manuscript Library, Yale University.
Cooley, Thomas. *Educated Lives: The Rise of Modern Autobiography in America.* Columbus: Ohio State UP, 1976. Print.
Cooppan, Vilashini. "The Double Politics of Double Consciousness: Nationalism and Globalism in *The Souls of Black Folk.*" *Public Culture.* 17.2 (2005): 299–318. *Duke UP Journals Online.* Web. 3 Jan. 2016.
Copeland, David. "The Innocent Children of *Nightwood* and Hayford Hall." *Hayford Hall: Hangovers, Erotics, and Modernist Aesthetics.* Eds. Elizabeth

Podnieks and Sandra Chait. Carbondale: Southern Illinois UP, 2005. 116–132. Print.

Coveney, Peter. *The Image of Childhood: The Individual and Society: A Study of the Theme in English Literature*. Baltimore: Penguin, 1967. Print.

Cox, Michael and R.A. Gilbert. Introduction. *Victorian Ghost Stories*. New York: Oxford UP, 1991. ix–xx. Print.

Crain, Patricia. *The Story of A: The Alphabetization of America from* The New England Primer *to* The Scarlet Letter. Stanford: Stanford UP, 2000. Print.

Crenshaw, Kimberle. "Mapping the Margins: Intersectionality, Politics, and Violence Against Women of Color." *Stanford Law Review* 43 (1991): 1241–1299. Web. 7 Jul. 2012.

Cross, Gary. *The Cute and the Cool: Wondrous Innocence and Modern American Children's Culture*. New York: Oxford UP, 2004. Print.

Curnutt, Kirk, ed. *The Critical Response to Gertrude Stein*. Westport: Greenwood P, 2000. Print.

---. "Inside and Outside: Gertrude Stein on Identity, Celebrity, and Authenticity." *Journal of Modern Literature*. 23.2 (1999): 291–308. *Project Muse*. Web. 26 Aug. 2010.

Cunningham, Hugh. *Children and Childhood in Western Society Since 1500*. 2nd ed. New York: Pearson, 2005. Print.

Daniel, Carolyn. *Voracious Children: Who Eats Whom in Children's Literature*. New York: Routledge, 2006. Print.

DeKoven, Marianne. *A Different Language: Gertrude Stein's Experimental Writing*. Madison: U of Wisconsin P, 1983. Print.

---. *Rich and Strange: Gender, History, Modernism*. Princeton: Princeton UP, 1991. Print.

de Lauretis, Teresa. "*Nightwood* and the 'Terror of Uncertain Signs.'" *Critical Inquiry*. 34 (2008): 117–129. *University of Chicago Press*. Web. 27 Mar. 2012.

de Man, Paul. *The Rhetoric of Romanticism*. New York: Columbia UP, 1984. Print.

Dickerson, Vanessa D. "W.E.B. Du Bois and the Victorian Soul of Black Folk." *Dark Victorians*. Urbana: U of Illinois P, 2008. 95–126. Print.

Dickson Jr., Bruce D "W.E.B. Du Bois and the Idea of Double Consciousness." *American Literature* 64.2 (1992): 299–309. *Academic Search Complete*. Web. 18 Apr. 2011.

Dillon, Elizabeth Maddock. *The Gender of Freedom: Fictions of Liberalism and the Literary Public Sphere*. Stanford: Stanford UP, 2004. Print.

Dodge, Mary Mapes. "Jack-in-the-Pulpit." *St. Nicholas: An Illustrated Magazine for Boys and Girls* 1 (November 1873): 46. Print.

Du Bois, Nina. Letter to W.E.B. Du Bois. 8–15 August 1914. W.E.B. Du Bois Papers: Series 1A (part 1). MS 312. Special Collections and University Archives. University of Massachusetts Amherst Libraries.

---. Letter to W.E.B. Du Bois. 31 October—15 November 1914. MS 312. Special Collections and University Archives. University of Massachusetts Amherst Libraries.

Du Bois, W.E.B. "As the Crow Flies." *The Brownies' Book* March 1920: 76–77; Jun. 1920: 183–184; Sep. 1920: 272; Oct 1920: 318 ; Nov 1920: 332–333; Dec 1920: 378–379; July 1921: 206–207. *Library of Congress: Digital Collections.* Web. 18 Apr. 2011.

---. "As the Crow Flies," *The Crisis* 36.6 (1929): 187. Print.

---. *The Autobiography of W.E.B. Du Bois: A Soliloquy on Viewing My Life from the Last Decade of Its First Century.* New York: International, 1968. Print.

---. "Children's Number." "Opinion of W.E.B. Du Bois." *The Crisis* July 1923: 103. Print.

---. "Consecration." "Editorial." *The Crisis* Oct. 1917: 284. Print.

---. "The Immortal Child." *Darkwater: Voices from Within the Veil.* 1920. Mineola: Dover, 1999. 114–127. Print.

---. "The Immortal Children." "Editorial." *The Crisis* Oct. 1916: 267–268. Print.

---. Letter to Yolande Du Bois. 10 November 1914. MS 312. Special Collections and University Archives. University of Massachusetts Amherst Libraries.

---., ed. "Men of the Month." *The Crisis* Oct. 1918: 282. Print.

---. "Of the Children of Peace." *The Crisis* Oct. 1914: 289–290. Print.

---. "Opinion of W.E.B. Du Bois" *The Crisis* Oct. 1922: 247–253. Print.

---. "Our Baby Pictures." *The Crisis* Oct. 1914: 298. Print.

---. *The Souls of Black Folk.* 1903. New York: Penguin, 1989. Print.

---. "The Talented Tenth." *The Negro Problem: A Series of Articles by Representative American Negroes of To-day.* New York, James Pott and Co., 1903. 33–75. *California Digital Archive.* Web. 15 Apr. 2012.

---. "The Training of Negroes for Social Power." *W.E.B. Du Bois Speaks: Speeches and Addresses, 1890–1919.* Ed. Dr. Philip S. Foner. New York: Pathfinder, 1970. 130–141. Print.

---. "The True Brownies." *The Crisis* 18.6 (1919): 285–286. Print.

---. "Worlds of Color." *Foreign Affairs.* 3.3 (1925): 423–444. Print.

Du Bois, Yolande. Letters to W.E.B. Du Bois. 12 January 1916 and February 1916. W.E.B. Du Bois Papers, General Correspondence. Part 1, Reel 5. Special Collections and University Archives. University of Massachusetts Amherst Libraries.

Eckstein, Barbara. "Unsquaring the Squared Root of *What Maisie Knew.*" *Henry James Review* 9.3 (1988): 177–187. *Project Muse.* Web. 27 Mar. 2012.

Edel, Leon. *The Treacherous Years: 1895–1901.* New York: Avon, 1969. Print. Vol 4 of *The Life of Henry James.* 5 vols. 1953–1972. Print.

---. "Introduction to *Tales of the Supernatural.*" *The Turn of the Screw.* Eds. Deborah Esch and Jonathan Warren. Norton Critical Edition. 2nd ed. New York: Norton, 1999. 191–192. Print.

Emerson, Ralph Waldo. *Nature. The Best of Ralph Waldo Emerson: Essays, Poems, Addresses*. Roslyn: Walter J. Black, 1941. 73–116. Print.
Felman, Shoshana. *Writing and Madness: Literature/Philosophy/Psychoanalysis*. Trans. Martha Noel Evans and Shoshana Felman. Palo Alto: Stanford UP, 2003. Print.
Field, Andrew. *Djuna, The Formidable Miss Barnes*. Austin: U of Texas P, 1985. Print.
Fineberg, Jonathan, ed. *Discovering Child Art: Essays on Childhood, Primitivism and Modernism*. Princeton: Princeton UP, 1998. Print.
Fleischer, Georgette. "Djuna Barnes and T.S. Eliot: The Politics and Poetics of *Nightwood*." *Studies in the Novel*. 30.3 (1998): 405–437. *Academic Search Premier*. Web. 27 Mar. 2012.
Foreign Slave Trade. London: Ellerton and Henderson, 1821. *JSTOR*. Web. 24 Jul. 2015.
Foster, Dennis. "Maisie Supposed to Know: Amo(u)ral Analysis." *Henry James Review*. 5.3 (1984): 207–216. *Project Muse*. Web. 27 Mar. 2012.
Galow, Timothy W. "Literary Modernism in the Age of Celebrity." *Modernism/modernity*. 17.2 (2010): 313–329. *Project Muse*. Web. 26 Aug. 2010.
Gargano, James W. "What Maisie Knew: The Evolution of a 'Moral Sense.'" *Nineteenth-Century Fiction*. 16. 1 (1961): 33–46. *JSTOR*. Web. 27 Mar. 2012.
Garlitz, Barbara. "The Immortality Ode: Its Cultural Progeny." *Studies in English Literature, 1500–1900*. 6.4 (1966): 639–649. *JSTOR*. Web. 15 Aug. 2009.
Gilligan, Carol. *In a Different Voice: Psychological Theory and Women's Development*. Cambridge: Harvard UP, 1982. Print.
Gilroy, Paul. *The Black Atlantic: Modernity and Double Consciousness*. Cambridge: Harvard UP, 1993. Print.
Ginsberg, Lesley. "Of Babies, Beasts, and Bondage: Slavery and the Question of Citizenship in Antebellum American Children's Literature." *The American Child: A Cultural Studies Reader*. Eds. Caroline F. Levander and Carol J. Singley. New Brunswick: Rutgers UP, 2003. 85–105. Print.
Glavey, Brian. "Dazzling Estrangement: Modernism, Queer Ekphrasis, and the Spatial Form of *Nightwood*." *PMLA*. 124.3 (2009): 749–763. Print.
Gray, William. *Fantasy, Art and Life: Essays on George MacDonald, Robert Louis Stevenson, and Other Fantasy Writers*. Newcastle upon Tyne: Cambridge Scholars, 2011. Print.
Green, Christopher. "Souvenirs of the Jardin des Plantes: Making the Exotic Strange Again." *Henri Rousseau: Jungles in Paris*. Eds. Frances Morris and Christopher Green. New York, Adams, 2006. 28–47. Print.
Gubar, Marah. *Artful Dodgers: Reconceiving the Golden Age of Children's Literature*. New York: Oxford UP, 2009. Print.
Habegger, Alfred. "Reciprocity and the Market Place in *The Wings of the Dove* and *What Maisie Knew*." *Nineteenth-Century Fiction*. 25.4 (1971): 455–473. *JSTOR*. Web. 27 Mar. 2012.

Harris, Andrea L. *Other Sexes: Rewriting Difference from Woolf to Winterson.* Albany: State U of New York P, 2000. Print.
Harris, Violet J. "African American Children's Literature: The First One Hundred Years." *The Journal of Negro Education* 59.4 (1990): 540–555. Print.
---. "Race Consciousness, Refinement, and Radicalism: Socialization in *The Brownies' Book.*" *Children's Literature Association Quarterly.* 14.4 (1989): 192–196. *MLA International Bibliography.* Web. 25 Mar. 2012.
Heckman, James J. and Yona Rubinstein. "The Importance of Noncognitive Skills: Lessons from the GED Testing Program." *The American Economic Review.* 91.2 (2001): 145–149. *JSTOR.* Web. 3 Jan. 2016.
Heinzelman, Kurt. "'Make It New': The Rise of an Idea." *Make It New: The Rise of Modernism.* Ed. Kurt Heinzelman. Austin: Harry Ransom Humanities Research Center, 2003. 131–134. Print.
Hemmings, Robert. "A Taste of Nostalgia: Children's Books from the Golden Age—Carroll, Grahame, and Milne." *Children's Literature.* 35 (2007): 54–79. *Project Muse.* Web. 24 Mar. 2012.
"Henry James's New Work: 'What Maisie Knew.'" Rev. of *What Maisie Knew*, by Henry James. *New York Times* 27 Nov. 1897: BR9. *ProQuest Historical Newspapers.* Web. 24 Oct. 2009.
Herring, Phillip. *Djuna: The Life and Work of Djuna Barnes.* New York: Penguin, 1995. Print.
Higonnet, Margaret R. "Modernism and Childhood: Violence and Renovation." *The Comparatist.* 33 (2009): 86–108. *Project Muse.* Web. 14 May 2010.
Honeyman, Susan E. "What Maisie Knew and the Impossible Representation of Childhood." *Henry James Review.* 22.1 (2001): 67–80. *Project Muse.* Web. 27 Mar. 2012.
Horner, Avril and Sue Zlosnik. "Strolling in the Dark: Gothic Flânerie in Djuna Barnes's *Nightwood.*" *Gothic Modernisms.* Eds. Andrew Smith and Jeff Wallace. New York: Palgrave, 2001. 78–110. Print.
Howells, William Dean. "Mr. Henry James's Later Work." *The North American Review* 26.554 (Jan. 1903): 125–137. *JSTOR.* Web. 29 Sep. 2015.
Hubbard, Dolan. Introduction. *The Souls of Black Folk: One Hundred Years Later.* Ed. Dolan Hubbard. Columbia: U of Missouri P, 2003. 1–17. Print.
Hughes, Langston. *The Big Sea.* New York: Hill and Wang-Farrar, 1968. Print.
---. "Books and the Negro Child." *The Collected Works of Langston Hughes: Essays on Art, Race, Politics, and World Affairs.* vol. 9. Ed. Christopher C. De Santi. Columbia: U of Missouri P, 2002. 49–51. Print.
---. *The Collected Poems of Langston Hughes.* Ed. Arnold Rampersad. New York: Vintage-Random House, 1994.
---. *The Dream Keeper and Other Poems.* New York: Scholastic, 1994.
---. "My Adventures as a Social Poet." *The Collected Works of Langston Hughes: Essays on Art, Race, Politics, and World Affairs.* vol. 9. Ed. Christopher C. De Santi. Columbia: U of Missouri P, 2002. 269–277. Print.

Hurd, Edith Thacher. "The World is Not Flat." *The World is Round*. San Francisco: North Point Press, 1988. 119–162. Print.

Hutcheon, Linda. *A Poetics of Postmodernism: History, Theory, Fiction*. New York: Routledge, 1988. Print.

"Innocence." *Oxford English Dictionary*. Web. 27 Mar. 2012.

Isle, Walter. *Experiments in Form: Henry James's Novels, 1896–1901*. Cambridge: Harvard UP, 1968. Print.

James, Henry. *The Notebooks of Henry James*. Eds. F.O. Matthiessen and Kenneth B. Murdock. New York: Oxford UP, 1947. Print.

---. "The Point of View." *Complete Stories of Henry James, 1874–1884*. Vol. II. Library of America, 1999. 519–564. Print.

---. "Preface." *What Maisie Knew, In the Cage, The Pupil*. Fairfield: Augustus M. Kelley, 1979. Print.

---. *A Small Boy and Others*. 1913. *Henry James: Autobiography*. Ed. Frederick W. Dupee. NeYork: Criterion, 1956. Print.

---. "To Dr. Louis Waldstein." 21 October 1898. *The Letters of Henry James*. Vol. I. Ed. Percy Lubbock. n.p.: Elibron Classics, 2006. 304–305. Print.

---. "To William James." 17 October 1907. *The Letters of Henry James*. Vol. II. ed. Percy Lubbock. n.p.: Elibron Classics, 2006. 84–86. Print.

---. *The Turn of the Screw*. Eds. Deborah Esch and Jonathan Warren. Norton Critical Edition. 2nd ed. New York: Norton, 1999. Print.

---. *Two Magics; The Turn of the Screw; Covering End*. London: William Heinemann, 1898. Hathi Trust e-book.

---. *What Maisie Knew*. New York: Penguin, 1966. Print.

Jameson, Fredric. *The Modernist Papers*. New York: Verso, 2007. Print.

James, William. "Habit." *The Heart of William James*. Ed. Robert Richardson. Cambridge: Harvard UP, 2010. 102–115. Print.

---. "On a Certain Blindness in Human Beings." *The Heart of William James*. Ed. Robert Richardson. Cambridge: Harvard UP, 2010. 146–163. Print.

---. *The Principles of Psychology*. Vol. 1. New York: Henry Holt, 1931. Print.

---. *Talks to Teachers on Psychology and to Students on Some of Life's Ideals*. Mineola: Dover, 1962. Kindle e-book.

Johnson, Georgia Douglas. "Brown Eyes." *The Brownies' Book*. May 1920: 158. Print.

---. "Motherhood." *The Crisis*. Oct. 1922: 265. Print.

Johnson-Feelings, Dianne. Afterword. *The Best of The Brownies' Book*. Ed. Dianne Johnson-Feelings. New York: Oxford UP, 1996. 335–347. Print.

Jonsson, AnnKatrin. "*Nightwood* and the Limits of Representation." *Critical Studies*. 26 (2005): 263–279. *IngentaConnect*. Web. 27 Mar. 2012.

Kannenstine, Louis F. *The Art of Djuna Barnes: Duality and Damnation*. New York: New York UP, 1977. Print.

Kaplan, Amy. *The Anarchy of Empire in the Making of U.S. Culture*. Cambridge: Harvard UP, 2002. Print.

Kaivola, Karen. "The 'beast turning human': Constructions of the 'Primitive' in *Nightwood*." *Review of Contemporary Fiction*. 13.3 (1993): 172–184. *Academic Search Premier*. Web. 27 Mar. 2012.
Key, Ellen. *The Century of the Child*. New York: G.P. Putnam's Sons, 1909. Print.
Kincaid, James R. *Child-loving: The Erotic Child and Victorian Culture*. New York: Routledge, 1992. Print.
---. *Erotic Innocence: The Culture of Child Molesting*. Durham: Duke UP, 1998. Print.
Kinchin, Juliet and Aidan O'Connor. *Century of the Child: Growing by Design: 1900–2000*. New York: Museum of Modern Art, 2012.
Kingsley, Charles. *The Water Babies: A Fairy Tale for a Land-Baby*. Mineola: Dover, 2006. Print.
Knoepflmacher, U.C. "Spaces Within: The Portable Interiors of Childhood." *Secret Spaces of Childhood*. Ed. Elizabeth Goodenough. Ann Arbor: U of Michigan P, 2003. 297–308. Print.
---. *Ventures into Childland: Victorians, Fairy Tales, and Femininity*. Chicago: The U of Chicago P, 1998. Print.
Kory, Fern. "Once upon a Time in Aframerica: The 'Peculiar' Significance of Fairies in the *Brownies' Book*." *Children's Literature*. 29 (2001): 91–112. *Project Muse*. Web. 25 Mar. 2012.
Leick, Karen. *Gertrude Stein and the Making of an American Celebrity*. New York: Routledge, 2009. Print.
Lesinska, Zofia. "Gertrude Stein's War Autobiographies: Reception, History, and Dialogue." *LIT: Literature Interpretation Theory* 9.4 (1999): 313–342. *MLA International Bibliography*. Web. 24 Mar. 2012.
Levander, Caroline F. "The Child and the Racial Politics of Nation Making in the Slavery Era." *Cradle of Liberty: Race, The Child, and National Belonging from Thomas Jefferson to W.E.B. Du Bois*. Durham: Duke UP, 2006. 29–51. Print.
Levine, Caroline. *The Serious Pleasures of Suspense: Victorian Realism and Narrative Doubt*. Charlottesville: The U of Virginia P, 2003. Print.
Lewis, David Levering. "A Small Nation of People: W.E.B. Du Bois and Black Americans at the Turn of the Twentieth Century." *A Small Nation of People: W.E.B. Du Bois & African American Portraits of Progress*. Library of Congress. New York: Amistad, 2003. 23–49. Print.
Locke, John. *Some Thoughts Concerning Education. Some Thoughts Concerning Education and Of the Conduct of the Understanding*. Eds. Ruth W. Grant and Nathan Tarcov. Indianapolis: Hackett, 1996. Print.
Lorde, Audre. "Man Child: A Black Lesbian Feminist's Response." *Sister Outsider*. Berkeley: Crossing P, 2007. 72–80. Print.
Lustig, T. J. *Henry James and the Ghostly*. New York: Cambridge UP, 1994. Print.
MacDonald, George. *At the Back of the North Wind*. Philadelphia: J.B. Lippincott, 1909. Google Play e-book.

---. "The Child in the Midst." *Unspoken Sermons Series I, II, and III*. 1867. NuVision, 2007. 7–16. Web. 15 Apr. 2012.
---. "The Fantastic Imagination." *Fantastic Literature: A Critical Reader*. Ed. David Sandner. 1890. Westport: Praeger, 2004. 64–69. Print.
MacKay, Marina. *Modernism and World War II*. New York: Cambridge UP, 2007. Print.
MacLeod, Anne Scott. *American Childhood: Essays on Children's Literature of the Nineteenth and Twentieth Centuries*. Athens: The U of Georgia P, 1994. Print.
Madden, Ed. *Tiresian Poetics: Modernism, Sexuality, Voice, 1888–2001*. Madison: Farleigh Dickinson UP, 2008. Print.
M. A. H. "Another Lynching." *The Crisis* Oct. 1916: 275–276. Print.
Makari, George. *Revolution in Mind: The Creation of Psychoanalysis*. New York: Harper Perennial, 2008. Print.
Malcolm, Janet. *Two Lives: Gertrude and Alice*. New Haven: Yale UP, 2007. Print.
Mao, Douglas and Rebecca L. Walkowitz, eds. *Bad Modernisms*. Durham: Duke UP, 2006. Print.
Mao, Douglas. *Fateful Beauty: Aesthetic Environments, Juvenile Development, and Literaure, 1860–1960*. Princeton: Princeton UP, 2008. Print.
Marcus, Jane. "Laughing at Leviticus: *Nightwood* as Woman's Circus Epic." *Silence and Power: A Reevaluation of Djuna Barnes*. Ed. Mary Lynn Broe. Carbondale: Southern Illinois UP, 1991. 221–250. Print.
Marcus, Leonard. *Margaret Wise Brown: Awakened by the Moon*. New York: William Morrow, 1992. Print.
Martin, Ann. *Red Riding Hood and the Wolf in Bed: Modernism's Fairy Tales*. Toronto: U of Toronto P, 2006. Print.
McCloskey, John C. "What Maisie Knows: A Study of Childhood and Adolescence." *American Literature: A Journal of Literary History, Criticism, and Bibliography* 36.4 (1965): 485–513. *Academic Search Premier*. Web. 27 Mar. 2012.
McCullough, John. Letter to Gertrude Stein. 9 October 1939. MSS 76, Box 131, Folder 2861. Gertrude Stein and Alice B. Toklas Papers. Yale Collection of American Literature, Beinecke Rare Book and Manuscript Library, Yale University.
McFarland, Thomas. *Romanticism and the Heritage of Rousseau*. New York: Oxford UP, 1995. Print.
McGavran, James Holt, ed. *Literature and the Child: Romantic Continuations, Postmodern Contestations*. Iowa City: U of Iowa P, 1999. Print.
McKeon, Michael. *The Secret History of Domesticity: Public, Private, and the Division of Knowledge*. Baltimore: Johns Hopkins UP, 2005. Print.
Mellow, James R. *Charmed Circle: Gertrude Stein and Company*. New York: Henry Holt, 1974. Print.
Meynell, Wilfrid. Preface. *The Child Set in the Midst by Modern Poets*. Ed. Wilfrid Meynell. New York: Charles Scribner's Sons, 1892. Print.

Miller, Tyrus. *Late Modernism: Politics, Fiction, and the Arts Between the World Wars*. Berkeley: U of California P, 1999. Print.
"Mind in Childhood." *Atchison Daily Champion*. 20 April 1888: 7. *19th Century U.S. Newspapers*. Web. 27 Mar. 2012.
Moebius, William. "Introduction to Picturebook Codes." *Children's Literature: The Development of Criticism*. Ed. Peter Hunt. New York: Routledge, 1990. 131–147. Print.
Morris, Frances. "Jungles in Paris." *Henri Rousseau: Jungles in Paris*. Eds. Frances Morris and Christopher Green. New York, Adams, 2006. 12–27. Print.
---. "Mysterious Meetings." *Henri Rousseau: Jungles in Paris*. Eds. Frances Morris and Christopher Green. New York, Adams, 2006. 156–167. Print.
"Mr. James' New Novel." Rev. of *What Maisie Knew*, by Henry James. *Current Literature: A Magazine of Contemporary Record*. Dec. 1897: 505. *American Periodicals Series Online*. Web 24 Oct. 2009.
M.S.C. "At the Back of the Child Mind." *The Living Age*. 293.3802 (May 19, 1917): 442. *American Periodicals Series Online*. Web. 27 Mar. 2012.
Natov, Roni. *The Poetics of Childhood*. New York: Routledge, 2003. Print.
Nesbitt, Elizabeth. "A Rightful Heritage." *A Critical History of Children's Literature*. Ed. Cornelia Meigs. New York: Macmillan, 1953. 313–326. Print.
"The Novels of Mr. Henry James." *The Living Age* 7 Mar. 1903: 577–595. *American Periodicals Series Online*. Web. 24 Oct. 2009.
Ohi, Kevin. *Innocence and Rapture: The Erotic Child in Pater, Wilde, James, and Nabokov*. New York: Palgrave Macmillan, 2005. Print.
Olson, Liesl. "Gertrude Stein, William James, and Habit in the Shadow of War." *Modernism and the Ordinary*. Oxford: Oxford UP, 2009. Print.
O'Neal. Hank. *"Life is Painful, Nasty, & Short ... in my Case it Has Only Been Painful & Nasty": Djuna Barnes, 1978–1981: an Informal Memoir*. New York: Paragon, 1990. Print.
Pater, Walter. "The Child in the House." *Miscellaneous Studies: A Series of Essays*. New York: Macmillan, 1895. 147–169. Print.
Pattison, Robert. *The Child Figure in English Literature*. Athens: U of Georgia P, 1978. Print.
Pearson, Maeve. "Re-exposing the Jamesian Child: The Paradox of Children's Privacy." *The Henry James Review*. 28 (2007): 101–119. *Project Muse*. Web. 27 Mar. 2012.
Pennington, Kenneth. "Innocent Until Proven Guilty: The Origins of a Legal Maxim." *The Jurist* 63 (2003): 106–124. *HeinOnline*. Web. 23 Dec. 2015.
Perosa, Sergio. *Henry James and the Experimental Novel*. Charlottesville: UP of Virginia, 1978. Print.
Petzold, Dieter. "A Race Apart: Children in Late Victorian and Edwardian Children's Books." *Children's Literature Association Quarterly*. 17.3 (1992): 33–36. *Project Muse*. Web. 28 Mar. 2012.

Pifer, Ellen. *Demon or Doll: Images of the Child in Contemporary Writing and Culture*. Charlottesville: UP of Virginia, 2000. Print.

Pippin, Robert. *Henry James and Modern Moral Life*. New York: Cambridge UP, 2000. Print.

Plain, Gill. *Women's Fiction of The Second World War: Gender, Power and Resistance*. New York: St. Martin's Press, 1996. Print.

Plotz, Judith. *Romanticism and the Vocation of Childhood*. New York: Palgrave, 2001. Print.

Posnock, Ross. "How It Feels to Be a Problem: Du Bois, Fanon, and the 'Impossible Life' of the Black Intellectual." *Critical Inquiry* 23.2 (1997): 323–349. *JSTOR*. Web. 18 Apr. 2011.

Rahn, Suzanne. "*St. Nicholas* and Its Friends: The Magazine-Child Relationship." *St. Nicholas and Mary Mapes Dodge: The Legacy of a Children's Magazine Editor, 1873–1905*. eds. Susan R. Gannon, Suzanne Rahn, and Ruth Anne Thompson. Jefferson: McFarland, 2004. 93–110. Print.

Rampersad, Arnold. *The Art and Imagination of W.E.B. Du Bois*. 1976. New York: Schocken, 1990. Print.

Reynolds, Kimberley. *Radical Children's Literature: Future Visions and Aesthetic Transformations in Juvenile Fiction*. New York: Palgrave Macmillan, 2007. Print.

Richardson, Alan. "Romanticism and the End of Childhood." *Literature and the Child: Romantic Continuations, Postmodern Contestations*. Ed. James Holt McGavran. Iowa City: U of Iowa P, 1999. 23–43. Print.

---. "Wordsworth, Fairy Tales, and the Politics of Children's Reading." *Romanticism and Children's Literature in Nineteenth-Century England*. Ed. James Holt McGavran, Jr. Athens: U of Georgia P, 1991. 34–53. Print.

Richardson, Robert D. *William James: In the Maelstrom of American Modernism*. Boston: Mariner-Houghton, 2006. Print.

Roberts, Lewis C. "Children's Fiction." *A Companion to the Victorian Novel*. Ed. Patrick Brantlinger and William B. Thesing. Oxford: Blackwell, 2005. 353–369. Print.

Rohman, Carrie. "Revising the Human: Silence, Being, and the Question of the Animal in *Nightwood*." *American Literature*. 79.1 (2007): 57–84. *Academic Search Premier*. Web. 27 Mar. 2012.

Rose, Jacqueline. *The Case of Peter Pan or The Impossibility of Children's Fiction*. 1984. Philadelphia: U of Pennsylvania P, 1992. Print.

Rousseau, Henri. *The Dream. Henri Rousseau: Jungles in Paris*. Eds. Frances Morris and Christopher Green. New York: Abrams, 2006. 12. Print.

Rousseau, Jean-Jacques. *Emile* or *On Education*. Ed and trans. Allan Bloom. New York: Basic Books, 1979. Print.

Rowe, John Carlos. "The Portrait of a Small Boy as a Young Girl: Gender Trouble in *What Maisie Knew*." *The Other Henry James*. Durham: Duke UP, 1998. 120–154. Print.

Rudd, David. "Children's Literature and the Return to Rose." *Children's Literature Association Quarterly*. 35.3 (2010): 290–310. Print.
Rukeyser, Muriel. "Effort At Speech Between Two People." *The Collected Poems*. Eds. Janet E. Kaufman & Anne F. Herzog. Pittsburgh: U of Pittsburgh P, 2005. 9–10. Print.
Santesso, Aaron. *A Careful Longing: The Poetics and Problems of Nostalgia*. Newark: U of Delaware P, 2006. Print.
Savoy, Eric. "France, French, and the French." Rev. of *Henry James Goes to Paris* by Peter Brooks. *Henry James Review* 30 (2009): 196–206. *Project Muse*. Web. 27 Mar. 2012.
Sawyer, Julian. Letter to Gertrude Stein. 5 August 1938. MSS 76, Box 123, Folder 2664. Gertrude Stein and Alice B. Toklas Papers. Yale Collection of American Literature, Beinecke Rare Book and Manuscript Library, Yale University.
Schoenbach, Lisi. "'Peaceful and Exciting': Habit, Shock, and Gertrude Stein's Pragmatic Modernism." *Modernism/modernity*. 11.2 (2004): 239–259. *Project Muse*. Web. 12 Sep. 2010.
"Shadows of Light." *The Crisis* Oct. 1916: 285–288. Print.
Sheppard, E. A. *Henry James and "The Turn of the Screw."* Auckland: Auckland UP, 1974. Print.
Shine, Muriel G. *The Fictional Children of Henry James*. Chapel Hill: U of North Carolina P, 1969. Print.
Shuttleworth, Sally. *The Mind of the Child: Child Development in Literature, Science, and Medicine, 1840–1900*. Oxford: Oxford UP, 2010. Print.
Sinnette, Elinor Desverney. "*The Brownies' Book*: A Pioneer Publication for Children." *Freedomways: A Quarterly Review of the Negro Freedom Movement* 5.1 (1965): 133–142. Print.
Smith, Katharine Capshaw. *Children's Literature of the Harlem Renaissance*. Bloomington: Indiana UP, 2004. Print.
Smith, Shawn Michelle. *Photography on the Color Line: W.E.B. Du Bois, Race, and Visual Culture*. Durham: Duke UP, 2004. Print.
Smuts, Alice Boardman. *Science in the Service of Children, 1893–1935*. New Haven: Yale UP, 2006. Print.
"Some Tendencies of Contemporary Fiction." *The Living Age* 2 Dec. 1899: 587–590. *American Periodicals Series Online*. Web. 24 Oct. 2009.
Spilka, Mark. "Turning the Freudian Screw: How Not To Do It." *Literature and Psychology*. 13.4 (1963): 105–111. Print.
Spufford, Francis. *The Child that Books Built: A Life in Reading*. New York: Picador, 2002. Print.
Starbuck, Edwin Diller. "The Child-Mind and Child-Religion." *The Biblical World*. 30.2 (1907): 101. *American Periodicals Series Online*. Web. 27 Mar. 2012.
Steedman, Carolyn. *Strange Dislocations: Childhood and the Idea of Human Interiority, 1780–1930*. Cambridge: Harvard UP, 1995. Print.

Stein, Gertrude and Carl Van Vechten. *The Letters of Gertrude Stein and Carl Van Vechten, 1913–1946.* vol. II. Ed. Edward Burns. New York: Columbia UP, 1986. Print.
Stein, Gertrude. "And Now." 1934. *How Writing is Written: Volume II.* Ed. Robert Bartlett Haas. Los Angeles: Black Sparrow P, 1974. 63–66. Print.
---. "The Autobiography of Rose." *How Writing is Written: Volume II.* Ed. Robert Bartlett Haas. Los Angeles: Black Sparrow P, 1974. 39–42. Print.
---. *Everybody's Autobiography.* 1937. Cambridge: Exact Change, 1993. Print.
---. *Geographical History of America or The Relation of Human Nature to the Human Mind.* 1936. *Gertrude Stein: Writings: 1932–1946.* Eds. Catharine R. Stimpson and Harriet Chessman. New York: Library of America, 1998. Print.
---. *Geographical History of America.* 1935. MSS 76, Box 23, Folder 447. Gertrude Stein and Alice B. Toklas Papers. Yale Collection of American Literature, Beinecke Rare Book and Manuscript Library, Yale University.
---. *The Gertrude Stein First Reader & Three Plays.* Dublin: Maurice Fridberg, 1946. Print.
---. *How to Write.* 1931. New York: Dover, 1975. Print.
---. Letter to John McCullough. N.d. MSS 76, Box 131, Folder 2861. Gertrude Stein and Alice B. Toklas Papers. Yale Collection of American Literature, Beinecke Rare Book and Manuscript Library, Yale University.
---. "The New Hope in Our 'Sad Young Men.'" 1945. *How Writing is Written: Volume II.* Ed. Robert Bartlett Haas. Los Angeles: Black Sparrow P, 1974. 142–145. Print.
---. *Paris France.* 1940. New York: W.W. Norton, 1996. Print.
---. *To Do: A Book of Alphabets and Birthdays.* New Haven: Yale UP, 2011. Print.
---. "A Transatlantic Interview." 1946. *A Primer for the Gradual Understanding of Gertrude Stein.* Ed. Robert Bartlett Haas. Los Angeles: Black Sparrow P, 1971. 11–35. Print.
---. *Wars I Have Seen.* 1945. London: Brilliance Books, 1984. Print.
---. "The Winner Loses, A Picture of Occupied France." 1940. *How Writing is Written: Volume II.* Ed. Robert Bartlett Haas. Los Angeles: Black Sparrow P, 1974. 113–132. Print.
---. *The World is Round.* 1939. New York: Harper Design, 2013. Print.
Sundquist, Eric J. *To Wake the Nations: Race in the Making of American Literature.* Cambridge: Belknap, 1993. Print.
Susina, Jan. "Children's Reading, Repetition, and Rereading: Gertrude Stein, Margaret Wise Brown, and *Goodnight Moon.*" *Second Thoughts: A Focus on Rereading.* Ed. David Galef. Detroit: Wayne State UP, 1998. 115–125. Print.
Tate, Claudia. Introduction. *Dark Princess.* By W.E.B. Du Bois. Jackson: Banner, 1995. ix–xxviii. Print.

Tribunella, Eric L. "Children's Literature and the Child Flâneur." *Children's Literature*. 38 (2010): 64–91. Print.
Viguers, Ruth Hill. "Childhood's Golden Era—Introductory Survey." *A Critical History of Children's Literature*. Ed. Cornelia Meigs. New York: Macmillan, 1953. 427–447. Print.
Wall, Cheryl A. "Resounding Souls: Du Bois and the African American Literary Tradition." *Public Culture* 17.2 (2005): 217–234. *Duke University Press Journals*. Web. 18 Apr. 2011.
Watts, Linda S. "Twice Upon a Time: Back Talk, Spinsters, and re-verse-als in Gertrude Stein's 'The World is Round.'" *Women and Language*. 16.1 (1993): 53–58. *Literature Resource Center*. Web. 26 Jan. 2006.
Weinbaum, Alys Eve. "Interracial Romance and Black Internationalism." *Next to the Color Line: Gender, Sexuality, and W.E.B. Du Bois*. Eds. Susan Gillman and Alys Eve Weinbaum. Minneapolis: U of Minnesota P, 2007. 96–123. Print.
Wells, Susan. "Discursive Mobility and Double Consciousness in S. Weir Mitchell and W.E.B. Du Bois." *Philosophy and Rhetoric* 35.2 (2002): 120–137. *Project Muse*. Web. 18 Apr. 2011.
Westover, Jeff. "Handing Over Power in James's *What Maisie Knew*." *Style* 28.2 (1994): 201–218. *Academic Search Premier*. Web. 27 Mar. 2012.
"What Maisie Knew." Rev. of *What Maisie Knew*, by Henry James. *The Literary World; a Monthly Review of Current Literature*. 2 Dec. 1897: 454–455. *American Periodicals Series Online*. Web. 24 Oct. 2009.
White, Walter F. "Chicago and Its Eight Reasons." *The Crisis* Oct. 1919: 295. Print.
Whittier-Ferguson, John. "The Liberation of Gertrude Stein: War and Writing." *Modernism/modernity*. 8.3 (2001): 405–428. Project Muse. Web. 26 Aug. 2010.
Will, Barbara. "'And Then One Day There Was a War': Gertrude Stein, Children's Literature, and World War II." *Children's Literature Association Quarterly*. 32.4 (2007): 340–353. *Project Muse*. Web. 14 Jun. 2011.
---. *Unlikely Collaboration: Gertrude Stein, Bernard Faÿ, and the Vichy Dilemma*. New York: Columbia UP, 2011. Print.
Wilson, Edmund. "The Ambiguity of Henry James." Eds. Deborah Esch and Jonathan Warren. Norton Critical Edition. 2nd ed. New York: Norton, 1999. 170–173. Print.
Woolf, Virginia. "Lewis Carroll." *The Moment and Other Essays*. New York: Harcourt Brace, 1947. 81–83. Print.
---. "Mr. Bennett and Mrs. Brown." *Essentials of the Theory of Fiction*. Eds. Michael J. Hoffman and Patrick D. Murphy. Durham: Duke UP, 1996. 2–35. Print.
Wordsworth, William. "My Heart Leaps Up." *The Norton Anthology of Poetry*. 3rd ed. New York: Norton, 1983. 285. Print.

---. "Ode: Intimations of Immortality from Recollections of Early Childhood." *The Norton Anthology of Poetry*. 3rd ed. New York: Norton, 1983. 286–289. Print.

Zelizer, Viviana A. *Pricing the Priceless Child: The Changing Social Value of Children*. Princeton: Princeton UP, 1985. Print.

Zipes, Jack. *When Dreams Came True: Classical Fairy Tales and Their Tradition*. New York: Routledge, 1999. Print.

Index

A

Adorno, Theodor, 92–5, 105
African-American children's literature
  and adult-rearing, 24–9
  and black childhood, 119–21, 124, 126–9, 132, 135, 138–41, 145–56
  and de-romanticizing of childhood, 29–31, 128–31, 142–57
  and double-consciousness, 5, 10, 15, 39, 119–26, 141, 148, 152–5, 161n34, 185, 207n15
  and racial infantilization, 127–8
  and physical representation, 132–43
  see also Baldwin, James; *Brownies' Book, The*; *Crisis, The*: "Children's Numbers"; Du Bois, W. E. B.; Fauset, Jessie; Hughes, Langston

B

Baldwin, James, 24–5
Barnes, Djuna: *Nightwood*, 5, 9, 15, 22–3, 91–117
  animal innocence in, 98–100, 104
  and anti-nostalgia, 30, 92, 98, 103
  child characters in, 22, 92, 96, 100, 108, 110–13, 117n15
  critical history of the text, 104–6, 114n1, 115n5–6, 116n10
  and cult of the child/childhood, 91–5, 100–7, 110–11
  and cult of the new, 92–5, 100–7, 111, 113–14, 115n2, 115n4
  and dispossession, 9, 92, 96, 113
  and innocence re-invented, 95–100, 109
  and late modernism, 91–5, 105, 113–14, 115n6
  and performance of childhood, 92, 95–7, 100, 104, 113

Note: Page numbers followed by 'n' refer to notes.

Barnes, Djuna: *Nightwood (cont.)*
   and perpetual childhood, 92–9,
      105–6, 109, 113
   role of art within, 94, 100–6, 113–14
   toys/dolls in, 95–7, 100, 113
   transitional status of, 94, 115n6
Barrie, J. M., 4, 8, 39, 65, 68
   Peter Pan (also *Peter and Wendy*),
      2–3, 6–7, 40, 65–6, 68, 71,
      87n1–3, 106, 178–9, 207n11
Baudelaire, Charles, 92–3
Benjamin, Walter, 93, 100, 115n2
Black Renaissance, 24. *See also individual authors*
Blake, William, 20, 71, 74
Bond, Horace Mann, 139–40
Bontemps, Arna, 24, 26
Brooks, Gwendolyn, 24
Brown, Margaret Wise, 207n15
Brownies' Book, The, 3–5, 10
   and "As the Crow Flies" (Du Bois),
      120, 144–57, 160n23, 160n26
   and Brownie figure, 147
   contributors to, 4, 145–7
   critical history of, 147, 158n4,
      158n6, 159n12
   mission of, 145, 148–9
   publication history of, 26–7, 120,
      144–7
   readership, 3
   relationship to *The Crisis*:
      "Children's Numbers", 120–1,
      126, 144–8, 156–7
   and *St. Nicholas Magazine*, 147–8,
      159n12, 160n26, 168
Burnett, Frances Hodgson, 39
   Secret Garden, The, 2

C

Carroll, Lewis, 20, 23, 30, 39–40, 71, 167
Cerf, Bennett, 3, 169

Child and childhood
   black childhood, 119–21, 124,
      126–9, 132, 135, 138–41,
      145–56
   and blank slate/blank paper, 9, 43,
      45, 48, 52, 73, 80, 85, 93, 95,
      104–11
   child in the midst, 8, 18–23, 41–2,
      50, 68, 114
   and child study movement, 1, 11n1,
      17, 67
   and death, 10, 44, 78, 97, 113,
      135–7, 143, 164–6, 169–74,
      177, 190–2
   and disenchantment/
      disillusionment, 2–3, 9, 26,
      30–2, 91, 100, 111, 113–14,
      121, 125, 197
   divided (partagé) child, 8–9, 21,
      39–41, 45–6, 53–62
   and drowning, 10, 23, 164–5,
      169–74, 190–4
   and education, 2, 14–17, 26, 71,
      74, 76, 124–31, 144, 164–5,
      176–7, 207n12
   essentialist view of, 1, 3, 7–8,
      12–23, 26–30, 38–9, 68, 177
   idealized/idyllic, 1, 5, 14–15,
      19–22, 28–31, 34, 47, 68,
      70–2, 74, 81, 91, 127, 135,
      141–2, 176
   inner child movement, 21–2, 35n5
   and interiority, 1, 7–8, 16, 19–22,
      35n5, 43–62, 63n4, 94, 103,
      106–10, 127–31, 174, 177,
      195
   and language, 28, 34, 64n11,
      109–10, 128, 138, 142, 167–9,
      177–8, 194, 198–9, 201–2
   performance of, 66–9, 72, 92, 95–7,
      100, 104, 114
   perpetual, 16–19, 65, 70–1, 81,
      92–9, 105–6, 113, 127–8, 170

in the Progressive era, 2–3, 19, 92, 176–7
psychology of, 2, 7–8, 13–23, 27, 34, 61, 66, 121–2, 140, 163, 188, 207n12
Romantic ideals of, 1, 9, 13, 15–21, 27–8, 39, 47–8, 66, 88n7, 121–4, 128–9, 141–2, 152–3, 157, 176, 178–9
social construct of, 4, 7–8, 15, 30, 67, 69–70, 98, 104, 127, 130, 179
and Victorian literature, 3, 20, 57, 63n4, 68, 78–80, 87n2, 87n5, 105
see also Innocence
Child labor, 2, 125
Children's Bureau, The, 2
Children's literature
 alphabet books, 163–5, 167–77
 first readers, 166, 174–8
 golden age of, 2, 7, 18, 29–30, 39, 120
 magazines, 3–5, 10, 26–7, 120–1, 126–56, 159n12, 160n26, 168
 Mother Goose, 32–3, 164, 180–3, 187–8, 194–5, 197, 202, 204, 205n1
 picture books, 139–40, 159n17, 159–60n18
 see also African-American children's literature; Fairy tales
Chopin, Kate: *The Awakening*, 166
Coates, Ta-Nehisi: *Between the World and Me*, 24–5, 28–9
Coleman, Emily, 116n12
Coleridge, Samuel Taylor, 88n6–7
Conrad, Joseph: *Chance*, 94
Crisis, The: "Children's Numbers", 4, 10, 120–1, 129–47, 149, 155
 comparison with *The Souls of Black Folk*, 137–43, 159n16
 and double consciousness, 120–1, 126, 141, 143, 148, 155

and dual (child and adult) audience, 121, 129–30, 138, 147, 158n8
and irony, 120, 134–5, 137, 140–1, 149
use of captions, 132, 135–40, 157–8n5
use of photographs, 120, 132, 135, 137–41, 149, 157–8n5
and violence, 129, 132–5, 139–43, 156
Cross-writing, 121, 138, 147, 158n8
Cullen, Countee, 11n2, 24
Cult of childhood, 13, 69–70, 72, 86, 91–5, 100–7, 110–11
Cult of the new, 92–5, 100–7, 111, 113–14, 115n2, 115n4

D
Dill, Augustus, 120
Double consciousness, 5, 10, 15, 39, 119–26, 141, 148, 152–5, 161n34, 185, 207n15
Du Bois, W. E. B., 4–5, 8, 10, 14
 and black childhood, 119–29, 132, 135, 138–41, 145–56
 Black Reconstruction, 120, 157n2
 and *The Brownies' Book*, 3–5, 10, 26–7, 120–1, 126, 141, 145–56, 157n4, 158n5–6, 159n12, 160n25–26
 and the color line, 5, 10, 121, 126–32, 155, 158n7, 161n33
 and *The Crisis* "Children's Numbers", 4, 10, 120–1, 126, 129–47, 149, 155
 Darkwater, 25, 120, 123–7, 129, 151, 154–5, 157n2–3, 158n7
 and double consciousness, 119–26, 141, 148, 152–5
 Dusk of Dawn, 120
 and modernism, 119, 121, 127, 140

Du Bois, W. E. B. (*cont.*)
  and politics of race, 126–31
  and problem of racial infantilization, 126–9
  "Strivings of the Negro People", 121
Du Bois, W. E. B.: "As the Crow Flies", 120, 144–57, 160n23, 160n26, 161n34
  and Crow persona, 120, 145, 148
  and double consciousness, 148, 152–5
  publication history of, 144–8
  and race representation, 149–50
  and war, 149–54
Du Bois, W. E. B.: *Souls of Black Folk, The*, 5, 14, 116n8, 119, 121–43, 148, 150–6, 157n2
  and the color line, 10, 126, 128–31, 155, 157n2–3, 158n7
  comparison with *The Crisis* "Children's Numbers": 137–43, 159n16
  and double consciousness, 119, 121–6, 161n34
  and politics of race, 126–31
  publication history of, 119–20
Du Bois, Yolande, 144, 147

E
Eliot, T. S., 94, 198, 204
  Old Possum's Book of Practical Cats, 6, 11n2, 198
  Waste Land, The, 166
Emerson, Ralph Waldo, 124
  Nature, 71

F
Fairy tales, 30, 33, 35, 92, 96, 100, 103, 111, 142–3, 159n12
  purpose of modern, 208n21

and Stein, 164–6, 168, 176, 178, 190, 193–4, 203–4, 206n2, 208n20, 210n29
  and *Turn of the Screw* (James), 78–80
Fauset, Jessie Redmond, 4, 24, 120, 145, 160n22
Ford, Charles Henri: *The Young and Evil*, 105
Ford, Ford Madox: *The Good Soldier*, 94
Frank, Joseph, 104, 116n10
Freud, Sigmund, 1, 11n1, 14–15, 18–19, 35n1–2, 74

G
Giovani, Nikki, 24
Goethe, Johann Wolfgang: *Wihelm Meister*, 16
Grahame, Kenneth: *The Wind in the Willows*, 2

H
Hall, G. Stanley, 14–17
Hemingway, Ernest, 116n7, 207n16
Hofer, Johannes, 29
Hoover, Herbert, 1
Hughes, Langston, 4, 8, 19, 24–8, 31, 163, 166
  Big Sea, The, 25–6
  Black Misery, 4, 26
  "Books and the Negro Child", 26
  Dream Keeper, The, 5, 27–8
  First Book of Jazz, 5
  First Book of Rhythms, 5
Hurd, Clement, 196, 209n26

I
Innocence
  and African American literature, 24–5, 28, 127, 129, 134–5, 142–3

animal innocence, 98–100, 104
counterfeit innocence, 68
and divided child, 21–2, 142–3
enduring innocence, 69–76
erotic innocence, 69–70, 87n2, 87–8n5
and essentialized childhood, 21–3, 42, 67
and evil, 9, 65–74, 81–6
"innocent until proven guilty", 74, 88n8
and irony, 43, 52
and late modernism, 33–4, 109, 114, 177
and modernism, 1, 3, 9–10, 21–2, 24–5, 28, 33–4, 65–6, 75, 94, 102, 104–5, 109–14
pattern of innocence lost and restored, 72–3, 81, 86
prolonging of, 74–8
re-invention of, 95–100, 109
and romanticized childhood, 1, 3, 9, 15, 39, 65–6
types of innocence, 70, 81, 86
and violence, 129, 134–5, 142–3
Intersectionality, 119, 157n1

J
James, Henry, 3–5, 9–10
and Du Bois, 14–15
Small Boy and Others, A, 40–1
James, Henry: *Turn of the Screw, The*, 5, 9, 65–86, 91, 93–6, 103–5, 110
compared with *Peter Pan*, 65–6, 68
and counterfeit innocence, 68
and cult of childhood, 69, 70, 72, 86
and dispossession, 85, 92, 96, 113
and erotic innocence, 69–70, 87–8n5
fairy tale in, 78–80, 85
ghost story in, 78–80, 82
and innocence, 67–74, 81, 85–6
innocence and evil in, 86
"innocent until proven guilty", 74, 88n8
pattern of innocence lost and restored, 72–3, 81, 86
performance of childhood, 66–7, 69, 73, 81
title, meaning of, 66–7, 79, 81–6, 89n12
types of innocence, 70, 81, 86
James, Henry: *What Maisie Knew*, 3, 5, 7–9, 15, 21–4, 37–62, 66–9, 91, 94
critical reception of, 57–8, 60–1, 64n10–11
and divided (partagé) child, 8–9, 21, 39–41, 45–6, 62
and emergence of modernist fiction, 53–62, 63–4n9
and "extraordinary ironic center", 40–5
and Maisie's limited/expanding consciousness, 51–62, 63n8
and Maisie's method of diversion, 48, 51, 59–60
and Maisie's method of secrecy, 46–8, 51, 53, 55, 57, 59–61
and Maisie's method of silence, 47–53, 55, 58–61
narrator of, 50–2, 56–62, 64n16
origins of the novel, 21–2, 40–1
role reversal of child and adult, 47, 52–3, 62, 63n6, 63n8
James, William, 13–15, 185
and modernism, 15, 17, 19
"On a Certain Blindness in Human Beings", 18
Pragmatism, 14–15
Principles of Psychology, 121, 207n15
on Rousseau, 13
stream of consciousness, 17–18
Talks to Teachers, 17–18
Johnson, Georgia Douglas, 24, 146

K

Key, Ellen, 2, 17, 75, 86
Kingsley, Charles: *The Water Babies*, 164–5

L

Late modernism
   and Barnes, 91–114
   and critique of modernism, 91–5, 165–6, 204–5
   and ideology of revision, 113–14
   radical conservatism of, 204–5
   and Stein, 5, 163–7, 177–8, 194–205
   and violence, 10, 163, 165–6, 190–4
Locke, John, 54, 63n5, 80, 159n13
Lorde, Audre, 25
   Sister Outsider, 28
Lost generation, 94, 116n7, 203

M

MacDonald, George, 19, 37–9
McCullough, John, 168, 174, 176, 195, 208n23, 208–9n25
Meynell, Wilfrid, 20–1
Milne, A. A.: *Winnie the Pooh*, 2
Modernism, 3–9, 15–35
   aesthetic, 5, 15, 18, 21, 30, 60–2, 92, 94, 97–8, 101, 104, 106, 109–14, 116n10, 119–21, 130, 137, 150, 155, 165–7, 181, 200, 204
   and ambivalence, 67, 79, 85, 87n2, 87n4, 104–5, 166, 185
   and anti-nostalgia, 29–35
   and childhood interiority, 1, 7–8, 16, 21, 127
   and child psychology, 15–23
   and children's literature scholarship, 3–8, 178–9, 206n4
   and cult of childhood, 13, 69–70, 72, 86, 91–5, 100–7, 110–11
   and cult of the new, 92–5, 100–7, 111, 113–14, 115n2, 115n4
   and deconstruction, 5, 166, 187, 207n12
   and divided child, 8, 21, 39–41, 45–6, 53–62
   early modernism, 31, 39–40, 53–62, 92–4, 205
   and essentialized childhood, 19–23, 26–30
   and innocence, 1, 3, 9–10, 21–2, 24–5, 28, 33–4, 65–6, 75, 94, 102, 104–6, 109–14, 127
   and irony, 7, 23, 26, 33, 40–5, 68, 80, 91, 107, 109, 120, 127,134–5, 137, 140–1, 149, 166, 176, 178, 205
   late modernism, 5, 10, 34, 91–5, 105, 114, 115n6, 163–7, 194–205
Montgomery, L. M.: *Anne of Green Gables*, 2
Morrison, Toni, 24
Mother Goose, 32–3, 164, 180–3, 187–8, 194–5, 197, 202, 204, 205n1

N

NAACP, 133–4, 142
Nesbit, Edith, 39–40
New psychology, 15, 18
Nostalgia, 8, 10, 19, 21, 61, 65, 92, 205
   anti-nostalgia, 29–35, 128–31, 195

P

Parents' Magazine, 2
Poe, Edgar Allan, 92–3
Pound, Ezra, 93, 204

R

Rose, Francis, 196
Rousseau, Henri: "The Dream", 101–2, 104, 116n9
Rousseau, Jean Jacques, 88n6
  Èmile, 13–14, 70
Ruskin, John, 20

S

St. Nicholas Magazine, 147–8, 159n12, 160n26, 168
Scott Publishers, 168–9, 174, 195, 196, 207n16, 208n23
Sendak, Maurice: *Where the Wild Things Are*, 159n18, 168
Stein, Gertrude, 3–6, 8, 10, 14–15, 19, 23, 116n7
  and Alice B. Toklas, 189, 193, 198–9, 209n28
  "And Now", 179–82
  and anti-nostalgia, 29–35
  Autobiography of Alice B. Toklas, The, 163, 177, 179, 182, 199, 201, 207n17
  and childhood death, 10, 164–7, 169–94
  and childlike language, 34, 177–8, 194, 198–9, 201–2
  and changing view of America, 197–8, 202–4
  and drowning, 10, 23, 164–5, 169–71, 175, 188–94
  Everybody's Autobiography, 32, 33, 181–2, 197, 204
  First Reader, The, 164–5, 174–7
  and "I am I because my little dog knows me," 164, 178–84, 186–8, 207n12
  and identity, 163–4, 174, 177–89, 193–5, 207n12
  and late modernism, 5, 34, 163–7, 177–8, 194–205
  and Mother Goose, 32–3, 164, 180–3, 187–8, 194–5, 197, 202, 204, 205n1
  Paris France, 171–2, 196–202, 209n27
  and politics, 166, 178, 194–205, 207n10, 208n20, 209n28, 210n30
  Wars I Have Seen, 31–2, 165, 172–3, 203–4, 208n20, 209n27
  and "What is the use of being a little boy if you are growing up to be a man", 164, 178, 182–4, 187–8, 207n12
Stein, Gertrude: *A Geographical History of America*, 182–90, 195–7, 199, 202
  connections with *The World Is Round*, 189–90, 195–6, 208n19
  critical reception of, 187, 192
  double-title structure of, 195–6
  and identity, 182–4, 186–9, 195
  and interiority, 195
  revision history of, 182–5
  role of children's narratives, 182–8
Stein, Gertrude: *The World is Round*, 5–6, 163–5, 168, 189–98, 202, 205n1, 208n21, 209n26
  allegorical journey in, 196
  connections with *A Geographical History of America*, 189–90, 195–6, 208n19
  critical reception of, 192–3
  and drowning, 164–5, 169–74, 190–4
  origins of, 189–90, 207n16
  publication history of, 168, 195–6, 207n16, 209n26

Stein, Gertrude: *To Do: A Book of Alphabets and Birthdays*, 3, 5, 163–5, 167–77, 210n29
  and alphabet book genre, 173–7
  and drowning, 169–71
  origins of, 167–78
  publication history of, 3, 168–9, 206n5
  and violence, 165, 167–76
  and wartime, 167–8, 171–3

T
Toklas, Alice B., 189, 193, 198–9, 209n28
Twain, Mark, 71

V
Van Vechten, Carl, 168–9, 206n5, 208n23

Violence, 10, 34, 48, 94, 98, 129, 132–5, 139–43, 156, 163–9, 177, 179, 185, 199, 205. *See also* Child and childhood: and death

W
Walker, Alice, 24
Wilde, Oscar: *The Picture of Dorian Gray*, 94
Williams, Margery: *The Velveteen Rabbit*, 2
Wilson, Edmund, 6, 87n4, 198–9, 205
Woolf, Virginia, 23, 30–1, 54, 167
Wordsworth, William, 20, 70, 74–5, 88n6–7, 136–7
World War I, 75, 143, 150–1, 154, 157n2, 158n7, 161n33
World War II, 9, 23, 31, 34–5, 93–4, 167, 173–4, 193, 198, 202–3, 206n4